POLITICS, POWER AND COMMUNITY DEVELOPMENT

This book is dedicated to the memory of
Martha Farrell (1959–2015),
who worked tirelessly and courageously for
community development and social justice

RETHINKING COMMUNITY DEVELOPMENT SERIES

Series editors: Mae Shaw,
Rosie R. Meade and Sarah Banks

Rethinking
Community
Development

Politics, power and community development, edited by Rosie R. Meade, Mae Shaw and Sarah Banks, is part of the Rethinking Community Development series from Policy Press.

This leading international monograph series brings together a variety of international, cross-generational and multidisciplinary perspectives to challenge readers to critically rethink what community development means in theory and practice.

Each book in the series:

- provides an international perspective on contemporary community development;

- theorises issues and practices in a way that encourages diverse audiences to rethink the potential of community development;

- encourages practitioners to engage more critically with their work.

The collection is essential reading for academics, upper level undergraduate- and graduate-level students in community development and related disciplines, including geography, social policy and sociology. The series will also appeal to practitioners and policy makers looking to explore the tensions between policy imperatives and the interests and demands of communities at grass roots level.

Forthcoming in the series:

Class, inequality and community development

Edited by Mae Shaw and Marjorie Mayo

September 2016
PB £24.99 ISBN 978-1-4473-2246-7
HB £70.00 ISBN 978-1-4473-2245-0
EPUB £22.49 ISBN 978-1-4473-2249-8
EPDF £90.00 ISBN 978-1-4473-2248-1

Available on **amazon**kindle

POLITICS, POWER AND COMMUNITY DEVELOPMENT

Edited by

Rosie R. Meade, Mae Shaw and Sarah Banks

Rethinking
Community
Development

First published in Great Britain in 2016 by

Policy Press
University of Bristol
1-9 Old Park Hill
Bristol
BS2 8BB
UK
t: +44 (0)117 954 5940
pp-info@bristol.ac.uk
www.policypress.co.uk

North America office:
Policy Press
c/o The University of Chicago Press
1427 East 60th Street
Chicago, IL 60637, USA
t: +1 773 702 7700
f: +1 773 702 9756
sales@press.uchicago.edu
www.press.uchicago.edu

British Library Cataloguing in Publication Data
A catalogue record for this book is available from the British Library

Library of Congress Cataloging-in-Publication Data
A catalog record for this book has been requested

ISBN 978 1 44731 737 1 paperback
ISBN 978 1 44731 736 4 hardcover
ISBN 978 1 44731 740 1 ePub
ISBN 978 1 44731 741 8 Mobi

Cover design by Liam Roberts
Front cover image: 'A city on a hill' by Ian Martin
Printed and bound in Great Britain by CMP, Poole
Policy Press uses environmentally responsible print partners

Contents

Rethinking Community Development

Communities are a continuing focus of public policy and citizen action worldwide. The purposes and functions of work with communities of place, interest and identity vary between and within contexts and change over time. Nevertheless, community development – as both an occupation and as a democratic practice concerned with the demands and aspirations of people in communities – has been extraordinarily enduring.

This book series aims to provide a critical re-evaluation of community development in theory and practice, in the light of new challenges posed by the complex interplay of emancipatory, democratic, self-help and managerial imperatives in different parts of the world. Through a series of edited and authored volumes, Rethinking Community Development will draw together international, cross-generational and cross-disciplinary perspectives, using contextual specificity as a lens through which to explore the localised consequences of global processes. Each text in the series will:

- *promote critical thinking,* through examining the contradictory position of community development, including the tensions between policy imperatives and the interests and demands of communities;
- *include a range of international examples,* in order to explore the localised consequences of global processes;
- include contributions from established and up-and-coming new voices, from a range of geographical contexts;
- *offer topical and timely perspectives,* drawing on historical and theoretical resources in a generative and enlivening way;
- *inform and engage a new generation of practitioners,* bringing new and established voices together to stimulate diverse and innovative perspectives on community development.

If you have a broad or particular interest in community development that could be expanded into an authored or edited collection for this book series, contact:

Mae Shaw	Rosie R. Meade	Sarah Banks
mae.shaw@ed.ac.uk	r.meade@ucc.ie	s.j.banks@durham.ac.uk

Acknowledgements

We are very grateful to all the contributors to the book for their commitment to the project and willingness to tailor their writing to the theme. We would also like to thank Anna Lopes at Sally Walker Language Services, who translated Chapter Thirteen from German into English, and Ian Martin who generously offered one of his original paintings for the front cover. We also wish to acknowledge the support and advice of Oga Steve Abah, Tom O'Connell, Andrea Cornwall and Gary Craig, who offered very helpful suggestions regarding the development of the book series as a whole. Finally, we would like to thank Isobel Bainton, our editor at Policy Press, and the anonymous referees whom she engaged, for their helpful advice and enthusiasm for this project.

Notes on contributors

Sarah Banks is professor in the School of Applied Social Sciences and co-director of the Centre for Social Justice and Community Action at Durham University, UK. She researches and teaches in the fields of community development and professional ethics, and has a particular interest in community-based participatory research. Her publications include *Ethics and values in social work* (4th edition, 2012), *Critical community practice* (2007, with H. Butcher, P. Henderson and J. Robertson) and edited collections on *Managing community practice* (2nd edition, 2013, with H. Butcher, J. Robertson and A. Orton) and *Practising social work ethics around the world: Cases and commentaries* (with K. Nøhr, 2012).

Lucius Botes is professor in development studies and dean of the Faculty of Humanities at the University of the Free State, South Africa. His areas of research and teaching include development studies, sociology of development, alternative development, local economic development and participatory development. He publishes extensively in this field. He was elected associate academic fellow of the World Economic Forum (2001–06). He was director of the Centre of Development Support (1999–2009), initiated the post-graduate programme in development studies and is currently the programme director.

Colin Cameron is a senior lecturer in disability studies and social work at Northumbria University, UK. He has been active in the disabled people's movement since 1992, involved in areas including disability arts, collective advocacy and independent living. He is a board member of the disabled people's organisations Disability Arts Online, Shaping Our Lives and Lothian Centre for Inclusive Living. His research interests centre around everyday disablism, disability and existentialism, and the affirmation model.

Yi-Ling Chen is associate professor in global and area studies/ geography at the University of Wyoming, USA. Her research is on how disadvantaged groups or regions are affected by economic liberalisation and political democratisation in Taiwan. She is also interested in comparative urban studies in East Asia. She has written chapters in *Globalizing Taipei* (2005), *Women and housing: An international analysis* (2011), *Locating neoliberalism in East Asia* (2012), and *Housing East Asia: Socioeconomic and demographic challenges* (2014). She has also published several journal articles on housing, gender, urban movements and regional development in Taiwan. She is currently editing a book, *Contesting urban space in East Asia: Recasting neoliberalism upon housing*.

John Clarke is emeritus professor of social policy at The Open University, UK, where he worked for more than 30 years. His research centres on questions of politics, power and culture in struggles over welfare states and citizenship. His recent publications include *Disputing citizenship* (with K. Coll, E. Dagnino and C. Neveu, 2014) and *Making policy move: Towards a politics of translation and assemblage* (with D. Bainton, N. Lendvai and P. Stubbs, 2015).

María Teresa Martínez Domínguez combines research, community development work and activism. For the last 18 years she has been working for environmental justice in Latin America, Spain and Scotland, especially looking at how over-consumption patterns in the North affect communities in the Global South, and supporting marginalised indigenous communities to achieve self-determination. Currently she works as development manager for The Fife Diet, the largest local food movement in Europe. She has also worked as an international development consultant for various organisations, including Friends of the Earth and UNICEF. Her main interests are indigenous resistance, food sovereignty, 'big oil' and the state, climate justice, and corporate accountability.

Martha Farrell was an adult educator, feminist practitioner and champion of gender equality. Her practice, writings and workshops inspired many students and activists to pursue efforts at engendering development and institutions. She was a director at PRIA, India, since 2000. While training Afghan practitioners on understanding gender, Martha was killed by a terrorist attack in Kabul on 13 May 2015.

Niamh Gaynor is a political sociologist and lecturer in development studies in the School of Law and Government in Dublin City University, Ireland, where she is currently also director of the MA in Development and the MA in International Relations. Prior to joining Dublin City University in 2008 she worked for a number of years in Bénin, West Africa, and then as a freelance researcher with non-governmental organisations and community groups in both Ireland and Africa.

Manish K. Jha is professor (Centre for Community Organisation and Development Practice) and dean (School of Social Work) at Tata Institute of Social Sciences, India. His research interests and writings include development and governance, poverty and migration, social exclusion, human rights and human security. He teaches social policy and planning, social action and movement, and community organisation and development practice. He has been a recipient of the Commonwealth Academic fellowship (2009) at the School of Oriental and African Studies, London, UK; the Erasmus Mundus fellowship (2011) at University College Dublin, Ireland; and a UKIERI visiting fellowship (2013) at Durham University, UK. He is a member of several research organisations and has been actively engaged with development practice, policy advocacy, and relief and rehabilitation work in post-disaster situations.

Sue Kenny is emeritus professor in the Faculty of Arts and Education at Deakin University, Australia. She has written extensively on tensions and issues in community development and the ways in which community development is practised in different settings. Recent books include *Developing communities for the future* (4th edition) and *Challenging the third sector: Global prospects for active citizenship*, co-authored with Marilyn Taylor, Jenny Onyx and Marj Mayo.

Brigitte Kratzwald is a social scientist and commons activist living in Graz, Austria, dealing with the currently emerging new forms of collective production and bottom-up strategies of reorganising society in a way conducive to both human beings and our non-human environment.

Niamh McCrea is a lecturer in youth and community work in the Institute of Technology Carlow, Ireland. She completed her doctoral thesis on the politics of philanthropy and community development at University College Dublin. Prior to this she worked in the area of development and anti-racist education with the National Youth Council of Ireland where she co-authored practice resources on global justice issues. She is a member of the editorial board of the *Community Development Journal* and is active across a number of campaigns on financial justice issues.

Rosie R. Meade is a lecturer in the School of Applied Social Studies in University College Cork, Ireland. She has written on issues related to state/community sector relationships, the governmentalisation of civil society and collective action and protest in Ireland. She has a particular interest in the theory and practice of cultural democracy and has a long-standing involvement with Cork Community Artlink. Her most recent book, co-edited with Fiona Dukelow, is *Defining events: Power, resistance and identity in twenty-first century Ireland* (2015).

Helen Meekosha is honorary associate professor in the School of Social Sciences at University of New South Wales, Australia. Previously she worked as a community worker in both England and Australia. Her primary research is located at the intersection between race, gender and disability relations. Her work in critical disability studies has broken new ground in setting disability in a context of neoliberalism and globalisation.

Janet Newman is emeritus professor in the Faculty of Social Sciences, The Open University, UK. She has written widely about questions of governance, politics and power, public policy and management, activism and participation, and the transformation of welfare states. Her most recent book is *Working the spaces of power: Activism, neoliberalism and gendered labour* (2012).

Eurig Scandrett is a lecturer in sociology at Queen Margaret University, Edinburgh, Scotland. After an initial career as a plant ecologist, he spent 15 years in community education including as head of Community Action at Friends of the Earth Scotland. He works on popular education for gender justice and learning in environmental justice movements. He contributed to *Bhopal survivors speak: Emergent voices from a people's movement* (2009), *Learning and education for a better world: The role of social movements* (2012) and *Environmental Nakba: Environmental injustice and violations of the Israeli occupation of Palestine* (2013). He is a trade union official and chair of Friends of the Earth Scotland.

Mae Shaw is a senior lecturer in community education at the University of Edinburgh, Scotland. She has worked as a community development practitioner in a variety of settings and now teaches and publishes extensively on the history, policy, politics and practice of community development. She is a long-standing member of the editorial board of the *Community Development Journal* and co-founder of *Concept*, the online practice/theory journal. She is a member of the international Popular Education Network. Her co-edited publications include *The community development reader: History, themes and issues* (2011).

Russell Shuttleworth is a medical anthropologist and social worker by training and is currently senior lecturer in social work at the School of Health and Social Development at Deakin University, Australia. He has been a social worker and support worker for disabled persons and older adults and has conducted disability-related research on issues such as sexuality, gender, leadership, access to healthcare contexts for persons with speech impairment and aged care.

Rajesh Tandon is founder-president of PRIA (Participatory Research in Asia), New Delhi, India. He is a pioneer of participatory research methodology, and has written extensively on these themes. He is UNESCO co-chair on Community-based Research and Social Responsibility in Higher Education. He is co-editor of the fifth edition of the GUNi (Global University Network for Innovation) report on higher education (*Higher Education in the World 5*, 2014).

Alison Wannan is undertaking her PhD at the University of New South Wales, Australia, on everyday life and participatory approaches to working in social housing estates. She has a background as a community worker in the non-government sector as well as in policy development and service delivery in government agencies.

ONE

Politics, power and community development: an introductory essay

Rosie R. Meade, Mae Shaw and Sarah Banks

Introduction

This chapter offers a critical overview of the main theme of the volume: the complex and constant interplay between the processes of community development, politics and power. After discussing in turn the contested concepts of 'community development', 'politics' and 'power', we discuss particular challenges for the global practice of community development in an increasingly neoliberalised context. Against the dominance of managerialism and the fracturing of solidarity between citizens, we highlight the importance of a critical vision of community that supports diversity while promoting dialogue across distance and difference. This chapter also introduces and summarises the varied perspectives offered throughout the volume, which draw on experiences from around the world. We conclude by reasserting our hope that despite, and maybe even because of, its critical orientation this volume can prove to be a politically useful and emboldening resource for its readers.

United and divided by a common language

Given its disparate provenance and contested history, it is hardly surprising that the concept and practice of community development has been subject to much interpretation over time and place. Changing political, economic, cultural and social conditions, which are played out locally and globally, mean that the expectations and aspirations invested in communities change over time. The concept of community itself is nebulous and difficult to trace. 'Community' embodies conflicting ideas and emotions: evoking notions of place, identity and interest; and drawing potency from nostalgia, romanticism, solidarity, fear, frustration and hope. It is not always apparent whether community is something that we already have or that we want to build; whether it is a prescription for ourselves or for others. As a political idea 'community' chimes with concepts of democracy, mutuality, autonomy, but it is just as likely to manifest as exclusivity, surveillance or control (Bauman, 2001). In this respect, O'Carroll (2002: 15) finds within it 'an inflexible notion of boundary between similarity and difference'. Ultimately, as Plant (1974) proposes, it may only be possible to figure out what community is by analysing the specific ways in which the term is deployed in different settings, and from that to extrapolate its meanings and its functions within the wider socioeconomic context.

Inherent ambiguities and contradictions notwithstanding, an interest in communities is a continuing focus of public and social policy worldwide: indeed, its very plasticity might be what renders the idea of community so appealing across time, context and space. 'Community development' – referring broadly to a democratic process concerned with the demands and aspirations of people in communities – is equally enduring. Its global relevance was first endorsed by the United Nations (UN) in the 1955 publication *Social Progress through Community Development*, where it was 'tentatively' defined as 'a process designed to create conditions of economic and social progress for the whole community with its active participation and the fullest possible reliance on the community's initiative' (United Nations, 1955: 6). While primarily framed with reference to rural communities that were not reaping the rewards of 'economic, social and technological change' (1955: 5), the UN also affirmed the potential benefits of community development for urban areas, where 'the most acute problems of disintegration of community and family occur'. Notably, this publication also asserted that 'the first projects should be initiated in response to the expressed needs of people' (1955: 8).

Across the intervening decades, and despite various setbacks and revivals, community development has continued to be a 'world-wide trend' (1955: 14). Although situated somewhere between rhetoric and reality, actuality and aspiration, generally speaking 'community development' can be described as a process through which 'ordinary' people collectively attempt to influence their life circumstances. It is premised on the belief that citizens can, or at least should, be active agents of social, economic, political or cultural change. Their collective agency may be expressed via localised forms of organisation or through expressions of solidarity and shared purpose that transcend geography. Beyond this descriptive account, community development is also seen to host evaluative meanings, which reflect particular political investments and which are often expressed as values (CDX, n.d.; Community Workers Co-operative, 2008; Meade, 2009; Banks, 2011). Here people self-consciously involve themselves in processes which are (claimed to be) democratic, participatory, empowering and inclusive, and where the changes being sought are oriented towards achieving greater equality, social justice, or other progressive outcomes.

As an edited collection with international reach, the authors in this volume draw on the particularities of their own diverse settings in order to elaborate significant concepts, theories and critical questions for contemporary community development. If the collection seeks to make horizontal connections across place, it also traces vertical connections that run across time and generation. It explores long-standing themes such as the deployment of community development for ideological purposes, and its diverse articulations in state policy; but it also explores some distinctly new tensions and common experiences, particularly those linked to the growing influence of neoliberalism, managerialism and market rationalities.

Despite this shared commitment to transnational exchange and dialogue, very real contextual and conceptual differences are navigated by the authors. For example, in Chapter Thirteen Brigitte Kratzwald observes that the term 'community development' is not widely recognised in German-speaking regions. As might be expected, there is no easy equivalence across place and culture. In addition, as many chapters illustrate, within policy, professional and popular discourses internationally, a range of alternative terms evoke or capture particular aspects and forms of the community development process. Terms such as *local development*, *rural extension*, *participatory development*, *community work* and *community organising* are frequently used interchangeably with *community development* while terms such as *community practice* appear to embrace community development as well as and alongside other kinds of community-based interventions.

Against these looser applications, the term *community development* has historically been deployed in a more specialised sense to distinguish a very specific kind of social practice or intervention that takes place in communities. In this reading it is one of several alternative approaches to community work, and its values, techniques and processes are seen as discrete, albeit overlapping in certain contexts, from those associated with other community work approaches; for example, *community action*, *community service delivery* or *community planning* (Thomas, 1983; Popple, 1995; Banks, 2011). While *community action* may involve working for radical social change, and *community service/planning* aims to develop community-oriented policies, services and organisations, *community development* is concerned with promoting community self-help and citizen participation. Community development in this sense is short for 'community development work', which may be regarded as a practice, and/or as an occupation, undertaken by community activists and/or paid workers. However, when we use the term 'community development' in this introductory essay, we are referring to it as a process – specifically a process through which ordinary people collectively attempt to influence their life chances. We use the term 'community development practice' to denote the purposefully applied values, knowledge and skills underpinning the process, and 'community development work' when referring to the occupation practised by community development workers.

Clearly this plurality of meanings and usages has the potential to generate considerable confusion and contestation. Consequently, in this volume we have decided to approach the term 'community development' in as open and inclusive a way as possible while still retaining some sense of conceptual coherence. With our selection of contributions from different parts of the globe, we want to acknowledge at least some of the variety of processes and practices that are involved when people work together to influence change in their communities, whether those communities are centred on place, shared interest or identity.

In the interests of clarity, within their respective chapters authors have been encouraged to explain how they are framing community development and whether and how the term is understood within that national or regional context. In all cases they describe and analyse practices that are aligned to a broad ideological commitment to community, that are collective rather than individual in focus, and that contain a promise of more genuinely participatory spaces for citizens. Beyond this, the chapters reveal varying roles for the state, national governments, political parties, local government, professionals, activists, local administrators, social movements, international donors, non-governmental organisations (NGOs), international governmental organisations (IGOs), private businesses, corporations and philanthropic foundations. And as different purposes, contexts and actors interact, the political and power relations that are always inherent in community development processes take shape.

Rethinking community development: a dialectical approach

While acknowledging its long-standing association with progressive ideas and values, the series *Rethinking Community Development* and this, its first book, take a somewhat more circumspect view of community development, contending that both in theory and practice, it is contested and malleable. Indeed we appreciate that the very concept of 'development', like community, is elusive and merits some scrutiny in its own right. For example, Escobar (1995: 6) characterises development as a 'historically produced discourse', observing a contingent relationship between the 'modernisation' of poverty through the creation of an interventionist social sphere in the West during the 19th century, and the invention and implementation of the development paradigm in the so-called 'Third World' after the Second World War. Consequent on the rise of development as the ultimate measure of human aspiration, in the wake of US President Truman's 'launch' of the concept in 1949, the lifestyles and production patterns of a majority of the world's population were defined by default as deficient (Nandy, 1987; Esteva, 1992; Escobar, 1995). Moreover, to this foundational framing of local populations as the obstacles to or objects of development, has been added a new and more disturbing dimension. Over time, the dominant paradigm of development has come under sustained critique for its singular emphasis on market integration (Selwyn, 2014). According to Bernstein (2005: 119), what has been lost to development thinking due to the hegemony of neoliberal economics is 'the wider intellectual, and political, understanding of development as a process of struggle and conflict'.

In the colonialist imaginary, the promise of 'civilisation' had long been used to mask or legitimise exploitation, appropriation and control, and the discourse of development would come to serve similar ideological functions in the 20th and 21st centuries. Kothari (2005: 432) reveals 'the similarities between colonialism and development as projects of modernity and progress', with their shared 'reassertion of dichotomies of the "modern" and the "traditional" and the "West" and the "rest"'. Significantly, Mayo (2011: 75) argues that community development was 'concocted' by British colonial authorities in the period between the First and Second World Wars in order to serve distinctive political and economic purposes – a dual mission which she characterises as 'civilising whilst exploiting'. As international liberation struggles began to gain traction during the mid-20th century, older imperialist administrations and an increasingly powerful US became concerned about the form that post-colonial independence might take in Africa, India, Malaysia and later Vietnam, Cambodia and Laos (Mayo, 2011). For the UK and US the fear of communism manifested as an interest in creating new democratic institutions, mass literacy programmes, rural or village development and targeted financial aid: in these, its nascent forms, 'the political implications of community development' were revealed with the building or bolstering of 'local bulwarks (and vested interests) opposed to communism' (Mayo, 2011: 77).

Notwithstanding legitimate scepticism regarding the self-evidence of development as 'progress', we would nevertheless argue that community development should be regarded as a dialectical process that hosts both progressive and regressive possibilities. If in their (post-) colonial formations, community development initiatives were deployed to shut down dissent or to foreclose on radical political ideologies, historical and contemporary experience also suggests that they have been positioned at the vanguard of revolutionary politics. For example, The Black Panther Party, established in Oakland California in 1966, developed an extraordinarily varied menu of community programmes, which included a 'Community Learning Centre', 'People's Free Medical Research Health Clinics', 'Free Breakfast for Schoolchildren Program', and 'Intercommunal Youth Institute'. Explicitly named as 'survival strategies' rather than as development objectives in their own right – this was 'survival pending revolution' – these programmes were expected to 'serve as a model for all oppressed people who wish to begin to take concrete actions to deal with their oppression' (The Dr. Huey P. Newton Foundation, 2008: 3–4).

Similarly, in the UK context, community development projects were, in many places, the focus for concerted political action around housing, health, planning and welfare (for example Bryant, 1979; Cowley et al, 1977; O'Malley, 1977). And in Australia, community development provided scope for constructive alliances between the building workers' union and working class communities around 'green-bans' in the defence of jobs and homes (Mundey and Craig, 1978).

These examples, ranging from the integrative to the radical, do not exhaust the possibilities of community development, and this volume explores a variety of manifestations from the Amazon to Australia. Albeit raising critical questions about the politics of contemporary neoliberalised community development in particular, there is nonetheless broad agreement among authors that projects and processes retain valuable scope to speak to people's real concerns, perhaps even cultivating prefigurative relations where ideals of justice and equality are lived out in the here and now. At the very least, community contexts can still offer increasingly rare and unsequestered spaces of conviviality and solidarity. In challenging and demoralising times, they can inspire resistance, creativity and critical insights into the public and private dimensions of exploitation and oppression. But thinking dialectically about community development means recognising that it is always a historically situated, ideologically contested and contextually specific set of practices. It is simultaneously formal and informal; of the state and beyond the state; concerned with the individual and with the collective; an expression of popular politics and a policy intervention or governmental strategy. Therefore, it occurs at the interface of divergent, and even competing, actors, rationalities, disciplinary interests, professional identities and epistemological fields.

Subsequent texts in the book series will continue to make such intersections explicit and *Politics, Power and Community Development* introduces key themes that will be picked up and expanded on in later volumes. Contributors to this, Volume One, include authors who may already be familiar as part of the international community development 'fold'; others come from backgrounds in social policy, commons activism and scholarship, international development, environmental justice or social movement theorising, geography and disability studies. The shared starting point is an acknowledgement that, while community development is a global practice, it is done, talked and thought about in different ways in different settings (Abah, 2007). Taken together, the chapters of this volume also propose that this ambivalence and plurality is what makes it distinctive and promising, creating space for reflexivity, strategic dialogue and critical inquiry.

Power in community development

As its title suggests, this volume highlights and critically examines some key political themes and issues, and the associated power relationships that are shaping contemporary community development. Not least because of its semantic connection with the concept of 'empowerment', community development generally comes with an explicit commitment to the reshaping of power relationships. However, when empowerment is promised, it is not always obvious what form power is presumed to take, what might be the optimal ways of unleashing it, or whether its pursuit involves a direct confrontation with the sources of conflict and inequality in our social world (Reed Jr., 2000). As with many of the shibboleths of community development, there are abiding questions about whether claims of empowerment should be abandoned, reclaimed or challenged to live up to their promise.

To make empowerment meaningful, we need to actively theorise and analyse the politics of power. As the chapters in this volume illustrate, empowerment in community development can variously translate as: successful demands for identity recognition or limited material redistribution; demonstrations of self-help and mutual aid; confrontations with oppressive or constraining state and market forces; the building of skills, education and 'marketability' of community members; mobilising communities as some kind of untapped economic resource; or people creatively reimagining their place in the wider economy, culture and society. It can manifest in policy and political change or emerge through resistance and struggle. Consequently the authors necessarily conceive of power in divergent ways, and thereby reflect and contribute to the unfinished and ongoing sociological debate that surrounds this concept.

In sociology, power is often regarded as a 'capacity', which allows actors to limit the actions or interests of other actors, and arguably it is this idea of power as 'power over' that figures most prominently in the discourse and practice of community development internationally (Takhar, 2011: 345–6). When conceptualised in this way, power may be seen to have different 'dimensions', which reflect varying degrees of accountability and transparency in its deployment (Powercube, n.d.; Bacharach and Baratz, 1962; Lukes, 2005). On the first dimension is visible power that operates in public contexts, and which requires communities to organise or mobilise strategically in order to effect their will. On its second dimension, power operates in hidden ways, to circumscribe agendas, silence actors and keep issues off the table in public and private contexts. And finally there is a third dimension where power is invisible and operates insidiously, obscuring our real interests while locking us into the dominant value consensus (Powercube, n.d.; Bacharach and Baratz, 1962; Lukes, 2005). This multi-dimensional conception implies that one of the central purposes of community development is to lay claim to some of the kinds of power that shape personal and social lives, and it is around such a project of claims-making that communities converge and collective action is organised.

In contrast, writers like Michel Foucault (1978: 93–4) argue that power is mobile and omnipresent, that it is 'not something that is acquired, seized or shared; something that one holds on to or allows to slip away' but instead it is 'exercised from innumerable points' in all kinds of social relationships. This alerts us to the prospect that power is present not only in public domains, but also in our private lives and most intimate encounters. It is a feature of all manner of family, community, institutional, governmental and professional interactions.

Nor does it merely constrain the actions and interests of ourselves and others; in fact it constitutes our identities and brings behaviours into being (Foucault, 1978). For example, and as Barbara Cruikshank (1999) argues, the very naming of communities as disempowered or as requiring the intercession of a facilitating actor – *qua* the community development worker – is itself an expression of power. The identities and subjectivities of the powerless, poor, socially excluded or disadvantaged on whom community development is so typically focused are thus constructed, mobilised and recruited to participate in its processes. Such a focus on the constitutive potential of community development supports an interrogation of the rationalities, judgements and assumptions that precede and legitimise its associated actions. It also raises questions about democratic accountability, about the comparative status of citizen knowledge and professional judgement, and about empowerment as a 'power relationship' that can be 'used well or badly' (Cruikshank, 1999: 86). In this volume, related themes are explored in chapters by Janet Newman and John Clarke (Chapter Two), Manish Jha (Chapter Four), and Niamh McCrea (Chapter Six).

Politics and community development in the age of neoliberalism

Politics is a key organising concept in this volume. In its broadest sense, politics is about the affairs of state and the actions and interventions that are linked to government; it relates to how citizens are constituted by society. But the term is also used to refer to a discipline, a topic of study, and an arena for action and critical thinking. It is this idea of politics as an arena for action and critical thinking that interests us and it 'entails that we ... ask why and how particular social formations have a specific shape and come into being, and what it might mean to rethink such formations in terms of opening up new sites of struggles and movements' (Giroux, 2004: 133).

This volume emerges partly from our acute unease about the global hegemony of neoliberalism, and the authors collectively trace whether and how its influence is felt in community development internationally. Brenner, Peck and Theodore (2010: 230) explain that neoliberalisation, a process rather than an actor, 'produces geo-institutional differentiation across places, territories, and scales; but it does this systemically, as a pervasive, endemic feature of its basic operational logic'. In other words, even as its intensity and extensity diverges according to context, there is still an underlying coherence behind this global ideological and political project. Consequently, tendencies towards the privatisation of public services, commodification of natural resources, deployment of managerialist rationalities, pursuit of competitiveness, promotion of financialisation and the redrafting of the boundaries of the social are replicated across nations.

Furthermore the enactment of these 'reforms' or adjustments, within state institutions and civil society, has been actively enforced through the funding regimes of global actors such as the World Bank and International Monetary Fund (IMF) (Kothari, 2005; Gaynor, Chapter Ten). Nonetheless, there remain significant local and regional variations in how citizens and publics respond to such transformations. Different traditions of democracy, leadership, welfare delivery, collectivisation, politicisation, public service, statecraft, industrialisation and 'modernisation' inflect really existing neoliberalisms. And, as the chapters in this volume show, for community development workers and activists too, there are varying degrees of critique, resistance and acquiescence (Chen, Chapter Five; Gaynor, Chapter Ten; Kenny, Chapter Three; Kratzwald, Chapter Thirteen; Martínez Domínguez and Scandrett, Chapter Nine; McCrea, Chapter Six; Newman and Clarke, Chapter Two).

Inevitably then, the volume explores the tensions and possibilities for community development practice that are emerging in the face of diminishing resources, new power alignments, and changing relationships between state and market. Significantly, neoliberalisation has not heralded the complete negation of the state or its relevance, even though its efficiency and its capacity to provide public welfare services have come under sustained attack from the cheerleaders of the so-called 'free' market (Crouch, 2011; Mirowski, 2013). In some contexts, it may in fact have succeeded in exposing the pressing necessity to 'conserve' those democratic impulses and values which have also found expression in state formations, by making demands on the state to resist the market (Judt, 2010). Peck (2010: 106) describes complex state transitions 'from dogmatic deregulation to market-friendly reregulation, from structural adjustment to good governance, from budget cuts to regulation-by-audit, from welfare retrenchment to active social policy', all of which point to neoliberalism's 'shape-shifting' propensities, where new roles and responsibilities for states emerge in different contexts, and in turn states formulate new expectations and demands of citizens.

Unsurprisingly, because of the 'dominance of the state as the provider that sets the overall framework for community development practice' (Chile, 2006: 423) in many jurisdictions, the texture and tone of relationships between the state and community-based projects have been long-standing preoccupations for commentators globally

(Arnstein, 1969; London Edinburgh Weekend Return Group, 1979; Kenny, 2002; Chile, 2006; Cornwall, 2008; Shaw, 2011). As sponsors, enablers and initiators of community development programmes, policy makers and governments have often struggled to move beyond a control or disciplinary style of engagement to a more democratic one. For example, in 1979 (n.p.) the London Edinburgh Weekend Return Group highlighted how 'the state also seems to represent our problems to us in a way that muddles us as to what is problematic for us and what is problematic for the state'. More recently, in the shadow of neoliberalism, nation states have become fixated on modernisation and managerialist agendas, so that public sector employees and funded projects are relentlessly pushed to demonstrate efficiency, performativity and compliance with centrally determined indicators of competency and achievement (Shaw, 2011; Rosol, 2012).

Nor is the imposition of bureaucracy and surveillance the function of nation states alone, it is also a by-product of the sponsor/donor relationships being promulgated by IGOs, private foundations and 'Big' NGOs. Consequently, following research with South African NGOs, Mueller-Hirth (2012: 656) contends that 'accountability is one of the key concerns of neoliberal development', where the onus is less on democratic oversight by communities and populations, and more on the creation of 'calculable spaces that can be made governable through experts and expertise' (also McCrea, Chapter Six). In this volume, contributors broadly agree that the role and identity of the (funded) community development worker is being fundamentally refashioned in this climate. But if surveillance cultures are becoming normalised, there is also evidence that some community development workers recalibrate, creatively comply with, and even resist managerial ordinances in order to minimise their impact (Mayo, Hoggett and Miller, 2007; Mueller-Hirth, 2012; Newman and Clarke, Chapter Two).

Outside the internal structures of community organisations, the impacts of neoliberalised social policies are felt in communities, by people 'on the ground', as policy makers promote the virtues of 'voluntarism' and meld rationalities of 'self-responsibilisation' with those of 'neo-communitarian ... active citizenship' (Rosol, 2012: 251). Albeit to varying degrees, people are exhorted, induced or coerced to fill gaps in welfare delivery and to contend with the consequences of austerity, deindustrialisation and the flexibilisation of work (Botes, Chapter Twelve; Kenny, Chapter Three; Meekosha, Wannan and Shuttleworth, Chapter Eight). And still they are asked to demonstrate innovation and entrepreneurship, to gentrify or exploit their living environments as 'places' that can compete in the global market (Rosol, 2012; Chen, Chapter Five; Martínez Domínguez and Scandrett, Chapter Nine).

As authors reflect on whether and how state policies are being transformed in line with market imperatives, other chapters assess the growing influence of private corporations over community development internationally (Martínez Domínguez and Scandrett, Chapter Nine; McCrea, Chapter Six). Arguably, through foundation funding and experiments in venture philanthropy, the corporate sector is at last displaying a willingness to become 'citizenship oriented' or 'socially responsible' (Marsden and Andriof, 1998); but again, such claims merit closer inspection and analysis. 'Philanthrocapitalism' (see Edwards, 2008) potentially offers alternative resource streams to hard-pressed communities that are otherwise denied public subsidy, and may even support a measure of independent activism where states actively repress or demonise dissent. Evidence so far suggests that community development organisations have had varying success in their efforts to encourage corporations to become publicly accountable or to abandon deleterious and invidious business practices (Ottinger, 2013; Martínez Domínguez and Scandrett, Chapter Nine; McCrea, Chapter Six). At the same time, the movement to philanthropy could be seen to further legitimise state disinvestment from welfare and service delivery, and to perpetuate the hegemony of quantitative conceptions of project efficiency and accountability. Through their application of business metrics to social justice contexts, corporations and foundations may in their own fashion discipline community development projects. As Edwards (2008: 45) explains: 'It is easy to identify quick fixes in terms of business and market criteria, only to find out that what seemed inefficient turns out to be essential for civil society's social and political impact'.

Drawing together these diverse themes and trends, neoliberalism emerges as a common denominator that is moulding and mobilising contemporary community development work internationally. Paradoxically perhaps, there may never have been another time in its global history when there has been such a degree of homogeneity across context; where people are experiencing some of the same kinds of conditions throughout the world. But rather than reduce us to defeatism or political quietude, we wonder if that insight might nourish some optimism too. Hardt and Negri (2000) characterise global neoliberalism as a de-centred 'Empire' which, precisely because it is everywhere at once, can be confronted from innumerable vantage points. The remaking of the status and coherence of the state, along with virtually unstoppable patterns of movement and migration across national frontiers, may create new possibilities for a progressive, cosmopolitan politics to emerge (Morell, 2012; Kenny, Chapter Three). Hardt and Negri (2000), for example, have denoted the 'Multitude' as the politically conscious and transformative actor of the moment, in which the promise of an inclusive and variegated resistance to the current political configuration resides. Their privileging of 'Multitude' over other subject categories such as 'class' is itself a reaction to the perceived limitations of Marxist orthodoxy, implying a more heterogeneous and poly-vocal movement that incorporates but is not restricted to peasants, indigenous communities, the non-working poor, women, migrants and *sans papiers*.

Notwithstanding some scepticism as to the efficacy or viability of the Multitude and its capacity to function strategically or to sustain itself politically, it is apparent that the globalisation of media, oppression, resistance and knowledge engenders new prospects for transnational solidarity and dialogue. This volume, and those that follow in the series, frame that dialogue through the lens of community development and its possible meanings. At the very least, we hope that common, or at least comparable, encounters with neoliberalised globalisation might inspire a measure of consensus regarding the necessary reassertion of a democratic, politically robust and inclusive version of community development; one which is critically engaged and posits alternatives to the current hegemony by drawing on its distinctive connections to and relevance for people's everyday lives in communities. But despite our hope, we cannot pretend that such a project is either inevitable or easy.

Solidarity across distance and difference

Of course we are aware that neoliberalism is not the only political or ideological game in town. Accentuating and intersecting it are other axes of oppression or exclusion, some contextually specific, some more generalisable (for example, imperialism, racism, sexism, homophobia), against which community development practitioners could feel impotent. Nonetheless, a willingness to oppose, transcend or transform those inequalities and misrecognitions animates multiple forms of collective action today. Even though there has been an abject failure to fundamentally destabilise capitalism as a system, throughout the 20th century (especially since the 1960s) progressive movements have sought to redefine both the substance and practice of progressive politics. Such movements speak of 'anti-racism, anti-imperialism, anti-war, the New Left, second-wave feminism, LGBT liberation, multiculturalism, and so on' (Fraser, 2013: 131). Chapters in this volume identify and explore some localised forms of cultural and social struggle, mainly centred on issues of access, autonomy, identity and self-expression, where fruitful alliances are already being made with community development practitioners. Others, however, show that such creative dialogue and mutual support remain largely absent but ongoing necessities (Botes, Chapter Twelve; Cameron, Chapter Eleven; Farrell and Tandon, Chapter Seven; Jha; Chapter Four; Kratzwald, Chapter Thirteen; Meekosha, Wannan and Shuttleworth, Chapter Eight).

Clearly politics are plural; inequalities are discrete *and* overlapping. The urgency of a critical politics of diversity that is founded on a commitment to empathy and solidarity has, if anything, intensified since the beginning of the 21st century. Paul Gilroy (2004: 1–6) analyses the conflicted character of the contemporary backlash against multiculturalism and cosmopolitan sensibilities: the 'resurgent imperial power of the United States ... Xenophobia and nationalism are thriving ... any open stance toward otherness appears old-fashioned, new-agey and quaintly ethnocentric' and there is 'a habitual resort to culture as unbridgeable division'. In many of the countries of the Global North, anti-immigrant and racist posturing is becoming normalised in politics. LGBT rights and freedoms are on the advance but there are significant setbacks too as political leaders cultivate homophobia and rationalise legal restrictions on sexual diversity (United Nations Development Programme, 2011). In this volume Helen Meekosha, Alison Wannan and Russell Shuttleworth (Chapter Eight) describe how in Australia, the hard-won rights and entitlements of women, disabled people and Aboriginal communities are being unpicked by reactionary forces. They acknowledge that over the course of their respective histories both social work and community development work have too often met racism, discrimination and exclusion with paternalism and charity. And, as Colin Cameron (Chapter Eleven) compellingly argues with reference to the cultural and social status of disabled people, such tendencies have not gone away. Similarly, in their respective chapters Manish Jha (Chapter Four) and Martha Farrell and Rajesh Tandon (Chapter Seven) consider how 'mainstream' or official models of community development in India have disregarded the rigidity of caste and gender hierarchy within communities of place, with profoundly negative consequences for poorer women and Dalits in particular.

Chapters across the volume highlight the continuing legacies of patriarchy, environmental destruction, racism, individualised constructions of disability, and caste- and class-based inequality, as forces with which community development practitioners must reckon.

Clearly poverty, oppression, misrecognition and alienation take their toll so that building community responses from the ground up, especially in compromised times, is never straightforward. However, our contributors describe original efforts to vitalise democratic principles and recreate community development practice. Through, for example, protest (Botes, Chapter Twelve), commoning (Kratzwald, Chapter Thirteen), culture and the arts (Cameron, Chapter Eleven), people co-produce countervailing forms of power and new ways of being or belonging. If communities are, however unwittingly or unwillingly, adopting and adapting to market values and processes, they are also germinating alternatives with varying degrees of confidence and success.

Finally, it would of course be possible to add to the litany of political concerns and crises that are explored in the chapters of this volume. Politics must be regarded 'not as a stable field but as a field whose form and content are continually re-defined' (Amin and Thrift, 2013: 6) and this inevitably makes it impossible to produce a representative inventory of issues that holds across place and time. We could equally and legitimately assess the way community development practice engages with and responds to: war and violence; ethnic and religious conflict; migration and displacement of populations; imperialism; homophobia and repressions of sexual freedoms; urbanisation or rural depopulation. While we appreciate the partiality and necessarily limited scope of this volume, as the series develops we want to create an intellectual space within which these and other issues and concerns can be paid the critical attention they deserve.

This volume's purpose and structure

This volume sets the tone for the *Rethinking Community Development* series as a whole by probing some fundamental challenges and dilemmas for community development today. At the same time, it is sufficiently open and generative to encourage different or even divergent responses. As contributors address the volume title, *Politics, Power and Community Development*, they raise issues of international relevance but which are, nonetheless, specific in their consequences. Across the 12 chapters that follow, we find critical reflections on policy and practice in Taiwan, Australia, India, South Africa, Burundi, Germany, the US, Ireland, Malawi, Ecuadorian and Peruvian Amazonia and the UK. No more than they can be expected to capture the 'essential' character of community development within a particular nation state, these cases do not claim to be representative of some kind of universal 'glocal' reality.

While all authors direct their chapters explicitly towards community development, in some cases their contributions are informed by a particular policy interest or political question. For example, individual chapters focus on global governance and the (post-)Washington Consensus; disability arts and the affirmation model; reversals to diversity and egalitarian policies; environmental justice in the context of oil exploration; gender equality and the successes and limitations of India's *Panchayat* system; service delivery protests and democratic deficits; and the remaking of place in the name of cultural specificity and economic competitiveness.

Thinking politically

The volume is divided into three main parts, although there are thematic overlaps across their individual chapters. Part 1, 'Thinking politically', raises fundamental theoretical questions regarding the form and substance of community development practice in the contemporary policy field. Janet Newman and John Clarke (Chapter Two) address the complicated 'politics of deploying community' when this attractive but elusive concept is burdened with contradictory expectations. Rather than present an account of community as unilaterally imposed from above – by the state or by other powerful actors – they are mindful that in the micro-contexts of practice the worker has agency and scope for negotiation or refusal. Official policies and discourses are never simply 'delivered' in pure unmediated form to communities by neutral or passive practitioners. Instead, they are subject to a 'politics of translation', through which actors exercise 'interpretation, creativity and judgement'. As community development practice migrates between organisational or institutional settings, and as it crosses national and local borders, it is repeatedly redefined and renegotiated.

This point is further underlined in Newman and Clarke's unpacking of 'the politics of articulation', which refers to the ways in which 'community' is inflected by its association with other concepts and ideas. They argue that the soldering of 'community' to words and policies that signify antagonistic or incompatible political aspirations means there can be no guarantee of predetermined outcomes. With so many diverse actors and agendas interacting in practice, there are borrowings and reclamations, inversions and reimaginings, all of which ensure that community development practice remains both unpredictable and an ongoing site of struggle.

Sue Kenny (Chapter Three) explores alternative constructions of the community development worker's role, which are themselves framed by the rationalities and assumptions that inform the establishment of community development processes. Highlighting and questioning the presumed divergence between 'facilitative' and 'leadership' approaches to the work, she suggests that in both theory and practice such distinctions become blurred. She further argues that practitioners and activists need to interrogate the models of leadership/facilitation being practised and promoted *as* community development, not least because of their implications for how visions of empowerment are enacted on the ground. In any event, new and problematic forms of professionalism and managerialism are inflecting the roles being asked of workers, potentially inhibiting more critical praxis. Kenny therefore considers innovative ways of thinking about practice that may relieve the stifling spirit of conformity that managerialism cultivates. Notably, and in the spirit of dialectical analysis that informs the volume, her chapter points to the transcendent possibilities of cosmopolitanism for a creative (re) engagement with the political and social realities of globalisation.

Manish Jha (Chapter Four) looks at policy and practice as it has evolved in post-independence India, to tease out how 'community development' and 'community organisation' have emerged as distinct governmental strategies that have experienced varying fortunes over time. Here government is understood in the Foucauldian (2009) sense as entailing a concern with the creation of particular kinds of subjects, an enterprise not exclusively linked to the programmes, actions or 'mentalities' of *the* government and the state. NGOs, professionals, political parties, micro-movements and grassroots activist groups also seek to mobilise and call particular kinds of 'subject' into being. In India the forms of community subjectivity that have been sanctioned and supported by the state are those most closely reconciled with the nation's wider modernisation project: in the past its successive five-year plans and, more recently, its status as a centre of competitive neoliberalised capitalism. However, against these dominant models of community development, Jha also traces the emergence of a more activist-led model of community organising, that challenges established political truths and, in particular, caste norms. He thus emphasises the hold of diversity and division within community; that there is no universal Indian community development subject. Instead inequalities linked to class, caste, religious affiliation, migration, gender or esteem intersect with governmental strategies; and people demonstrate their capacity for agency through distinct models of collective self-organisation.

Practising politics

The second part of the volume is more explicitly concerned with how the politics of community development and power relations unfold in specific contexts. Chapters include case studies with a geographical focus, in that they are based in particular countries, but they are also thematic, highlighting issues and concerns that have a more generalisable international significance. Yi-Ling Chen (Chapter Five) reflects on the peculiar salience of locality in this era of globalisation, whereby cities must become entrepreneurial as they seek competitive advantage in the international market place. Within post-industrialising nation states, competition is enacted across regions, as national development policies responsibilise cities to find unique selling points. In Taiwan's evolving democracy, a particular emphasis is placed on 'culture', both as a signifier of national identity and as a marketable resource. Meanwhile, processes of community development and community participation are being invited by policy makers in order to popularise and embed this project of cultural and spatial renewal. For example, communities have mobilised to regenerate historic buildings and decommissioned industrial plants in Hualien City, on the east coast of Taiwan. The depth of community participation varies within and between these 'places' but Chen alerts us to the pivotal role that communities play in the government's reconstruction of the nation.

Niamh McCrea's analysis of philanthropy and its expanding role in the resourcing of community development (Chapter Six) brings some other consequences of neoliberalism into sharp relief. In the Republic of Ireland, where community development has been funded almost exclusively by the state, private foundations have begun to establish a significant presence. The history and scale of philanthropic funding to social justice causes varies considerably between nation states. However, as national governments increasingly divest themselves of responsibilities for welfare delivery, community organisations' dependence on private sector resources is likely to deepen. Like Jha, McCrea adopts a Foucauldian approach as she analyses the political nuances of this transition. Foundations can seek to impose distinctive kinds of organisational rationalities, especially those linked with performance management, on grantees. Yet, while allowing for critiques of the associated de-radicalisation and depoliticisation of community development, McCrea's account of the experiences of the Migrants Rights Centre Ireland cautions against a deterministic appraisal of those trends. Evoking indirectly the politics of articulation and translation as defined by Newman and Clarke (Chapter Two), she finds that community organisations may in their turn destabilise the rationalities of funder organisations, prompting new understandings of social issues and of organisational cultures.

Some problems inherent to top-down, government-mandated forms of community development are profiled by Martha Farrell and Rajesh Tandon (Chapter Seven). They chart the historical evolution of participatory approaches in India, where community development-type activities and programmes have been incorporated within successive five-year plans since the late 1940s. The promotion of rural modernisation, agricultural extension and, from the 1950s, new community-based democratic institutions (the *Panchayat* system), spawned an extensive community-based development infrastructure. However, the disregarding of and lack of engagement with the politics of class, caste and religious hierarchy ultimately reinforced established social relations and ways of doing things. Specifically, Farrell and Tandon testify to the resilience of patriarchy as a regime of oppression that inhibits development and continues to undermine women's participation in the public sphere. The chapter concludes with some learning from the campaigning and capacity-building work of Participatory Research in Asia, which mobilises and supports Indian women to confront everyday patriarchy in its various guises.

In Chapter Eight, on the 'politics of diversity in Australia', Helen Meekosha, Alison Wannan and Russell Shuttleworth focus their attention on community practice – incorporating community development and other (professionalised) interventions. Their chapter strongly evokes the dialectical character of community practice as they cite the historical complicity of community and social workers in the systemic oppression of Aboriginal and disabled communities. Underpinning their analysis is a concurrent recognition that social movements, community activists and, in some exemplary cases, professional workers, have secured important welfare, social and political advances for minority groups in Australia. However, empowerment and social rights can be built on fragile foundations, particularly where the advocates of neoliberalism, reactionary political agendas and new kinds of nationalist insularity seek to roll back progress, discredit multiculturalism and legitimise inequality. Thus these writers describe a conflicted public sphere, where community practitioners work within increasingly straitened financial circumstances and where state-sponsored community programmes champion bland 'capacity-building' approaches at the expense of more democratic forms of engagement.

Against these trends, the chapter presents two more promising case studies that suggest positive expressions of solidarity are being created within and between diverse social groups: one focused on disability politics and new alliances between activists and professionals; the other analysing efforts to vitalise cultural diversity, democratic engagement and cross-community alliances within public housing estates. Their chapter ultimately calls for a politics of diversity that is necessarily inclusive of difference and that is expansive enough to forge solidarity between oppressed communities that may be fractured or suspicious of each other.

Analysing the contemporary politics of environmental justice, Teresa Martínez Domínguez and Eurig Scandrett (Chapter Nine) circle some issues also highlighted by Niamh McCrea. Their chapter explores another dimension of corporate or private sector sponsorship of community development: the enactment of Corporate Social Responsibility programmes in the Ecuadorean and Peruvian Amazon. Here the oil industry seeks to legitimise its appropriation of natural resources, and the consequent social and environmental damage, via community development initiatives. This incorporation of community development is not entirely new: historically, and as noted already, its practices have been implicated in, for example, the politics of colonialism, anti-communism and social control. In Latin America, where national and transnational oil companies extract resources with virtual impunity in the absence of state regulation and oversight, community development programmes are deployed to mitigate the associated environmental contingencies and to override conflict with 'good neighbour agreements'. When not posing as neighbours, however, the oil companies can also engage in manipulation and coercion to establish economic control. In their most conventional forms, community development processes and practices are deployed in service of corporate interests, yet the authors do acknowledge more hopeful variants. They propose that the concept of 'ecological debt' may provide an alternative framework for understanding the real costs and legacies of oil exploration, a framework that also supports mobilisations by indigenous communities against the exploitation of their lands and cultures.

As we reflect on the politics of community development it is tempting to centre our gaze on the familiar or the proximate: on what is happening in local government, regional agencies or national government departments. Niamh Gaynor (Chapter Ten) alerts us to the wider or distal politics of globalisation and the ever-encroaching influence of IGOs. She is attentive to the threat of manipulation and top-down agendas as institutions such as the IMF, World Bank and World Trade Organization cultivate an interest in communities.

Pledges to empower and engage civil society feature prominently in the rhetoric and funding strategies of the World Bank as it tries to obviate the public relations crisis precipitated by its allegiance to neoliberal orthodoxies – often referred to as the Washington Consensus because of its and the IMF's operational base in Washington DC. These sister organisations' combined championing of structural adjustment policies and rigid fiscal indicators during the 1980s and 1990s has generated widespread economic, social and economic devastation. In order to re-establish credibility and appease critics, the World Bank has been party to an ideological shift – towards a post-Washington Consensus – that Gaynor compares to the supposedly middle-ground politics of the 'Third Way'. While attuned to the risks and realities of co-option present for civil society in the associated development infrastructure and consultative forums, Gaynor nonetheless identifies opportunities for resistance. Drawing on examples from Malawi and Burundi, she observes how participating communities have challenged their own representatives to better articulate their interests and how they have subverted structures and processes by demanding real institutional accountability and enhanced democratic oversight.

Politicising the future

The final section of the volume turns towards contexts and issues which may seem relevant and promising for community development theory and practice, but where there is at best limited engagement and at worst outright estrangement. These three chapters detail innovations and forms of activism which progress outside and in parallel to mainstream community development programmes, even though they have much to contribute to the formulation of a more pluralistic, critically engaged and creative model of practice.

Like Yi-Ling Chen, Colin Cameron (Chapter Eleven), emphasises the central role that culture plays in the building and mobilisation of community. In his detailing of the symbiotic relationship between the disability movement and disability arts, Cameron describes a cultural project that proudly and defiantly rejects mainstream constructions of disabled people and their identities. The disability arts movement is an activist-artist-led force for social change that raises profound questions for individuals, communities, institutions and legislators about how we view capacity or agency. Reflecting on the work of the poet Sue Napolitano, Cameron illustrates how poetry – in content, form and expression – gives voice to alternative values that may effect transformations in the political consciousness of disabled people. He thus raises a red flag for much community development practice, where the rhetoric of community participation and ownership may disguise a deeply rooted paternalism (see also Jha, Chapter Four). Mainstream conceptions of development often pivot on what Nikolas Rose (2000: 331) denotes as constructions of 'excluded populations' as people who 'have either refused the bonds of civility and self-responsibility, or they are unable to assume them for constitutional reasons, or they aspire to them but have not been *given* the skills, capacities and means' (emphasis added). Cameron sets out a progressive agenda for practitioners of community development who may wish to engage with the vital insights of disability activism. In his reckoning the adoption of an 'affirmation model' of disability by community practitioners, might support a praxis that consciously resists and replaces the disabling structures, institutions and processes that manifest in everyday contexts in communities.

Lucius Botes (Chapter Twelve) analyses forms of community action, organisation or mobilisation that consciously identify as political. He details the emergence of service delivery protests on the South African landscape since 2004. These protests are inspired by and reflect people's everyday lives in community contexts, highlighting gaps in basic services such as electricity, water and sanitation, and the poor quality of infrastructure such as housing and roads. Post-apartheid governments have stewarded the country's transition to democracy and provided much-needed investment in civic and public amenities. However, this has not been sufficient to override historical legacies of racism and inequality or indeed more localised patterns of brokerage and exclusion in the determination of access to services. Botes details the various tactics adopted by participants in such protests, which have become violent in some instances. Given that the protests are enacted in distinct geographical places and speak to such everyday concerns, there is a notable absence of community development practitioners in mobilising citizens or in brokering agreements. Botes thus alerts us to a defining problematic for community development in South Africa, but one that has a wider relevance too. Community development practice may exhibit its own democratic deficits when it is primarily responsive to external donors or statutory agencies, but lacks a popular mandate.

The global hegemony of neoliberalism privileges an economic model that cultivates individualism, competitiveness and a disconnection between production and consumption. Brigitte Kratzwald (Chapter Thirteen) explores whether and how the participatory ethos of community development might be linked to alternative economic rationalities. In so doing, she acknowledges that alternative economics is itself a contested field, with some versions attempting to complement or mitigate market ideology but with others expressly anti-capitalist in orientation. Furthermore, in German-speaking contexts, community development has been widely regarded as a social work methodology and has often been viewed sceptically as an abdication of state responsibility for service provision.

Extending her discussion to explore innovative ideas in action, Kratzwald reflects on the potential for correspondence and mutual learning between commons activism – often called commoning – and community development. There has been a recent renewal of interest in commoning (McDermott, O'Connell and O'Donovan, 2014), which had previously been widely dismissed as a moribund relic of pre-industrial society, and Kratzwald highlights precisely what commons processes have to offer in the face of our current global predicament. Drawing on examples from Germany, Detroit and the UK, Kratzwald highlights how people have united against marginalisation and urban decay to create commons that are respectful of local environments, that validate human sociability and that sustain principles of mutuality and cooperation. She also exposes some dilemmas that exercise commons activists but which resonate with the world of community development practice too: for example, ambivalences regarding the role and place of the state, whether it can become a partner in such processes or whether it should be regarded with suspicion and maybe even rejection. Nonetheless if community development and commons processes are to contribute to a progressive politics, they need to embrace and work with differences in social strata or world view. And Kratzwald concludes that there are already some exciting examples of such praxis from which we can learn and take inspiration.

Conclusion

Clearly, despite the very significant differences in focus and tone across its chapters, some unifying themes and concerns are being interrogated by the contributors to the volume. As a totality, *Politics, Power and Community Development* raises fundamental questions regarding the current form, status and future viability of the processes and practices of community development. We see that community development continues to occupy a contradictory position within the changing politics of various state formations. In many contexts agendas are imposed from the top and accountability is constructed as a system of control rather than as an expression of popular democracy. Yet in these disparate international examples there is also evidence that creative alliances are being forged between government agencies, professionals, activists and communities, as they seek to protect or to reassert more progressive visions of statehood and citizenship. There is much commonality in these chapters as they report on the commodification and marketisation of community development, and the parallel responsibilisation of communities to prove their competitive edge or to compensate for the residualisation of public services. Authors also alert us to some of the homogenising tendencies of neoliberalised globalisation. Against the market's promise of boundless choice, we see the stranglehold of managerialism internationally as funders, be they government, IGO or philanthropic, demand quantifiable outcomes and guarantees of performativity from civil society groups.

In drawing attention to such trends and issues, we hope to support a nuanced understanding of the inevitable tensions and challenges that characterise community development roles and relationships. Our purpose is not to castigate workers, activists or professionals for their 'failure' to deliver on community development's putative radicalism; we recognise that contexts are deeply compromised and obstacles are manifold. Instead, we want to encourage all those concerned with the democratic potential of community development, particularly practitioners, to use this volume as a resource for thinking critically and creatively about their work. Out of the contradictions, concepts, illustrations and questions that are presented by the authors, we hope that readers can trace new options and possibilities. And out of the apparent strangeness of different contexts and places, we hope that readers will be able to recognise the prospect of solidarity and new alliances.

References

Abah, O.S. (2007) 'Vignettes of communities in action: an exploration of participatory methodologies in promoting community development in Nigeria', *Community Development Journal*, 42(4): 435–8.

Amin, A. and Thrift, N. (2013) *Arts of the political: New openings for the Left*, Durham, North Carolina and London: Duke University Press.

Arnstein, S. (1969) 'A ladder of citizen participation', *Journal of the American Planning Association*, 35(4): 216–4.

Bacharach, P. and Baratz, M.S. (1962) 'Two faces of power', *The American Political Science Review*, 56(4): 947–52.

Banks, S. (2011) 'Re-gilding the ghetto: community work and community development in 21st century Britain', in M. Lavalette (ed), *Radical social work today*, Bristol: Policy Press, 165–87.

Bauman, Z. (2001) *Community: Seeking safety in an insecure world*, Cambridge: Polity Press.

Bernstein, H. (2005) 'Development studies and the Marxists', in U Kothari (ed) *A radical history of development studies*, London: Zed Books, 111–37.

Brenner, N., Peck, J. and Theodore, N. (2010) 'After neoliberalization?', *Globalizations*, 7(3), 327–45.

Bryant, R. (1979) *Dampness monster: Report of the Gorbals anti-dampness campaign*, SCVO, Edinburgh.

Chile, L. (2006) 'The historical context of community development in Aotearoa New Zealand', *Community Development Journal*, 41(4): 407–25.

CDX (Community Development Exchange) (n.d.), *What is community development?*, Sheffield: Community Development Exchange, www.iacdglobal.org/files/what_is_cd.pdf.

Community Workers Co-operative (2008) *Towards standards for quality community work practice*, www.cwc.ie/wp-content/uploads/2010/10/Towards_Standards.pdf.

Cornwall, A. (2008) 'Unpacking "participation": models, meanings and practices', *Community Development Journal*, 43(3): 269–83.

Cowley, J., Kaye, A., Mayo, M. and Thompson, M. (1977) *Community or class struggle*, London: Routledge and Kegan Paul.

Crouch, C. (2011) *The strange non death of neo-liberalism*, Cambridge: Policy Press.

Cruikshank, B. (1999) *The will to empower*, New York: Cornell University Press.

Edwards, M. (2008) *Just another emperor? The myths and realities of philanthro-capitalism*, The Young Foundation/DEMOS, www.futurepositive.org/edwards_WEB.pdf.

Escobar, A. (1995) *Encountering development*, New Jersey: Princeton University Press.

Esteva, G. (1992) 'Development', in W. Sachs (ed), *The development dictionary*, London: Zed Books, 6–25.

Foucault, M. (1978) *The Will to knowledge. The history of sexuality: volume one*, London: Penguin.

Foucault, M. (2009) *Security, territory, population: Lectures at the Collège de France 1977–1978*, Basingstoke: Palgrave Macmillan.

Fraser, N. (2013) 'A triple movement? Parsing the politics of crisis after Polanyi', *New Left Review*, 81 (May/June): 119–32.

Gilroy, P. (2004) *After empire – melancholia or convivial culture*, Abingdon: Routledge.

Giroux, H. (2004) *The terror of neoliberalism*, Boulder, CO: Paradigm Publishers.

Hardt, M. and Negri, A. (2000) *Empire*, Cambridge, MA: Harvard University Press.

Judt, T. (2010) *Ill fares the land*, New York: Penguin.

Kenny, S. (2002) 'Tensions and issues in community development: new discourses, new Trojans', *Community Development Journal*, 37(4): 284–99.

Kothari, U. (2005) 'Authority and expertise: the professionalisation of international development and the ordering of dissent', *Antipode* 37(3): 425–46.

London Edinburgh Weekend Return Group (1979) *In and against the state*, https://libcom.org/library/against-state-1979.

Lukes, S. (2005) *Power, a radical view*, Basingstoke: Palgrave.

Marsden, C. and Andriof, J. (1998) 'Towards an understanding of corporate citizenship and how to influence it', *Citizenship Studies*, 2(2): 329–52.

Mayo, M. (2011) 'Community development: a radical alternative?', in G. Craig, M. Mayo, K. Popple, M. Shaw and M. Taylor (eds) *The community development reader: History, themes and issues*, Bristol: Policy Press, 75–82.

Mayo, M., Hoggett, P. and Miller, C. (2007) 'Navigating the contradictions of public service modernisation: the case of community engagement professionals', *Policy and Politics*, 35(4): 689–704.

McDermott, M., O'Connell, T. and O'Donovan, Ó. (eds) (2014) *Commons sense: New thinking about an old idea – Community Development Journal Special Supplement*, 49 (Supplement 1).

Meade, R. (2009) 'Community development; a critical analysis of its keywords and values', in C. Forde, E. Kiely, and R. Meade (eds) *Youth and community work in Ireland – critical perspectives*, Dublin: Blackhall Publishing, 57–80.

Mirowski, P. (2013) 'The thirteen commandments of neoliberalism', *The Utopian*, www.the-utopian.org/post/53360513384/the-thirteen-commandments-of-neoliberalism.

Morell, M. Fuster (2012) 'The free culture and 15M movements in Spain: composition, social networks and synergies', *Social Movement Studies*, 11(3–4): 386–92.

Mueller-Hirth, N. (2012) 'If you don't count, you don't count: monitoring and evaluation in South African NGOs', *Development and Change*, 43(3): 649–70.

Mundey, J. and Craig, G. (1978) 'Joint union-resident action', in P Curno (ed) *Political Issues and Community Work*, London: Routledge and Kegan Paul, 199–218.

Nandy, A. (1987) *Traditions, tyranny and Utopias: Essays in the politics of awareness*, Delhi: Oxford University Press.

O'Carroll, P. (2002) 'Culture lag and democratic deficit in Ireland: or "dat's outside de terms of d'agreement"', *Community Development Journal*, 37(1): 10–19.

O'Malley, J. (1977) *The politics of community action: A decade of struggle in Notting Hill*, Nottingham: Spokesman.

Ottinger, G. (2013) *Refining expertise – How responsible engineers subvert environmental justice challenges*, New York: New York University Press.

Peck, J. (2010) 'Zombie neoliberalism and the ambidextrous state', *Theoretical Criminology*, 14(1): 104–10.

Plant, R. (1974) *Community and ideology*, London: RKP.

Popple, K. (1995) *Analysing community work: Its theory and practice*, Buckingham: Open University Press.

Powercube.net (n.d.) 'Strategize and act', www.powercube.net/strategize-and-act/.

Reed, A. (2000) *Class notes: Posing as politics and other thoughts on the American scene*, New York: The New Press.

Rose, N. (2000) 'Government and control', *British Journal of Criminology*, 40(2): 321–39.

Rosol, M. (2012) 'Community volunteering as neoliberal strategy? Green space production in Berlin', *Antipode*, 44(1): 239–57.

Selwyn, G. (2014) *The global development crisis*, Cambridge: Polity.

Shaw, M. (2011) 'Stuck in the middle: community development, community engagement and the dangerous business of learning for democracy', *Community Development Journal*, 46(S2): ii128–ii146.

Takhar, S. (2011) 'The construction of political agency: South Asian women and political activism', *Community Development Journal*, 46(3): 341–50.

The Dr. Huey P. Newton Foundation (2008) *The Black Panther Party: Service to the People Programs*, Albuquerque, NM: University of New Mexico Press.

Thomas, D. (1983) *The making of community work*, London: Allen and Unwin.

United Nations (1955) *Progress through community development*, New York: United Nations Bureau of Social Affairs.

United Nations Development Programme (2011) 'Homophobic hate crimes on the rise, UN human rights chief warns', 18 May, www.undp.org/content/undp/en/home/presscenter/articles/2011/05/18/homophobic-hate-crimes-on-the-rise-un-human-rights-chief-warns.html.

PART 1

Thinking politically

TWO

The politics of deploying community

Janet Newman and John Clarke

Introduction

Community development is understood – by practitioners and governments, by enthusiasts and critics – as an essentially *political* practice. In this chapter, then, we focus on the politics of deploying 'community' in programmes of development, empowerment and containment. Community development has been the focus of a series of attempted cooptions and reinventions as governments have sought to deflect its goals, incorporate its workers and depoliticise its activities. However, it has also been the focus of numerous reinventions as the political landscape has shifted and new generations of activists have aspired to bring about radical political and social change. The fracturing of the political settlements in many nations following the banking crisis of 2008 and the subsequent experience of austerity, coupled with images of popular uprisings in some of the nations of North Africa, Latin America and Eastern Europe, is producing new political aspirations and actions. Sometimes, these aspirations are understood through the distinctive entanglement of the romance of 'community' and the promise of 'development' (Ferguson, 1994; Escobar, 1995; Joseph, 2002).

However, the politics of community development are elusive. There are huge differences between community development in the US, the UK, India, Latin America, and other nations or regions. Time, as well as place, makes a difference: it is possible to trace the different national cycles of community development activity and draw attention to their different political aims, actions and outcomes. Time, we might suggest, itself carries ideological connotations: in some places community development signifies radical and new forms of political reinvention and renewal. However in others – not least the UK – it is associated with the discredited politics of the 1970s, and with the unfulfilled goals of numerous governmental programmes of renewal in the decades that followed. Nevertheless, notions of both 'community' and 'development' continue to serve as objects of political and governmental desire.

But this chapter does not aim to be comparative, nor do we set out to trace one particular history. Rather we seek to show how community development has been the focus of numerous political projects, and then go on to trace two crucial political processes that are in play in such projects. The first is the *politics of translation*. Here we argue that it is necessary to explore what happens as ideas and practices of community development move across national and/or institutional boundaries, and we draw attention to the importance of mediating actors – including, but not exclusively, community workers themselves. The second is the *politics of articulation*. We trace how some of the many possible meanings of 'community' and 'development' are selectively mobilised and articulated with other political concepts in ways that shape their meaning and that open – or close – political possibilities. The politics of articulation is crucial in understanding processes of cooptation, incorporation and managerialisation integral to programmes of neoliberalisation. However, as we argue, processes of articulation are never closed and complete. A focus on the *work* of community development enables us – and other contributors to this volume – to show how actors 'work the spaces' of would-be hegemonic projects in order to pursue alternative and radical goals of development and democratisation.

Community development as political projects: time, space and ideology

We begin by highlighting the multiplicity of political projects associated with the terms 'community' and 'development'. Community is, of course, a highly contested concept, and there is an extensive literature that highlights different perspectives, meanings and policy foci (Cohen, 1987; Rose, 1999; Amit and Rapport, 2002; Creed, 2006; Mooney and Neal, 2009). In *Keywords*, Raymond Williams identified the continuing attractions of community:

> Community can be the warmly persuasive word to describe
> an existing set of relationships, or the warmly persuasive
> word to describe an alternative set of relationships. What
> is most important, perhaps, is that unlike all other terms of
> social organization (*state, nation, society etc*) it never seems to
> be used unfavourably. (Williams, 1976/1986: 76)

Community has this long history of mobility and mutability of meanings. It is at one and the same time an ideal, a hoped-for way of living (for a civil society); the object of government enthusiasm (enabling and empowering communities, promoting economic development, offering a resource beyond the state); and the focus of anxiety (about social conflict and division, often between migrants and the imagined 'home' community). Such diverse connections render the idea of community ambiguous, able to be mobilised – and appropriated – within numerous and often antagonistic political projects. Political projects are not simply the programmes of particular political parties: they can be defined as 'more or less coherent efforts to bring ideas, interests, people and power together' (Newman and Clarke, 2009: 22).

Community development approaches in the global north, especially among former colonial powers, can be understood in a longer historical context of colonial struggles for independence. Craig (1989) notes the associations between community development and attempts by colonial powers to control, rather than liberate, local populations; but community development was also a central strategy in preparing former colonised populations for independence. These critiques of colonial rule are significant for our purposes since many who had participated as young people in the overseas service programmes of voluntary/NGO projects went on to help shape community development practices in their 'home' countries in the post-war years (Craig et al, 2011).

Community served as a device through which to fix governable identities among colonial populations (Pandey, 2005; 2006). Later, it also served as a device through which such 'backward' populations could be transformed through development and modernisation – towards a model of independence, both national and individual, decanted directly from the metropolitan imaginary. The combination of modernisation and development generates a dominant view of community as the space and as the relationships through which people might be improved (see, inter alia, Scott, 2004; Li, 2007a; 2007b).

These tensions between the 'empowerment' and 'control' of local populations also run through the urban social development programmes of industrialised nations – such as the UK – experiencing rapid economic and political change resulting from the decline or destruction of traditional industries in the 1970s and 1980s. The hardships that resulted generated the idea of community development as a form of class-based struggle, supported by trades unions, political parties of the left, and, crucially, radical community workers. In contrast, conservative political ideology tended to depict deficient communities peopled by poor families as the source of 'cycles of deprivation' linked to cultures of poverty (for example Rutter and Madge, 1976). A series of targeted programmes aimed to break such cycles, from the community development programmes of the late 1970s through to the social exclusion initiatives of the 1990s. In focusing on community as a spatially and culturally bounded entity, however, all failed to tackle the material roots of poverty and disadvantage.

A rather different set of political projects, often associated with the radical politics of Latin America, is directed to what Freire (1970) termed the 'pedagogy of the oppressed'. Here community is inflected with notions of a whole civil society rather than with a particular place-bound locality: a civil society that might, through processes of collective development and education, be the source of mobilisations on the part of the subordinated, impoverished and marginalised. Freirean approaches seek to challenge established ideological frameworks of domination, creating and embedding new conceptual frameworks through pedagogic practices that enable people to make sense of their lived experience and promoting new forms of participation and engagement. This transformative conception of development has been espoused by many community workers and community projects in the global north who view the problems of their communities as rooted in broader patterns of inequality and injustice. This was particularly the case where activists had been inspired by the rise of new social movements and the 'new left' of the 1970s (Newman, 2012).

This 'transformative' approach can be contrasted with the work of Saul Alinsky, which offered a more focused engagement with the mobilisation of particular disenfranchised communities in order to challenge dominant relations of power. Alinsky's model of community organising, originating in Chicago, worked through the activities of community organisers to promote broad-based alliances of existing community-based organisations. Through such alliances it proved possible to participate in the public decision-making arena and to negotiate with – or confront – power holders (Smock, 2004). The aim was to create 'a permanent diverse alliance of civil society institutions working in a specific location to effect social and economic change' (Jamoul and Wills, 2008: 209). This approach tended to be centred on the work of the organiser, and to be problem based rather than concerned with the building of long-term community strength (Minkler, 1997). However, it can serve to replicate – rather than challenge – dominant styles of politics. It may also exclude minority groups or fail to challenge social and economic polarisation.

The 'community-building' approach or 'asset-based community development' (ABCD) has also emerged from the US. This is focused less on securing concessions from the powerful through entry into the public sphere of decision making and more on developing and realising a community's own assets in order to enable it to solve its own problems. Community building is concerned with 'strengthening the internal social and economic fabric of the neighborhood itself' (Smock, 2004: 17) to counter the lack of internal capacity, people's isolation from mainstream political opportunity structures, and the erosion of more traditional forms of social cohesion in inner cities. This model can be criticised for its focus on enabling communities to realise their own assets from within rather than engage with 'external' structures of power and authority, including the state. It is, however, gaining popularity among think tanks and policy makers in mature welfare states as they seek to contain state expenditure, and increasingly look to communities to solve their own problems. It is an approach that may encourage the assumption that the problems belong to, and reside in, the community.

The ambiguities of earlier community development approaches in colonial and post-colonial nations can also be traced in the more recent approaches of the World Bank and other international agencies, which seek to 'empower' those in poverty and enhance participation in order to promote economic development agendas. As Craig et al (2011: 9) comment: 'Their programmes, better known for fiscal conservatism than for political and social risk-taking, frequently led, however, to the undermining of local community social and economic structures while appearing to advocate the importance of "community".' Cruikshank (1999), Sharma (2008), Brown (2005) and others have noted the significance of such agencies in promulgating technologies of neoliberal rule 'which help mold individuals into responsible citizen-subjects who fit the requirement of the prevalent governance regime and who participate in the project of rule by governing themselves' (Sharma, 2008:17).

We will return to these contradictions later in the chapter, but here want to note the particular significance attached to women in international development programmes. Women tend to be positioned as the *objects* of development: the source of unrealised assets, and the stabilisers of otherwise potentially unruly political forces. But they are also frequently the *agents* of development, building economic activity through micro finance schemes and entrepreneurial forms of production. This multiple positioning is carried into community development programmes in the global north. Some forms of feminist scholarship have focused on how women's agency is expressed in the 'liminal spaces' between public and private. This positioning, it is argued, enables women to focus on the everyday, the local and the pragmatic, and can be used strategically by women to develop community capacity and resources (Staeheli, 1996; Jupp, 2010).

Other feminist scholars show how community development programmes tend to rely on the work of women in partnering, joining up and reconciling difference (Larner and Craig, 2005). Newman (2012) explores the links between feminist activism and community politics. Many participants in her study had come to politics through an early involvement in community-based action. Some had been involved in anti-racist movements in India, the US, the Caribbean and the UK, and helped inflect the politics of community with a politics of race. Some, frustrated with the class-based politics of the left, had worked to build community capacities and resources in order to combat the poverty, poor housing and run-down estates that affected women's lives. Others created small-scale cooperative and neighbourhood projects that brought 'personal' issues of childcare, women's health or domestic violence into the public domain; yet others participated in community organising as a form of oppositional politics.

The gendering of community action underscores the dangers of viewing community as a cohesive entity, unmarked by social characteristics such as 'race', class, sexuality, disability, age and gender, and untouched by the political movements to which these gave rise. However, many community development initiatives have, as a more or less explicit aim, the promotion of 'social cohesion' in order to minimise possible tensions between different racialised groups. The community-mobilising and community-assets approaches outlined above frequently rely on churches, mosques and faith groups as a way of reaching out to untapped sources of social capital. But these in turn have been criticised for the suppression of potential political conflicts surrounding gender and sexuality in order to mobilise around supposedly 'common' issues and agendas. At the same time they implicitly look to women's labour as offering unrealised capacities and resources – the capacities of neighbourliness and care, the emotional labour of building networks and community links, and the capacity to link 'public' and 'personal' agendas.

In this section we have shown how community development is not a singular set of ideas and practices, but has been aligned to very different political projects. Such projects 'seek to remake the world (or part of it) in a different way: to give power to the people; to concentrate it in the hands of a deserving elite; to create social justice; or to spread market efficiencies' (Newman and Clarke, 2009: 22). In what follows, we seek to show how multiple projects are often uneasily combined and to highlight the tensions that are generated as would-be dominant forms have to cope with the insurgent power of other projects. The politics of community development cannot, we think, be contained by a reading of dominant ideologies and government projects. In the next two sections we explore this concern through the concepts of a politics of translation and a politics of articulation.

The politics of translation

The political projects we have outlined above do not exist in pure form: they are both mobile, moving from place to place as actors look elsewhere to seek new solutions, and are highly mediated as ideas are translated into social action. That is, they are subject to a *politics of translation*. This idea draws attention to

> the work of social actors – publics, professionals, front line workers, social entrepreneurs, managers, policy makers, civil society groups, voluntary organisations and many others – as mediators and translators of change. Processes of translation denote the creative and dynamic ways in which actors seek out, interpret and enrol ideas in new settings. Even where changes are experienced as imposed 'from above', actors have to find ways of translating them that are more or less congruent with 'local' contexts. (Newman and Clarke, 2009: 20)

Translation draws attention to human agency: the work of translators. And translators know that translation is not just a technical process; it involves interpretation, creativity and judgement (see, for example, Morris, 2006; Lendvai and Stubbs, 2007). As a consequence, translation, as we use it here, is fundamentally a *political* process (see Morris, 2006; Lendvai and Stubbs, 2007; Freeman, 2009; Clarke et al, forthcoming). We are not, then, merely concerned with how different linguistic meanings of community are translated, changed and modified in use; our focus is on how political projects move across boundaries, are modified, changed and (perhaps) become inscribed in practice. For example, we are interested in how a government agency might translate a community initiative (which they think offers a good model) into policy, and then how that policy is translated into action. Or we might point to how an activist visiting an exciting project overseas attempts to apply its principles back home; and what happens as they, and other actors, translate its practices and ideas to fit local circumstances. As states and NGOs have become more interested in community as a resource that can be mobilised, so the values and practices of community development have been translated into a succession of new state spaces: local government partnership bodies, neighbourhood management or community cohesion programmes. And workers have attempted to work 'in and against' the state, translating between different rationalities and purposes.

This view of translation as a political practice is important in at least three respects. First, it suggests the difficulty of working with concepts of discourse or ideology without paying empirical attention to how ideas are deployed and enacted by particular actors in specific contexts. This includes the drawing down of mainstream or governmental discourses and their deployment by community actors to legitimate strategies in local struggles. For example, when actors are seeking to 'represent' the views of a particular community to those in power – to secure funding, recognition or some form of policy shift – they may well recast the views of that community in the language of the powerful – the language of active citizenship, community cohesion, the 'Big Society', or economic development. Some things, of course, may be 'lost in translation' if community actors succeed in securing their goals, and the workers themselves may be vulnerable to cooption, learning the language of power too well – but they play crucial roles in mediating between the powerful and powerless.

Second, the idea of translation shows how ideas move – across cultural, linguistic and national boundaries – and draws attention to the agents and agencies who enable ideas to move from one setting to another. Many of those returning from newly independent countries in Africa, Asia and the Caribbean helped shape community development practices in their 'home' countries in the post-war years. The Latin American community development ethos of Paulo Freire inspired the beliefs and practices of many community development workers in the UK in the 1970s and beyond. One of the participants cited in Newman (2012) recounts how she had herself been inspired by the work of Freirean projects in a visit to Latin America, and later in her life, when working for a time in a government department anxious to promote community participation, had brokered meetings between senior civil servants (considered rather dour and unimaginative) and more radical theorists and practitioners. Freirean ideas of participation as radical pedagogy subsequently informed recommendations of 'best practice' in a handbook promoted by the UK civil service, but fared badly in their subsequent translation into the bureaucratic practices of local government and other agencies keen to foster managed forms of public participation.

In a different example, Jane Wills (2012) traces how models of community organising in the US, based on the ideas of Saul Alinsky, have been taken up in the UK, notably in the broad-based alliance London Citizens and subsequently in a national movement, Citizens UK. These have been remarkably successful in securing political concessions from government and local government, notably in the Living Wage campaign. However, these approaches were subsequently taken up and translated again by the Coalition government of 2010–15, which promoted the idea of a Big Society, by officially trained and appointed 'community mobilisers'. This typifies the ambiguous position of community in governmental approaches: both in mobilising communities to develop the resources and capacities for self-government, and as integral to initiatives to shrink the state and cut public services.

Third, notions of translation challenge rational-linear notions of policy making in which policy is viewed as separate from implementation. The idea of translation requires us to consider how policy is multiply reinterpreted and enacted in specific settings as it moves from national to local governments, from senior to front-line managers, from clients to contractors and so on. Such policy travels are often well illuminated by ethnographic studies, for example a study of neighbourhood and community development workers in local governance organisations in Salford in the UK (Durose, 2011). This traced how such workers interpreted and translated neighbourhood policies of the middle and late 1990s. Durose showed how government policies on neighbourhood work in that period opened up new spaces for front-line workers, and how the loose boundaries of such spaces created considerable space for innovation – what Durose, following Leadbeater and Goss (1998), termed 'civic entrepreneurship'. This, she argued, offered a more expansive and community-focused narrative of front-line work in local governance. Rather than simply 'interpreting' policy through the use of discretion, Durose (2011) sees the concept of the civic entrepreneur as offering a more dynamic sense of social and political agency. The research traced the roles of such workers in 'reaching out' to marginalised groups, in 'enabling' such groups to take action by building civic capacity, and in 'fixing' community problems. The latter in particular offers a classic example of translation, showing how front-line workers drew on government objectives and rules in ways that helped communities to seize opportunities and address their own priorities. A follow-up study (Durose, forthcoming) showed how those same workers had moved to translating 'austerity'. The cuts, downsizing and job losses that had taken place had, it was felt, undermined the conditions that had facilitated civic entrepreneurialism. Yet the workers she interviewed continued to act as brokers between austerity policies and local action: '[the community] rely on us really as almost a translator to explain to them what the [policy] changes are ... But then in the same token, we have to be able to translate what the community are telling us are their needs and priorities' (cited in Durose, forthcoming: 14).

Translation was something more than facilitating understanding and interpreting messages: it concerned the creative adaptation of policies and the stitching together of resources from multiple small pots in order to pursue what the workers felt were the most significant priorities. Austerity had dire consequences for the community development ethos, with interviewees reporting that rather than pursuing such an ethos they saw their role, in part, as supporting organisations to ensure they could survive financially in the market economy of public services. We can trace, in the extracts from interviews, a sense of strain between the workers' own continued commitments to community development and the actions they took to defend groups from the consequences of cuts in funding and new regimes of commissioning. In the following section, we suggest how our concern with the politics of translation leads to the politics of articulation.

The politics of articulation

Notions of community – and of development – retain their power not only because they speak to forms of popular common sense, but also because they 'connect vernacular discourses with governmental ones; political discourses with academic ones; emotional discourses with analytical ones; and nostalgic discourses with ones in which futures are imagined and anticipated' (Clarke, 2014: 54). This 'connective' work involves a politics of articulation in which notions of 'community' and 'development' are recruited to, and positioned in, different chains of meaning. It is through processes of articulation with other concepts that they come to take on new associations. Community, for instance, becomes articulated as community activism, community work, community assets, the 'community and voluntary sector', community as an element of the 'big society', community cohesion, community safety and so on. And development may signify the development of people, of places, of assets, of capacities, of economies and more. As a result, community development can be – and is – articulated into very different political projects. The processes of articulation we are concerned with here are not just about the translation of words and concepts, but the alignment of different and often antagonistic political projects. So we want to try to tease out attempted closures around dominant political-cultural projects, but also to show how these are not necessarily successful – dominant projects can be inflected and borrowed for other purposes.

What is sometimes termed the 'governmentalisation' of community signifies an uneasy articulation between government strategies and policies on the one hand, and, on the other, community as an 'authentic' space somehow beyond politics, associated with the personal, familial and relational dynamics of everyday life, or perhaps as a space of radical mobilisations that threaten the social fabric:

> What distinguishes the contemporary spaces of community [is that they] have been objectified by positive knowledges, subject to truth claims by expertise and hence can become the object of political technologies for governing through community. And these political technologies involve the constitution of new forms of authority of this new space of natural associations, and the instrumentalisation of new forces in the government of conduct. (Rose, 1999: 188–9)

From this perspective the emphasis on community engagement in many government programmes can be viewed as a way of tutoring citizens through forms of participative governing, rendering potentially unruly populations compliant through the production of new forms of self-governing subjects. For example Craig et al (2011) note how the liberatory education goals of Freire have been translated, in much of the global north, into forms of education designed to enhance employability. The slips and slides towards communitarian politics, the recasting of governance regimes to favour 'faith' communities, and the privileging of the 'local' community as the site of depoliticised forms of participative governance all make it difficult to imagine community as an autonomous space of political agency and antagonism. Rather, they show how deeply imbricated community activism and governmental projects and programmes have been, not only in the UK and some other European nations, but also in the development projects promulgated by the Word Bank, international NGOs and other agencies.

This has particular implications for community development workers, caught between competing logics and subject to new forms of discipline that challenge their capacity to engage in radical or transformative projects. However, this is not just a case of the imposition of new disciplinary logics that constrain community workers or indeed reshape their values and goals. What is at stake is the cooption and translation of the language and practice of community work by government programmes. Radical pedagogy becomes translated into bureaucratic programmes of public participation, replete with action plans, targets and evaluation mechanisms (Stewart, 2013). The empowerment of marginalised groups becomes translated as social cohesion programmes that tend to stigmatise those who fail to be properly assimilated. The result, Bunyan (2010: 125) argues, is a 'colonising by other professions of its language and practice, [and] the hollowing out of concepts such as "partnership" and "empowerment"' that have led to erosion of much of the radical edge and vitality of community development activity'.

These strategies of rule have been widely criticised (Rose, 1999; Newman and Clarke, 2009: chapter 3; Cruikshank, 1999). Less visible are questions of ambiguity and tension within and between a multiplicity of different governmentalities, rather than a singular form of rule. General narratives of incorporation and cooption, we suggest, are both politically immobilising and theoretically problematic. Activist commitments are not necessarily eroded: as Larner and Craig report in their work on partnerships in New Zealand: 'This gaining of professional and technical expertise was complemented by hearty political engagement, powerfully motivated by anger over the impact of neoliberalism' (Larner and Craig, 2005: 409).

This continued capacity for anger and engagement is often sidelined or ignored in the literature on managerialisation and professionalisation, where the politics of community development tends to be viewed through binary logics: community as authentic space/governmentalised space, invited space/popular space, professional/political, 'elsewheres' such as Latin America and 'here'. But more than two elements may be at stake in any one programme. In her study of gender and development programmes in India, Sharma points to four empowerment frames, which 'stem from different ideological perspectives and arose out of diverse spatial locations and historical moments' (Sharma, 2008: 22). In the Indian context these included a feminist strategy to engender social transformation; a Freirean liberatory struggle against oppression; a Gandhian conception of moral self-rule; and a neoliberal project that fosters individualising models of market empowerment in order to solve poverty and reduce big government. The articulation of these frames, she argues, serves to give neoliberalism, and the World Bank itself, a 'social and ethical spin' (2008: 20). But they diverged in terms of the social subjects and social relations they wished to create and the kind of society they sought to establish: 'Even as development attempts to create and regulate disciplined individuals and collective bodies, it also breeds subversive tactics and unruly subjects who protest their subjectification and subjection, who test the state and unbound it from presumed limits, and who resignify development' (2008: xxxv).

The value of Sharma's work is that, by drawing attention to four different ideological projects, she helps challenge the 'in or against' duality of activist politics and governmental power. In the context of the UK, we might point to forms of community activism inspired by Freirean notions of empowerment; to critiques of professional power and the shift, within many professions, towards notions of participation and co-production; to the movements demanding greater devolution and local control; to feminist practices of cooperative and collaborative working; to democratic movements advocating more associational or deliberative forms of engagement; and to communitarian ideas of interdependence and reciprocity. Each has offered ideas and resources that have been drawn on by regressive governmental programmes.

The multiplicity of different ideologies and projects condensed in governmental programmes of community development also opens up spaces of contradiction and contestation. Newman's study (2012) shows how participants have 'worked the borders' between activist commitments (inspired by both feminism and community politics) and governmental projects and programmes. By being drawn in to such programmes they may have become responsibilised for delivering governmental agendas and may have developed professional skill bases that distanced them from those they sought to represent or mobilise. But they did not thereby necessarily become depoliticised: the women participating in the study all spoke of continued activism and all carried strong political identities. They continued to look to what they often term the 'grassroots' for inspiration. The interviews indicated not only that radicalism was alive and well, but also that governmental programmes could offer resources and spaces of agency that could be used for alternative political projects; and that government can itself be challenged by new models of community organising. Neither governmental projects nor activist commitments are unchanging; each draws on, borrows and adapts to the other, and each is configured through wider social and political transformations.

Conclusion

In hard times, it is always tempting to look back to more expansive, more progressive or more highly politicised moments. However, we agree with Craig et al (2011: 7) when they argue that:

> There has never been a 'golden age' of community development ... It is perhaps better to see community development as an 'embodied argument', a continuing search for new forms of social and political expression, particularly at the 'grassroots' level (within a participatory paradigm) in the light of new forms of social and political control.

In the spirit of this continuing 'embodied argument', we have tried to offer a way of thinking about community development that resists simplifying distinctions – whether these are the contrast between a dire present and a more radical past; or between an independent and radicalising project of community development and the depoliticising cooption of the idea by governments and other centres of power. Instead, we have tried to use attention to the politics of translation and the politics of articulation as a way of making visible the shifting and contested alignments of community and development in fields of politics and power. Such an approach refuses the excesses of optimism and pessimism, claiming instead that community development is always contested by multiple projects, always draws on diverse political, social and cultural resources, and is always being reworked into different relationships to power and inequality. Such an approach is attentive to the spaces and conditions of political possibility (against pessimistic accounts) but is equally alert to the ever present dangers of the romance of community, the dominant definitions of development and the depoliticisation of community as a site of struggle.

References
Amit, V. and Rapport, N. (2002) *The trouble with community*, London: Pluto Press.
Brown, W. (2005) *Edgework: Critical essays on knowledge and politics*, Princeton, NJ: Princeton University Press.
Bunyan, P. (2010) 'Broad-based organizing in the UK: reasserting the centrality of political activity in community development', *Community Development Journal*, 45(1): 111–27.
Clarke, J. (2014) 'Community', in D. Nonini (ed), *The Blackwell companion to urban anthropology*, Oxford: Blackwell Publishers, 46–64.

Clarke, J., Bainton, D., Lendvai, N. and Stubbs, P. (forthcoming) *Making policy move: Towards a politics of translation and assemblage*, Bristol: Policy Press.

Cohen, A. (1987) *Symbolic construction of community*, London: Taylor and Francis.

Craig, G. (1989) 'Community work and the state', *Community Development Journal* 24(1): 1–19.

Craig, G., Mayo, M., Popple, K., Shaw, M. and Taylor, M. (eds) (2011) *The community development reader*, Bristol: Policy Press.

Creed, G. (ed) (2006) *The seductions of community*, Santa Fe, NM: School of American Research Press.

Cruikshank, B. (1999) *The will to empower*, Ithaca, NY: Cornell University Press.

Durose, C. (2011) 'Revisiting Lipsky: front line work in UK local governance', *Political Studies*, 59(4): 978–95.

Durose, C. (forthcoming) 'Neighbourhood working in austerity: where now for civic entrepreneurialism in front line work with local communities?' *Political Studies*, in press.

Escobar, A. (1995) *Encountering development*, Princeton, NJ: Princeton University Press.

Ferguson, J. (1994) *The Anti-politics machine: 'Development', depoliticization, and bureaucratic power in Lesotho*, Minneapolis, MN: University of Minnesota Press.

Freeman, R. (2009) 'What is translation?', *Evidence and Policy* 5(4): 429–47.

Freire, P. (1970) *Pedagogy of the oppressed*, New York, NY: Continuum.

Jamoul, L. and Wills, J. (2008) 'Faith in politics', *Urban Studies* 45(10): 2035–56.

Joseph, M. (2002) *Against the romance of community*, Minneapolis, MN: University of Minnesota Press.

Jupp, E. (2010) 'Private and public on the housing estate: small community groups, activism and local officials', in N. Mahony, J. Newman and C. Barnett (eds) *Rethinking the public*, Bristol: Policy Press 75–90.

Larner, W. and Craig, D. (2005) 'After neo-liberalism? Community activism and local partnership in Aotearoa New Zealand', *Antipode*, 37(3): 420–4.

Leadbeater, C. and Goss, S. (1998) *Civic entrepreneurship*, London: DEMOS.

Lendvai, N. and Stubbs, P. (2007) 'Policies as translation: situating transnational social policies', in S. Hodgson and Z. Irving (eds) *Policy reconsidered: Meanings, politics and practices*, Bristol: Policy Press 173–90.

Li, T. (2007a) 'Practices of assemblage and community forest management', *Economy and Society*, 36(2): 263–93.

Li, T. (2007b) *The will to improve*, Durham, NC: Duke University Press.

Minkler, M. (1997) *Community organizing and community building for health*, New Brunswick, NJ: Rutgers University Press.

Mooney, G. and Neal, S. (eds) (2009) *Community: Welfare, crime and society*, Maidenhead: Open University Press.

Morris, M. (2006) *Identity anecdotes: Translation and media culture*, London: Sage Publications.

Newman, J. (2012) *Working the spaces of power: Activism, neoliberalism and gendered labour*, London: Bloomsbury.

Newman, J. and Clarke, J. (2009) *Publics, politics and power: Remaking the public in public services*, London: Sage Publications.

Pandey, G. (2005) *The construction of communalism in North India* (2nd edn), Oxford: Oxford University Press.

Pandey, G. (2006) 'The politics of community: some notes from India', in G. Creed (ed), *The seductions of community*, Santa Fe, NM: School of American Research Press 255–78.

Rose, N. (1999) *Powers of freedom: Reframing political thought*, Cambridge: Cambridge University Press.

Rutter, M. and Madge, N. (1976) *Cycles of disadvantage: A review of research*, London: Heinemann.

Scott, D. (2004) *Conscripts of modernity: The tragedy of colonial enlightenment*, Durham, NC: Duke University Press.

Sharma, A. (2008) *Logics of empowerment: Development, gender and governance in neoliberal India*, Minneapolis, MN: University of Minnesota Press.

Smock, K. (2004) *Democracy in action: Community action and urban change*, New York, NY: Columbia University Press.

Staeheli, L. (1996) 'Publicity, privacy and women's political action', *Environment and Planning D: Society and Space*, 14(5): 601–19.

Stewart, E. (2013) 'What is the point of citizen participation in health-care?' *Journal of Health Services Research and Policy*, 18(2): 124–6.

Williams, R. (1976/1986) *Keywords*, London: Fontana.

Wills, J. (2012) 'The geography of community and political organization in London today', *Political Geography*, 31(2): 114–26.

THREE

Changing community development roles: the challenges of a globalising world

Sue Kenny

Introduction

In its broadest sense, community development practice can be understood as a way of empowering people in disadvantaged communities to act together for the purpose of influencing and exerting greater control over decisions that affect their lives (Craig, 1998: 15; Taylor, 2003: 3; Mayo, 2005: 101; Ife, 2010: 67; Gilchrist and Taylor, 2011: 3; Kenny, 2011: 8). Given this definition, it may appear that the roles expected of those who practise community development are relatively straightforward. They involve agents intervening in disadvantaged communities to assist members to identify their needs, goals and assets and to help in developing the knowledge, skills, confidence and resources to give them more control over their future. However, approaches to community development vary considerably. For example, roles differ according to whether community development is seen primarily as a process aimed at improving community welfare, as an activist endeavour or as a professional practice (although of course they overlap in particular contexts and settings). In any case, as socio-political contexts change, so do the policy and theoretical frameworks which set out the rationales for community development intervention.

This chapter begins by illustrating how community development roles can vary, through a discussion of potential distinctions between 'facilitation' and 'leadership' practices, and between 'external' practitioners and 'organic' practitioners. The chapter proceeds to a consideration of some of the complexities arising from different understandings of 'empowering communities', drawing on visions of community as object, subject and site of community development. While community development has always been a complex and contested field (Craig, 2007; Mayo, 2008: 13), today there are some quite distinct contexts and socio-political considerations, which pose new challenges for practice. Thus, the second part of the chapter explores ways in which emerging conditions and new ways of thinking, particularly those ideas associated with the concept of cosmopolitanism, might open up new possibilities for reframing significant aspects of community development practice, and reconfiguring community development roles.

Negotiating tensions between facilitation and leadership roles

Traditionally, a core theme in community development revolves around its commitment to recognising the agency and political legitimacy of disadvantaged and marginalised communities. This theme has gained succour from a variety of intellectual and political sources, including social movement theory (Touraine, 1981; Melucci, 1989) and feminism (Dominelli, 1995; Lister, 1997; Mayo, 1977), and also from observations of effective community self-organisation in many local social and political campaigns over the past four decades, around such issues as environmental degradation and women's rights.

Ife (2010: 67) describes community development as an approach to communities based on respecting and validating the knowledge and expertise in the community itself. Similarly, and as a critique of the focus in mainstream social policy on 'a community's needs, deficiencies and problems', Kretzmann and McKnight (1993: 1) argue for an approach based on commitment to discovering 'a community's capacities and assets'. For Craig (1998: 15), respecting the integrity of disadvantaged communities means that the collective needs and aspirations of community members should be placed 'at the front rather than at the end of political debate'. A corollary of this concern with upholding the wisdom, integrity, capacities and assets existing in a community is an added emphasis on facilitating roles. For example, community development practitioners will typically facilitate the identification of community needs and assets as perceived by a community. They will be accountable to the community and work to the community's agenda and terms of reference. Another approach, however, focuses on the need for practitioners to take more directive leadership roles, which might include the identification and clarification of community needs and the best way of fulfilling these.

The notion of community development practice as a form of leadership can be traced back to the 1960s and 1970s, when community development emerged as a significant aspect of 'nation building' in British colonies (Popple, 2008). This was in the context of the erosion of Western empires during the first half of the 20th century and attempts by colonial regimes to maintain power and influence during processes of decolonisation (Escobar, 1995; Mayo, 2008: 19). Yet development agendas during this period consisted of both genuine efforts to support the self-determination of post-colonial societies (Batten, 1957, 1974) and strategic endeavours to maintain Western power via the proxy of international development experts (Rist, 2008). Consideration of recent international development interventions, such as post-disaster reconstruction (Kenny, 2010), indicates a continuing story of tensions between facilitation and leadership, and being caught up in the efforts of Western countries to construct development roles to suit their own agendas (Nederveen Pieterse, 2001: 28).

Within the 'global North', there has also been a tradition of community development practitioners being identified as leaders with a responsibility to mobilise, inform and organise communities. This approach is, in part, a legacy of the structuralist critique advanced in the 1970s by socialist-leaning practitioners who saw their central role as raising the political consciousness of the working class (Corrigan and Leonard, 1978: 88). In this context, the community development role was conceived as more akin to activist leadership, and usually undertaken by men. However, this particular focus on leadership was not left unchallenged. Feminist analyses, in particular, pointed to the patriarchal nature of such leadership and the need to understand the gendered nature of power relationships (Dominelli, 1995).

By the 1980s there was interest in community development as leadership from an alternative quarter, in which community development practice was argued to be a legitimate profession (Waddington, 1979). The professionalisation trajectory has been primarily based on the idea that community development practice requires particular skills and expert knowledge that are not necessarily found in communities. One prevailing version, for example, holds that formal training and credentials are required for 'effective' community development practice and, since the 1980s, there have been continual and often uneasy forays into issues associated with professionalism. These highlight the tensions between those who advocate for professionalisation of community development, and those who argue that members of communities themselves are best placed to undertake community leadership (sometimes called organic practitioners). In the latter camp are those who argue that bringing in a professional 'external' community development practitioner can actually further disempower community members. For example, when leadership roles involve speaking *for* a community, or setting agendas and identifying needs as either external experts, or from a partisanship position within a community (Gilchrist and Taylor, 2011: 123), this can act to undermine community self-determination.

By contrast, in the US, Saul Alinsky's (1972) influential approach focused specifically on the role of external leaders in organising communities to mobilise, confront and resist powerful elites. Since the 1970s, both the conservative community economic development projects, such as the Community Development Corporations and the Alinskyite community organising approach, have emphasised the positive roles of external leaders, professionals or activists, albeit each tradition offering different rationales (De Filippis, 2007; Stall and Stoecker, 2007). In Latin America, even the 'critical pedagogy' of Freire (1972), while based on a critique of teaching as a domesticating process and emphasising the dialogical relationship between teacher and student, nonetheless also assumes the intervention of an external practitioner to reframe the experiences of powerless people in disadvantaged communities. It is apparent, therefore, that the politics of leadership, as reflected in community development practice and processes, relates to issues of democracy and participation and that this politics may transcend binary divisions between left and right or between reformist and transformative agendas.

A more recent dimension to the question of leadership and its optimal form in community development is evident in the interest in social enterprise, which has brought with it a focus on entrepreneurial practice (Bertotti et al, 2012; Eversole et al, 2013). When constructed as an entrepreneurial activity, roles might include the identification of socially useful projects, the fostering of initiative and innovation, and the establishment of self-sustaining community projects. However, while leadership of social enterprise activities can of course incorporate sensitivity to community views, a full embrace of enterprise culture can also act to reinforce the idea of individual leadership without the 'hindrances' of community interference (Hoogendoorn et al, 2007: 121).

One response to debates about facilitation and leadership roles, and about the 'organic' versus the 'external' practitioner, is to point to the ambiguities in all these terms. To begin with, community development roles tend to involve both leadership and facilitation. For example, Kretzmann and McKnight (1993: 8) assume the need for guidance to assist communities to identify assets, but this guide is intended to be facilitative – and might function as no more than a handbook to be used by community members themselves as they see fit, for their own self-directed development. Moreover, in everyday practice we can distinguish between different leadership styles, including leaders as consultants, partners or activists (Fletcher, 1988); hierarchically based leaders; team-based leaders; or transformative leadership 'which enables people to engage reality with new eyes' (Kirk and Shutte, 2004: 238). Similarly, the distinction between 'external' and 'internal' is not clear cut. So-called 'external' community development practitioners often move into the communities in which they are working and become 'part of' the community, while at the same time using their expertise to identify key contacts and resources which may benefit that community.

Notwithstanding such ambiguities, the ways in which community development practitioners situate themselves in relation to the community they are working with and for is important, and affects the roles they undertake. Perhaps, therefore, we need to be thinking about ways to move beyond dichotomous frameworks and binary constructions which do not express the diversity of practice. The final part of the chapter looks at how we might take a more nuanced approach to community development roles.

The complexities of 'empowering communities'

While community empowerment is supposedly at the heart of community development, the meanings of the terms 'empowering' and 'community' clearly raise significant questions. A detailed discussion is beyond the scope of this chapter, but we can perhaps explore the concepts sufficiently to illustrate how they might affect the ways in which community development is framed and practised.

In the preceding section it was pointed out that one, not uncommon, understanding of a community development practitioner is as an external leader. This construction can lead to 'the community' being viewed primarily as the 'object' of intervention, rather than as active subjects and agents of change. One of the attractions of a normative construction of community, however, lies in a second understanding of community, in which community members have the potential to be the agents of change themselves by challenging individualism, self-interest and competition, and providing alternative models of social and political life. The Transition Towns movement, for example, may offer one such model (Walker et al, 2007), based as it is on a vision of communities as self-sufficient entities organised around a low-energy, minimally polluting future (Connors and McDonald, 2011). Here, communities conceive of themselves as the agents of change. This imagery of community as organic and active, rather than as a contrived artifice of government strategy, makes for community development roles that begin by recognising the legitimacy and authenticity of the views and concerns of local communities.

The normative construction of community has perhaps found its strongest expression in the communitarian tradition, whereby inclusiveness and solidarity offer refuge from increasingly fragmented lives (Etzioni, 1995). As Bauman (2001 : 1–2) critically observes, such a normatively constructed notion of community is like a 'warm and cosy' home. Indeed, many commentators have emphasised the problematic nature of some established community discourses and practices, such as the way in which the inclusionary intent of community membership can also involve exclusionary politics. Furthermore, the ideological recycling of 'community' in government policy can signal the ways in which community-based practices can serve to gloss over inequalities experienced at community level (Repo, 1977; Bryson and Mowbray, 1981; Bauman, 2001; Shaw, 2008). Bauman (2001: 3), rehearsing earlier analyses of the positive sheen given to community (for example Williams, 1976), argues that the normative conception expresses a yearning for a comforting world of order and certainty: he contends that this world is a 'paradise lost' or 'still hoped for', but not available to us. From this perspective, we can no longer afford to seek shelter from the threats, uncertainties and risks of contemporary life in an idealised world of community.

Such critiques draw attention to the need to clarify the concrete reality of real communities. Descriptively, the term 'community' generally refers to groups and social relations based on some form of recognised commonality such as geographical location, class position, demography or specific common interest. The default position, however, is to define community spatially, identifying it with local neighbourhoods, for example. In each of these constructions, distinct community identities and clear community boundaries are assumed to exist. Hence, the role of community development practitioners is to work with people sharing a common identity and within bounded communities, by undertaking such tasks as identifying needs and assets, developing strategies for change and organising community events. But delineating the empirical object of community and its boundaries brings with it another set of problems, which are discussed in the final part of the chapter.

Like the concept of community, 'empowerment' is also normatively charged. In particular, the task of empowering communities seems to be full of transformational promise. A key question facing community development practitioners, therefore, (whether they identify as part of a community or as external professionals) is the efficacy of working at the community level for transformational change, particularly when community effort is conflated with localist effort. In other words, to what extent can the empowerment of disadvantaged communities be achieved through policies for local social amelioration, or should community development focus on more ambitious structural change that is explicitly transformative? One response is that, because the root causes of disadvantage lie in the deep structures and ideologies prevailing in a society, then it is only by challenging and changing structures and ideologies that power relations can be transformed. An alternative view is that large-scale structural change is largely unattainable and small interventions do matter. Indeed, the literature in this field is full of examples of the ways in which people's lives are affected positively by small projects contributing to incremental change: co-operative ventures that challenge local multinational retailers, or participatory forms of decision making to challenge top-down government policies. The point is that problem definition and practice roles are logically connected, either explicitly or implicitly.

While there is considerable theoretical literature concerned with the overall aims of community development, the purpose of the discussion here is to note the implications of different ways of framing the aims of community development for the construction of community development roles. For example, as Gilchrist and Taylor (2011: 22) point out, if social amelioration within the existing system is taken as the goal of community development, then it will be framed as an activity oriented to making 'existing structures work more smoothly'. If community development is framed as an intervention that brings about small but incremental change, then the roles of community development practitioners are more likely to focus on capacity building, advocacy, research and negotiation. Conversely, if the framing of community development prioritises large-scale transformation based on the redistribution of power through structural change, then dealing with the conflicts resulting from challenges to existing power structures becomes part of the community development repertoire. That is, practitioners might identify alliances and activities that can mobilise communities to undertake acts of protest and resistance, with the aim of dislodging the power of existing structures, systems and elites. Of course the different roles can overlap, and indeed, roles which at face value seem to be ameliorative can develop into far-reaching resistance to government policy.

Regardless of which roles prevail, there is a view that the goal of empowerment, whether expressed as small 'victories', or larger confrontations with power structures, has been challenged in powerful ways over the past few decades. In the Anglo world in particular, funded community development projects, particularly those linked to welfare delivery, have been required to operate through market rationales, leading to a reframing of community development in significant ways. In some cases, community development projects have been contracted out to groups on the basis of competitive tender. In this contract culture, community development practitioners are often compelled to prioritise managerial capabilities, risk management strategies and financially efficient organisation over more transformative purposes.

Within managerial frameworks, the dominant preoccupation with top-down organisational efficiency and performance management has placed practitioners in particularly difficult and compromising positions, opening the way to new forms of cooption whereby community activities and agendas are constructed around state and business needs, with little or no reference to the views or aspirations of communities. This has, arguably, resulted in the (further) depoliticisation of community development (Gaynor, 2011). For example, in the 'global South', community development projects funded by international agencies have increasingly been required to embrace new narrowly focused accountability regimes. Here, community development roles are often constructed around technical procedures involving evaluation, audit and reporting systems designed to suit the requirements of funding bodies, rather than facilitating community initiatives. As a consequence of these processes, the goal of 'empowering communities to control their own future' is continually undermined by the wider imperative to ensure compliance (Mowbray, 2004). Such forms of cooption can be usefully explored through governmentality theory. Governmentality describes those processes whereby society is rendered 'governable terrain' by subtle techniques and forms of knowledge, through which members of a community unknowingly practise self-management (Rose, 1999). Its relevance to community development lies in the way in which it can help to explain why communities are invariably hailed as active self-determining subjects, while, in reality, they are often unwitting objects of state policy.

New contexts, new insights?

Reflecting on such processes helps us to understand the difficulties of considering community development practitioners, in any decisive sense, as agents of transformational change. In fact Miller (2004: 148) observes that community development is more often than not constructed around what he calls 'tragic, rather than heroic feats', involving struggles against overwhelming forces. From this perspective, the 'eternal optimism' of community development practitioners is continually undermined by the daily grind of operating in communities which are invariably in social and economic decline. Given the urgency of responding to need in such communities, it may be tempting to focus on those roles oriented to 'social rescue' rather than social transformation (Miller, 2004: 149). Operating within frameworks of tragedy, heroism and social rescue, however, can leave practitioners continually confronted with disillusionment and burn-out. It is the argument of this chapter that there are possible alternatives to these established ways of framing community development. This section, therefore, highlights particular frameworks that draw attention to changing socio-political conditions, and which might offer ways of reframing community development practice and rethinking community development roles.

We begin with the argument that past certainties are under challenge in new ways. Bauman (2000) uses the term 'liquid modernity' to describe how our lives today are being continually reshaped. For example, new technologies, particularly new global information and communication technologies, have transformed the ways in which we access information and communicate with each other. Not only are our lives being continually reshaped, but the communities in which we live and work are likewise being recast. From the perspective of liquid modernity, communities are loose and fluid: as populations become increasingly mobile, more and more of them are made up of people with different, multifaceted and shifting identities and loyalties, thereby challenging the traditional idea of community as a clearly defined place of belonging and a source of stable solidarity.

Now, while the metaphor of liquidity reinforces the ubiquity of change, its use is not unproblematic. For example, in arguing that Bauman overstates the case for liquid modernity, Elliott (2009: 302) reminds us that there are also many enduring structural elements of existence, including millions of people trapped in cycles of poverty and war. At the same time, the nation-based realms of authority are being confronted by new forms of transnational activity and political engagement. In turn, these emerging forms of transnational and transcultural activity are reshaping established relationships and identities, further problematising traditional ways of framing community relations and boundaries. As Gaventa and Tandon (2010: 3–4) remark, such new political configurations can be understood as the outcome of changing patterns of global governance, involving different layers, arenas and jurisdictions. Sometimes these configurations open up opportunities for diverse visions, and allegiances, facilitated by global networks; at other times global influences affect forms and prospects for national and local engagement by adding layers of power which limit possibilities for local action.

Furthermore, the fluid and multifaceted nature of communities prompts discussion of what kinds of solidarity are now possible. One framework which offers the potential for reconstructing solidarity in this context is based on the concept of cosmopolitanism. The term cosmopolitanism is, like community development itself, a contested idea which variously describes: a quality of experience; a political project; a form of relationship; a set of competencies; a socio-political condition (Vertovec and Cohen, 2002; Beck, 2006; Delanty, 2006; Fine, 2007). A starting point for all these descriptions, however, is acknowledgement of the global interconnections and interdependencies between human beings which provide key foundations for human solidarity. For Beck (2006: 3–7) the cosmopolitan outlook involves what he calls the '*melange* principle', in which all aspects of life interpenetrate, interconnect and intermingle. Fine (2007: x) argues that cosmopolitanism 'has to do with the idea that human beings can belong anywhere, humanity has shared predicaments and we find our community with others in exploring how these predicaments are faced in common'. In other words, within a cosmopolitan framework, shared humanity does not necessarily mean denial of difference. Rather, recognition of our commonality, interconnections and diversity is central to a cosmopolitan outlook.

Like the concept of liquid modernity, cosmopolitanism is not without criticism. For example, the *melange* principle tends to assume a cross-fertilising osmosis where all traditions have equal power. It can be blind to the reality of global dominance by certain economic and political forms and traditions, particularly those emanating from Western precepts. From the perspective of community development, there is also the problem of how enjoinders to acknowledge human interdependencies and mutuality might serve to gloss over inequalities of resources and power.

Reframing community development?

This final section of the chapter identifies some of the ways in which community development theory and practice might be reframed through these ways of thinking about changing socio-political conditions. First, from the perspective of liquid modernity, community development practitioners are increasingly engaging with loose networks and solidarities, rather than with traditionally stable and homogeneous communities. So, while the concept of community might retain descriptive resonance, it may be better conceived as an elastic entity, shaped by changing membership and identities. In other words, communities form, change, disperse and re-form.

In a context where boundaries and identities are loose and shifting, the idea of fixed or polarised categories of facilitator and leader, community development practitioner and community becomes even more complex and problematic. For example, the binary distinctions between practitioner/community member and external/ internal worker are more permeable. When such distinctions dissolve, community development practice becomes an activity that can be undertaken by anyone who identifies as part of a particular community. Indeed in this scenario, all members of a particular community are potentially community development practitioners. In terms of democratising community development practice there is considerable appeal in such a reconceptualisation. However, such recasting would also undermine the construction of community development as a distinctive professional practice in two ways. First, and perhaps most importantly, it assumes that all community members have the skills, beliefs and dispositions to be effective practitioners, thus rendering redundant the view that community development requires specific sets of skills and experiences. Second, it challenges the idea of community development as a specialised and distinct job, enhanced by formal training.

What would a cosmopolitan framing of community development look like? As with liquid modernity, a cosmopolitan frame extends the object/subject of community development intervention beyond the bounded or local community. Rather than rejecting the notion of community development as a localist endeavour, it would stretch community development roles to include empowering activities in communities that are transnational and transcultural. In preceding discussions it is argued that community development actions, in communities of locality or other forms of commonality, do not alone have the power to challenge entrenched structures of inequality or the hegemony of dominant groups. Community development, constructed as a cosmopolitan project, working with and across spaces and diverse groups, potentially offers a more powerful collective force, and could open up paths to transformational change at both local and transnational levels.

Cosmopolitan endeavours, of course, can nudge community development into the domain of social movements. For practitioners, the extended scope of their roles would require expanding their repertoire in order to connect different local projects cross-nationally, and to begin organising for transnational mobilisation – for example through advocacy for refugees or exploited workers, or campaigns for debt relief and environmental justice. We are already seeing some of these roles being enacted by community development practitioners in a variety of contexts (Sites et al, 2007: 45). At the same time, the physical sites of community development are becoming more diverse. To the more traditional 'invited spaces', such as community halls, offices and shopfront premises provided by various organisations, can be added the 'claimed spaces' of streetscapes and the virtual spaces of internet-based mobilisation, advocacy and agitation. Such claimed spaces have included the physical landscapes for the activities of the World Social Forum and the virtual landscapes for online activism, such as Avaaz. Within a cosmopolitan framework, such expanded roles would become a central part of everyday community development activities.

Recognition of the interplay between commonality, interconnection and diversity has many implications for community development roles. For example, a major shift of emphasis from 'the community' would involve assistance in giving voice to diverse groups, and to the facilitation of discussion and debate between groups. In diverse cultural contexts, practitioners need to be able to move between cultures. A recent approach to cross-cultural communication draws on the idea of interculturalism, which offers a way of understanding how we can relate to each other in the context of diverse cultural encounters. Interculturalism foregrounds the need for recognition of diversity as an ongoing feature of society, while at the same time emphasising how human relations are based on concepts of interdependency and interconnectedness (Cantle, 2012). An intercultural approach involves curiosity and dialogue to establish areas of mutuality. It requires reciprocal respect, but it does not preclude drawing out contradictions and critical judgements of different cultural traditions, including one's own cultural background(s) (Turner, 2006: 144). Key roles for community development practitioners working interculturally would include networking across traditional boundaries and negotiating around conflict; facilitating new networks, organising new multi-ethnic activities and assisting in processes for deliberative democracy.

Now, while arguments for boundarylessness, interculturalism and transnationalism might open up new thinking about community development roles at one level, they leave us with further issues at another level. If dissolving boundaries simply means discursively airbrushing out class and gender categories, for example, it does nothing to eliminate the reality of power inequalities organised around such boundaries. From a community development standpoint, therefore, it is imperative that such inequalities are not ignored. One resolution may be to take a dualist perspective: acknowledging the power of categories and binary constructs to maintain inequalities, while also identifying and acting on elements of mutuality and solidarity. This self-critical, reflexive approach is now being practised in some indigenous programmes in Australia. For example, in reflecting on her engagement with indigenous Australians and the power of 'white privilege', Land (2015: 23) describes how she tries to navigate her own colonial complicities without taking a confessional or redemptive path. Taking a dualist perspective also suggests that acknowledegment of power differentials and the cosmopolitan principles of interdependence and interconnectedness are reconcilable.

It should be acknowledged that some view the idea of a cosmopolitan trajectory for community development as misplaced. Such a view holds that, like the elusive searches for community (Bauman, 2001) and global citizenship (Falk, 1994: 139), cosmopolitanism is no more than an aspiration. For example, citizenship, described as the rights and obligations of members of society (Marshall and Bottomore, 1992), is still largely state bounded. Indeed, the nation state remains central to the well-being of human beings, both in guaranteeing rights and perpetuating oppressive practices. Clearly, people's identities are shaped by their positions as members of societies, ethnic groups and local communities and through existing concepts of 'us' and 'the Other'. Our lives are so embedded in our experiences at an introverted local level, and our discourses are so permeated by essentialised categories such as Western and non-Western, that it is naive to believe that we can really think and practise as freestanding or unencumbered cosmopolitan actors. Certainly, cosmopolitan relations are severely constrained by existing social structures. The quest for relations of respect, trust and mutuality between groups is always, and everywhere, undermined by those persistent structural inequalities found in and between societies. Moreover, resourcing community development projects, particularly in the global North, has been largely dependent on the state, and nation states are rarely enthusiastic about funding transnational programmes unless such funding is clearly in their interests. Transnational cosmopolitan projects may therefore need to look to other sources of funding, such as social enterprises and international agencies.

At one level, then, it would seem that cosmopolitanism can be no more than a desired or limited add-on. Nonetheless, cosmopolitanism is an evolving concept, and there is substantial evidence of inexorable shifts in how people relate to each other as active citizens, and new ways in which they challenge power relations within local areas, across regions and transnationally. Community development roles are in any case being pushed in a cosmopolitan direction through, for example, involvement in global communications networks, joint projects of people who have met as local and regional volunteers, and through global protest movements, expressing what Beck (2006: 5) calls cosmopolitan empathy. In some ways then, the framing of community development as a cosmopolitan endeavour is already on us.

Conclusion

How should we frame the roles of community development practitioners in the second decade of the 21st century? This is especially important because it goes to the heart of the future of community development. As we have seen, at one level there is an argument that the survival of community development may be resolved by a dramatic bifurcation of community development roles, in which one path largely involves social amelioration programmes based around capacity building, social inclusion and welfare delivery, while the other path takes community development in the direction of a social movement. Another view is that, as a theory and practice constructed in the years following the Second World War, a period in which the dominance of Western economies and cultures largely prevailed, community development is losing its way. It continues to operate through confused concepts and binary divides which are inadequate for responding to contemporary challenges. Yet, rather than jettisoning the key precepts of community development or succumbing to arguments for the bifurcation of community development practice, the chapter concludes with a call for a sustained and open investigation of how the precepts of community development can be applied in a diverse, fluid and globalising world. One starting point for this investigation is cosmopolitanism, and would include consideration of ways in which community development practice might be framed as a cosmopolitan endeavour. Of course, community development has always been a contested and dynamic field, which should equip it for these new challenges and engagements in the 21st century.

References

Alinsky, S. (1972) *Rules for radicals*, New York, NY: Vintage.

Batten, T.R. (1957) *Communities and their development. An introductory study with special reference to the Tropics*, London: Oxford University Press.

Batten, T.R. (1974) 'The major issues and future direction of community development', *Community Development Journal*, 9(2): 96–103.

Bauman, Z. (2000) *Liquid modernity*, Cambridge: Policy Press.

Bauman, Z. (2001) *Community. Seeking safety in an insecure world*, Cambridge: Policy Press.

Beck, U. (2006), *Cosmopolitan vision*, Cambridge: Policy Press.

Bertotti, M., Harden, A., Renton, A. and Sheridan, K. (2012) 'The contribution of a social enterprise to the building of social capital in a disadvantaged urban area of London', *Community Development Journal*, 47(2): 168–83.

Bryson, L. and Mowbray, M. (1981) '"Community": the spray-on solution', *Australian Journal of Social Issues*, 16(4): 255–67.

Cantle, T. (2012) *Interculturalism: Era of cohesion and diversity*, Basingstoke: Palgrave Macmillan.

Connors, P. and McDonald, P. (2011) 'Transitioning communities: community, participation and the Transition Town movement', *Community Development Journal*, 46(4): 558–72.

Corrigan, P. and Leonard, P. (1978) *Social work practise under capitalism. A Marxist approach*, London: Macmillan.

Craig, G. (1998) 'Community in a global context', *Community Development Journal*, 33(1): 2–17.

Craig, G. (2007) 'Something old something new …', *Critical Social Policy*, 38(3): 335–59.

De Filippis, J. (2007) 'Community control and development: the long view' in J. De Filippis and S. Saegert (eds) *The Community Development Reader*, New York, NY: Routledge, 28–35.

Delanty, G. (2006) 'The cosmopolitan imagination: critical cosmopolitanism and social theory', *British Journal of Sociology*, 57(1): 25–47.

Dominelli L. (1995) 'Community: feminist principles and organising in community work', *Community Development Journal*, 30(2): 133–43.

Elliott, A. (2009) *Contemporary social theory. An introduction*, Abingdon: Routledge.

Escobar, A (1995) *Encountering development: The making and unmaking of the third world*, Princeton, NJ: Princeton University Press.

Etzioni, A. (1995) *The Spirit of Community*, London: Fontana.

Eversole, R., Barraket, J. and Luke, B. (2013) 'Social enterprises in rural community development', *Community Development Journal*, doi: 10.1093/cdj/bst030.

Falk, R. (1994) 'The making of global citizenship', in B. van Steenbergen (ed) *The condition of citizenship*, London: Sage, 127–40.

Fine, R. (2007) *Cosmopolitanism*, London and New York, NY: Routledge.

Fletcher, E. (1988) 'The change agent as a catalyst in community education: leadership styles and roles', *Community Development Journal*, 23(2): 107–9.

Freire, P. (1972) *Pedagogy of the oppressed*, Harmondsworth, Middlesex: Penguin.

Gaventa, J. and Tandon, R. (2010) 'Citizen engagements in a globalizing world' in J. Gaventa and R. Tandon (eds) *Globalizing citizens: New dynamics of inclusion and exclusion*, London: Zed Books, 3–30.

Gaynor, N. (2011) 'In-Active citizenship and the depoliticization of community development in Ireland', *Community Development Journal* 46(1): 27–41.

Gilchrist, A. and Taylor, M. (2011) *The short guide to community development*, Bristol: Policy Press.

Hoogendoorn, B., Pennings, E. and Thurik, R. (2007) 'Conceptual overview of what we know about social entrepreneurship', in J. De Filippis and S. Saegert (eds) *The community development reader*, New York, NY: Routledge, 117–23.

Ife, J. (2010) 'Capacity building and community development', in S. Kenny and M. Clarke (eds) *Challenging capacity building. Comparative perspectives*, Basingstoke: Palgrave Macmillan, 67–84.

Kenny, S. (2010) 'Reconstruction through participatory practice?', in M. Clarke, I. Fanany and S. Kenny (eds) *Post-disaster reconstruction. Lessons from Aceh*, London: Earthscan, 79–106.

Kenny, S. (2011) *Developing communities for the future*, 4th revised edn, South Melbourne: Cengage Learning.

Kirk, P. and Shutte, A. (2004) 'Community leadership development', *Community Development Journal*, 39(3): 234–51.

Kretzmann, J. and McKnight, J. (1993) *Building communities from the inside out: A path toward finding and mobilizing a community's assets*, Evanston, IL: Institute for Policy Research, Northwestern University.

Land, C. (2015) *Decolonizing solidarity: Dilemmas and directions for supporters of indigenous struggles*, London: Zed Books.

Lister, R. (1997) *Citizenship: Feminist perspectives*, Basingstoke: Macmillan.

Marshall, T.H. and Bottomore, T. (1992) *Citizenship and social class*, London: Pluto Press.

Mayo, M. *(ed)* (1977) *Women in the community. Community work 3*, London: Routledge.

Mayo, M. (2005) *Global citizens. Social movements and the challenge of globalisation*, London: Spokesman.

Mayo, M. (2008) 'Community development. Contestations, continuities and change', in G. Craig, K. Popple and M. Shaw (eds) *Community development in theory and practice. An international reader*, Nottingham: Spokesman, 13–27.

Melucci, A. (1989) *Nomads of the present: social movements and individual needs in contemporary society*, London: Hutchinson.

Miller, C. (2004) 'Community development as the pursuit of human rights: the new direction of travel? Community development, human rights and the grassroots', Conference Proceedings, Centre for Citizenship and Human Rights, Deakin University, Melbourne, 141–58.

Mowbray, M. (2004) 'The new communitarianism: building great communities or brigadoonery?', *Just Policy*, 32: 11–20.

Nederveen Pieterse, J. (2001) *Development theory, deconstructions/reconstructions*, London: Sage.

Popple, K. (2008) 'The first forty years: the history of the *Community Development Journal*', *Community Development Journal*, 43(1): 6–23.

Repo, M. (1977) 'The fallacy of community control', in J. Cowley, A. Kaye, M. Mayo and M. Thompson (eds) *Community or class struggle*, London: Stage 1.

Rist, G. (2008) *The history of development: From Western origins to global faith*, 3rd edn, London: Zed Books.

Rose, N. (1999) *Powers of freedom: Reframing political thought*, Cambridge: Cambridge University Press.

Shaw, M. (2008) 'Community development and the politics of community', *Community Development Journal*, 43(1): 24–36.

Sites, W., Chaskin, R. and Parks, V. (2007) 'Reframing community practice for the 21st century. Multiple traditions, multiple challenges', in J. De Filippis and S. Saegert (eds) *The community development reader*, New York, NY: Routledge, 38–48.

Stall, S. and Stoecker, R. (2007) 'Community organizing or organizing community? Gender and the crafts of empowerment', in J. De Filippis and S. Saegert (eds) *The community development reader*, New York, NY: Routledge, 241–48.

Taylor, M. (2003) *Public policy in the community*, Basingstoke: Palgrave Macmillan.

Touraine, A. (1981) *The voice and the eye: An analysis of social movements*, Cambridge: Cambridge University Press.

Turner, B.S. (2006) 'Classical sociology and cosmopolitanism: a critical defence of the social', *British Journal of Sociology*, 57(1): 133–51.

Vertovec, S. and Cohen, R. (2002) *Conceiving cosmopolitanism: Theory, context and practice*, Oxford: Oxford University Press.

Waddington, P. (1979) 'Looking ahead – community work into the 1980s', *Community Development Journal*, 14(3): 224–34.

Walker, G., Evans, B., Devine-Wright, P., Hunter, S. and Fay, H. (2007) 'Harnessing community energies: explaining community based localism in renewable energy policy in the UK', *Global Environmental Politics*, 7(2): 64–82.

Williams R. (1976) *Keywords: A vocabulary of culture and society.* London: Fontana.

FOUR

Community organising and political agency: changing community development subjects in India

Manish K. Jha

Introduction

The trajectory of community development has been a tumultuous one: a path defined by radical potentialities yet able to claim only limited success. Even during those phases when radical philosophies were less prominent in community development, it stood for relatively 'fair' and 'just' processes and outcomes. Arguably, we have witnessed a simultaneous expansion and constriction in our understandings of the transformative potential of 'community' over several decades, and this in turn necessitates a closer examination of the changing expectations and make-up of community development's subjects. This chapter highlights the evolution and maturation of community development in India. It attempts to explain how 'community' has been variously construed in India's processes of community development and how those constructions have been challenged, revised and improvised by practitioners and activists. The chapter thus emphasises that community development's subjects have shown a potential for transformation and agency. For example, subjects have questioned the idea of 'community development' itself and, through self- and collective organising, they have become more 'political'. This phenomenon is referred to here as 'community organising' (CO) and by that I mean organising and collectivising processes that redefine power relationships in society. In India, the conception of CO has evolved away from a model of community development that was critiqued as statist, and that mainly referred to government- and/or NGO-guided or facilitated development programmes. CO, on the other hand, has been regarded as far more progressive, with mobilisation and collectivisation generating strategies of contestation, along with the potential for collaboration with the state and its agencies.

The chapter analyses community development from the standpoint of its constituents, that is its subjects. By 'subject', I am referring to two contrasting situations: the first, where the 'subject' is seen as dissolving into a non-sovereign product of social and discursive construction, devoid of any stability, autonomy or unity of self; the second, where the 'subject' can be regarded as self-sufficient, enduring and sovereign, from which all consciousness and action springs. Since 'subject' implies both an actor and one who is acted on, this chapter traces movements from one situation to another. More specifically, it is interested in the processes that have led to the emergence of 'political subjects' who demonstrate a capacity to influence their lives and circumstances. Communities, acting as 'political subjects', consciously challenge the situations whereby they are made subjects of power, asserting their rights, entitlements, freedom and dignity instead.

It is important to acknowledge that while the community development paradigm has evolved differently in varied socioeconomic and political contexts, fundamentally it is concerned with engaging communities towards addressing their needs, problems and demands (Moffatt et al, 2011). Ideas such as participation, self-help and mutual cooperation are embedded in its claims and discourses. While this chapter acknowledges such aspirations, it goes on to suggest that interventions have often fallen short of these progressive intentions. By drawing on the Indian context, the chapter problematises and draws attention to those hegemonic processes whereby intervention is being initiated, facilitated, anchored and monitored by state agencies and NGOs. Such interventions typically lack a nuanced understanding of power and its performance and they rarely interrogate if and how subjects may act against or dissent vis-à-vis prescribed programmes and policies.

Community: meaning and manifestation

The conception of 'community' in community development has been a dynamic one. Over the past two centuries 'community' has changed in scope, perspective and outlook with ever fluctuating social realities. A great deal of scholarly engagement towards defining its meaning, nature and character has been carried forth, yet the concept of community within community development remains fiercely debated, discussed and contested. For example, Eileen and Stephen Yeo's (1988) survey of the use of community unravelled three different and competing meanings. Beginning around the 16th century the usage of community meant 'holding something in common, a feeling of common identity and most positively, a quality of mutual caring in human relations' (Yeo and Yeo, 1988: 231). This characterisation was formulated by the Diggers in 17th-century England and by socialists such as Robert Owen and William Morris in the 19th century. This community of mutual caring 'made by people for themselves' (Yeo and Yeo, 1988: 231) with its 'vision of a fully liberated humanity living in supportive social relations' (Yeo and Yeo, 1988: 232) can be contrasted with two alternative approaches – 'community as service' and 'community as the state'. According to Yeo and Yeo (1988) the former developed in the 19th century as a middle class ideal of service to the poor, thereby displacing a less easily managed practice of working class mutuality and solidarity. On the other hand, community as target of state intervention formalises and institutionalises 'the community', and 'community interests' are interpreted by the state, in the process undermining independent working class action (Yeo and Yeo, 1988).

Contemporary authors like Bauman (2001: 1) critically analyse the positive connotations of community – '"Community" feels good because of the meanings the word "Community" conveys – all of them promising pleasures, and more often than not the kinds of pleasure we would like to experience but seem to miss.' For Banks and Butcher (2013: 9) such positive value connotations ignore the potential for stifling conformity, exclusiveness and resistance to innovation and change. Paradoxically, Clarke (2009) also observes 'a combination of mobility, inequality, vulnerability and insecurity' for which community has come to stand as a kind of shorthand – so that communities are widely regarded as being composed of 'problem' people (Shaw, 2011: ii 134). The widespread ambivalence, ambiguity and divergence in the meaning and manifestation of community are aptly summed up by Tett et al (in Shaw, 2011: ii 129):

> Communities are confused. On the one hand they're told they can have their say through community learning and development and then they are confused when they're told that what they say is wrong, or it isn't taken up. The main problem [within such a frame] is that it purports to be bottom-up and ticks all the boxes for bottom-up, but it's actually top-down.

This confusion is amplified by the actions of the state and its agencies as they promote community development processes. The agency of communities themselves is often ignored and/or undermined; as a consequence they are treated as subjects under the control of others.

This chapter attempts to unravel the process whereby this control is challenged, negotiated and, ultimately, facilitated towards the making of community organisation subjects, through an experiential consciousness connected with others.

Community development, state and civil society: politics and practice

In many case, communities view state institutions, including state-led community development programmes, with a mixture of hope for service delivery and mistrust at the failure to deliver (Westoby and Botes, 2013: 1295). Although the diversity among and within NGOs makes it difficult to identify their common strengths and limitations, clearly there are distinctions between such organisations and more direct agents of the state (Kang, 2011: 224). Nonetheless, whether facilitated by government, NGOs, social activists or others, community development as a socio-political process potentially enables people to come together, develop analyses and plan collective action for enhancing capability and functioning. However, unequal power relations, embedded social hierarchy and inequality clearly complicate the processes of participation, engagement and action by the subjects of community development. For example, there has been a conspicuous absence of critical discourse through which communities might comprehend the political significance of their socio-cultural locations and how they are made to provide consent to development experiences which are not necessarily emancipatory. There are innumerable instances where community development practice has seemed oblivious to state–market coalitions and the development decisions and practices emanating from their shared agendas. In India, a case in point is the Special Economic Zones (SEZs) that are being set up by corporations, and for which land is provided by the state at throwaway prices, leading to the dispossession of communities and a loss of sovereignty over natural resources (Jha, 2012).

Here we can draw on scholars such as Bachrach and Baratz (1972) and Lipsky (1968) who have demonstrated in other contexts the relative powerlessness of low-income communities in influencing resource allocations where agendas are already set. Powerlessness and lack of influence accentuate the experiences of social exclusion among community development subjects whose voices and concerns do not even receive any acknowledgement and are thus invisibilised. In consequence, their lack of representation in formal decision-making bodies, lack of control over resources, and exclusion from critical social and institutional networks renders them dependent on sympathetic third parties to influence resource allocation decisions (Thomson, 2011: 568). This puts community development in an ambivalent position when it operates on behalf of government and NGOs through the interventions of professional agents.

Fook (2002: 104) argues that professionalism maintains power relations through many levels of discourse and this holds true for community development practitioners as well. Incongruity is particularly manifest when community development professionals, working within what are conflictual and contested political spaces (Boyte, 2008), 'read' situations critically at the personal level but nonetheless authorise actions that are only consonant with officially sanctioned 'co-ordination and collaboration' roles. Such actions encourage communities towards a conformity that turns out to be ultimately disempowering. In India, several 'development projects' have been initiated in conflict-ridden central tribal regions where radical left movements are strong; likewise in the Jammu and Kashmir regions, where autonomy struggles have been sustained for over six decades. Such projects are simply regarded as state-sponsored diversionary tactics by which both overt and covert political agendas are operationalised through policies and programmes that render communities apologetic and silenced.

Community development in India

India has a chequered history of community development. Its first organised endeavours were initiated after independence and can trace their ideological genesis to the Gandhian conception of constructive work. They were premised around the notion of village self-reliance and localised development, which Gandhi saw as an antidote to the corrosive effects of modernisation and colonial rule (Mansuri and Rao, 2004: 4). Over the years, the practice of community development has acquired new meanings in India where different forms of collectivisation and mobilisation thrive amidst hierarchy, marginality and acute deprivation. Indeed Mayer and Rankin's (2002) observation that community development flourished with the support of government and international bodies such as the World Bank, the Ford Foundation and the European Union, formalised around the concept of social capital, holds true also in the context of India.

From the outset, the subjects of state-run development programmes were mainly the rural poor who were to be supported by basic services, although these were not guaranteed as rights or entitlements. The initial paradigm was not one which encouraged people and communities to understand how 'what they were' was made possible by 'who they were'. Nor did it facilitate a pedagogy that might link their poverty and powerlessness to socio-cultural and political roots. At the time of independence from British colonial rule, over 90% of the population lived in rural areas, where socioeconomic inequalities were severe and agriculture was dependent on the vagaries of the weather. The people's overall standard of living was very low. Based on the USSR model of centralised planning, it was envisaged that five-year plans would benefit India and, beginning in March 1950, a planning commission was set up. The first five-year plan, initiated in 1952, brought forward the idea of community development projects, which aimed at increasing production though agriculture and allied activities. Following these initial thrusts, the second plan laid more stress on training urban people who would in turn train rural people. In theory, rural people were to be incorporated and involved as 'planners', but the parallel creation of an educated task force of trainers introduced governmental hierarchy to an already deeply entrenched hierarchical society. Plans rarely took account of the fissures and divisions that existed in the village, conceiving it as one 'happy' unit, and this later became an impediment to community mobilisation, as the people's own consciousness of differences was deep rooted.

By the third five-year plan (1961–66) major achievements included the introduction of the *Panchayat Raj* (PRIs)[1] legislation, which initiated democratic decentralisation. Community development programmes were planned, perceived and implemented with an emphasis on poverty alleviation – mainly led by governmental agencies with a specific focus on rural communities. However, they idealistically assumed that communities were homogeneous, and that any interventions or services provided would more or less be beneficial to all. That never was remotely true, especially in India, with its mix of landless, nearly landless, subsistence tenants, owner-producers and semi-commercial farmers (Jones and Wiggle, 1987: 107–8). Conventional understandings of *the* community – as a social group with a common territorial base and shared interests and spirit of belonging – were bereft of an acknowledgement of power dynamics and political nuances. Besides, the sense of superiority demonstrated by educated community development professionals in relation to illiterate communities, their bureaucratic administrative approaches, persistent social hierarchy and the nexus between government officials, feudal interests and the political class, further restricted the success of community development initiatives. Ultimately, their failure to impact on the poverty levels of people excluded from health, education, housing, sanitation and infrastructure forced some social workers and community organisers to re-examine the programmes' excessive emphasis on local development issues: workers began to recast their work to recognise those structural factors that shape local realities (Andharia, 2009: 277).

It should be acknowledged that such problems with bureaucracy and control are not exclusive to India, or indeed to the historical past. Banks and Orton (2007), writing from the contemporary UK context, for example, observe that various forms of community development are centrally implicated as strategic agents of the managerialist or modernisation agenda: facilitating partnership working, applying set standards for community engagement, capacity building around predetermined outcomes and managing the performativity culture.

India's programmatic approach to community development shifted somewhat in successive five-year plans to include the Green Revolution (1968),[2] the slogan of *garibi hatao* (abolish poverty) (1971),[3] 20-point economic programmes (1975), the Integrated Child Development Scheme (1975), urban development projects, food for work, special development programmes for the hill and tribal areas, and tribal sub-plans. In most of these programmes individuals and households, rather than communities, were made the target of intervention. In the sixth five-year plan (1980), special component plans were formulated to enable Scheduled Castes (SCs) families to cross over the poverty line. Significantly, this was an era in which a shift towards identity politics and social movements changed the direction of state intervention from its charity orientation to the process of development and empowerment. It is against this backdrop that the targeted programmes for SCs and Scheduled Tribes (STs)[4] were conceived as a supplement to the total development effort under general sectors of development. Influenced by the idea of distributive justice for marginalised communities, special schemes and programmes were initiated to cater to the SCs and STs.

Subsequent five-year plans (from 1985 onwards) gradually moved their policy frame towards opening up the market economy and this brought new challenges for deprived communities. Ostensibly depoliticised forms of community development facilitated the entry of neoliberal agendas, by allowing the state to either delegate its responsibilities to NGOs or use the processes of community development to coopt people for agendas decided by the state–market nexus. The homogenised and totalising concept of community, and the idea of development it embraced, was now premised on the construction of communities as passive objects rather than thinking and acting subjects. Ironically, the state's attempts to depoliticise community development in this way also produced counter movements that mobilised at the micro level with a sharper political focus.

The trajectory of community development in India so far has been marked by the somewhat hollow rhetoric of equality of opportunity which, more often than not, masked the precarious practices underneath. Awareness that community implies similarity *and* difference as well as inclusion *and* exclusion (Kaplan, 1993) has now, arguably, become the foundational premise to capture the changing contours of community development subjects in India. This brings us to the central theme of this chapter: who are the changing community development subjects in India? How do these subjects assert their agency? What are the issues around which one observes the active engagement of subjects, where one can see the emergence of political subjects in the process of collectivisation and mobilisation?

Transformation of subjects: from development to organising

In the Indian context, the constituents or subjects of community development are typically identified as experiencing poverty, deprivation, exclusion and marginality, characteristics that can be attributed to social structures and dominant development processes. Birth-based virtues and ascribed statuses still dominate the normative social structure of Indian society. Widening disparities in development outcomes, coupled with socio-historical legacies and political processes, have created further ruptures in relationships across socio-religious communities (Shahid and Jha, 2014: 24). A large proportion of India's community development subjects are Muslims, women or members of SCs or STs and they have brought issues of identity and their own marginality as subjects to the forefront of activist discourses and practices. Communities in India are now frequently referred to as deterritorialised groups of people sharing an identity or at least the perception of a shared identity (Jha, 2009: 307). A case in point is the positive identity assertion by Dalit (SCs) communities, which were formerly known as the 'untouchables'. The Dalit community emphasises the intersectionality of its deprivation, as exclusion and multidimensional poverty interact with its caste identity; collectivisation is mostly based on this understanding.

Premised on multiple and intersecting experiences of subordination, identity-based community mobilisation started catching the imagination of subjects in the mid–1970s when the political dominance of upper caste elites began to dwindle. Caste-based dominance and exclusionary practices; the communal ruptures and splits experienced by minority communities; the displacement and deprivation experienced by indigenous tribal populations; and manifestations of patriarchy in everyday life, demonstrate the pluralised locations and forms of power and powerlessness encountered by subjects. Through the more nuanced formulation of CO, the processes of social exclusion of communities could be better understood, revealing, for example, that deprivation and disempowerment are imposed on Dalit (SCs) and Adivasi (STs) communities as a whole, and not only on individual members. Though upper caste dominance was nothing new for Indian society, a novel desire to resist and alter life circumstances was reflected in the transformative collectivisation of their subjects. In the 1970s the Dalit Panthers, a movement of urban slum-dwelling Dalit youths in Maharashtra, explicitly rejected the caste system and organised in alternative community formations to break existing socioeconomic hierarchies. Innumerable instances of collective organisation against identity-based discrimination became discernible. Processes of defining and redefining identities, and claims making that was based on specific experiences of humiliation or deprivation, became instrumental in subject formation. For example, the objectivising of subjects through 'legitimate' power was countered by a growing awareness of the historical roots of present circumstances. Castes were no longer exclusively talked about by reference to the frameworks of hierarchy and rurality associated with government-sponsored development programmes or schemes. In this sense, through the reconceptualisation and positive assertion of their identities and their collective mobilisation around issues of indignity, displacement, rights and entitlements, Dalits, women, Adivasis, Muslims and other communities elevated CO beyond the language and practice of development economics, the language through which the needs and problems of people had thus far been articulated. The power of hegemony in legitimising the inhuman and making 'people hold views at odds with their interests' (Ives, 2004: 78) was challenged by these transformative subjects. In a society where caste configurations, religious affiliations, linguistic commonalities, gender, sexual orientation and multiple other divisions have the propensity to become the natural parameters of segregation or exclusion, new subjects have shaped the contours of community organisation by engaging with substantive structural issues that influence power and hegemony.

Policy shift and its implication for community development subjects

Far-reaching policy shifts from the beginning of the 1990s have had an impact on and accentuated the vulnerability and marginality of disadvantaged groups and communities in India. The last three decades have witnessed fundamental changes in the nature, character and modus operandi of the Indian state, as new economic policies and programmes have been triggered by developments on the global stage (Jha, 2012). The state–community–civil society interface has been altered by the Indian state's decision to connect itself with neoliberal global economic processes in the last decade of the 20th century. Economic 'reforms' brought about by globalisation have included the disciplining of labour to benefit the financial sector, privatisation of public companies and resources, and the weakening of state intervention in social welfare (Parada, 2007). These policy shifts were balanced by a parallel process of enhanced people's participation through democratic decentralisation following the enactment of the 73rd and 74th constitutional amendments.[5] Around the same time, rights-based approaches (RBA) to development were being advocated and implemented across civil society. However, the simultaneous process of engagement around RBA and the weakening of CO processes and action can be observed. With the blurring of boundaries between market and state, the subjects of community organisation began to find the avenues of struggle and resistance more and more complicated.

On the other hand, globalisation has also had the effect of bringing together a range of organisations under analogous forums and alliances. Alliances such as the National Alliance for People's Movement have launched, supported and coordinated campaigns to protest against government and multinational corporation programmes that represent the policies of hegemonic globalisation (Sheth, 2004: 51). These campaigns have raised issues such as displacement due to big projects, access to natural resources for tribal communities and housing rights for the urban poor. Viewed together, these diverse developments amplify already paradoxical situations: on the one hand it looks as if civil society is getting stronger, while on the other, CO subjects are becoming increasingly marginalised and further made vulnerable. Due to dominant development processes – involving dams, mining, steel plants or infrastructure projects – they are displaced from their habitats, their livelihoods are affected and they are converted into the urban poor, the homeless, 'footloose labour' and so on.

While it is important to acknowledge that contemporary societies continue to produce struggles against direct domination and capitalist exploitation, increasingly they also manifest social struggles against the forms of subjection that people themselves experience in their everyday lives (Jha et al, 2013: 49). The Indian state, which in turn is being influenced by corporate interests, finds itself dealing with rather more conscious political subjects. Against the frame of neoliberal development, there has been a spurt of mass-based grassroots mobilisations across the length and breadth of the country, mainly led by community activists. These mobilisations have facilitated the transformation of 'deficit subjects' into 'political subjects'. The next section explains the nature and character of subjecthood and draws on a case study that captures some of the processes that have led to this transformation.

Case study: towards collective and political subjects?

The transformative potential of subjects is reflected through the act of assertion itself: to speak as an act of public life and as an expression of a collective/political existence. The community development subject, from the standpoint of government and NGOs, may have been conceived as apolitical, having been defined primarily in economic terms. More often than not, class dynamics, issues of social hierarchy (read caste), religious cleavages and concomitant vulnerabilities, patriarchy and its interplay on gender discrimination have been misrecognised. With the emergence of identity- and interest-based community mobilisation and conscientisation, however, issues of exclusion, discrimination, power and authority have started to be articulated through community organisation.

One illustration of the changing role of community organisation subjects can be found in a forum known popularly as Gram Vikas Sansthan (GVS). However, before explaining the emergence of political subjects through GVS, it is important to first clarify what we mean by this term, which clearly encompasses different levels of action:

> At one level the political subject is the citizen-militant fighting at the barricades, raising manifestos, assembling crowds, organising parties, writing and speaking on behalf of collectives, ... organising peasant demonstrations ... At another level, the political subject is less of a citizen because s/he has either opted out, or s/he has not been taken in as a legitimate member of the political society ...

> At the third level, we can see how the political subject is 'subject' to given politics, but aware that subjection wants to subject politics to its own visions, that is authoring politics. (Samaddar, 2010: xix)

In this conception of political subject, Samaddar explains the identity of action and demonstrates the emergence of collective sense among the subjects. The figure of the subject symbolises resistance and desire for a new mode of life. Desire and effort to transform life can be understood through the case of GVS. GVS, a grassroots community-based organisation, works for social inclusion of the excluded Dalit community in two districts of India's largest province, Uttar Pradesh.[6] GVS's endeavour is supported by the Poorest Areas Civil Society (PACS)[7] Programme. The Dalit community, with which GVS engages, has historically been subject to caste-based exclusion, discrimination, exploitation, abuse, violence and victimisation. For Dalits, exclusion means that their opinions are not sought and do not count. In fact they are considered incapable of having an opinion; rather they are expected to trust the opinions of those higher in the echelons of power. Set against this backdrop of exclusion and un-freedom, GVS works mostly with Dalit women, organising them to assert their rights and entitlements. This collective assertion of Dalit women challenges and opposes casteist slurs and everyday experiences of humiliation. Within the GVS programmes, such humiliations are critically deliberated on to expose the socioeconomic and political contexts of oppression.

Revitalisation of a shared spirit of collective agency has been accomplished through conscientisation processes. The power of this sense of political agency has encouraged Dalit women to assume leadership positions, to use their strength against dominant castes and to challenge their caste/class interests. The tangible outcome of such processes is to demand their rights through social protection programmes: for work under the National Rural Employment Guarantee Act (NEGRA),[8] better healthcare through the National Rural Health Mission (NRHM),[9] employment possibilities in the Mid Day Meal Scheme (MMS),[10] and use of the Right to Information Act.[11] In all of these cases, women have invariably taken the lead. Taking strength from Ambedkar's strategic slogan 'educate, agitate and organise' (Rodrigues, 2007), GVS's motto is to transmit 'governments' vision to [the] poor and [the] poor's dream to government'.[12] Since state-led development programmes are the biggest source of livelihood, community organisation subjects find it essential to engage with the state and its agencies, by using multiple strategies to leverage power.

It could be argued that this grassroots activism and mobilisation is made possible only by transforming Dalit women into active political subjects. It is also significant that Uttar Pradesh has the distinction of being led by a Dalit woman as Chief Minister of the state for four terms and that 33% of seats in decentralised governance institutions are reserved for women. The transformation of excluded communities into political subjects has, in addition, been firmed up and given strength through mass politics and mobilisation by Dalit-led organisations such as GVS. More subtle forms of discrimination when accessing welfare services – such as when a Dalit cook is not allowed to prepare food, or Dalit children are made to sit separately while being served food in the school – are collectively resisted by Dalit women activists. The strategies of Dalit women also demonstrate that the politics of expert knowledge and professional power that are situated within the distinct and highly specialised 'social sphere' (Meade, 2011: 890) are assiduously confronted. In contrast to governmentalised forms of community development discussed above, Dalit women demonstrate that 'the public enactment of power does not occur in crudely hierarchical ways, with the state as sole determining arbiter, but that individuals, families and communities absorb, assume, resist, claim and interface with power' (Meade, 2011: 891) in myriad ways.

The mobilisation of Dalit women can also be understood from an epistemological standpoint. Guru (1995: 2549) claims, for example, that the less powerful members of a society have a more encompassing view of social reality because their disadvantaged position grants them a certain epistemic privilege over others. Though one would refrain from romanticisation of the transformative potential of Dalit women, it is undeniable that hitherto invisible subjects have started speaking out and found affirmation through claims making. Through the mobilisation of communities for their overall development, GVS challenges exclusion and devises processes to guarantee their inclusion in society as a whole. However, dominant class and caste interests invariably find it intolerable to accept such resistance to their entrenched positions of power and respond with newer, more insistent forms of oppression or strategies of exclusion.

The simultaneous act of resistance and insistence makes CO extremely dynamic and complex. The shift in the political responses of subjects is located in the realisation that, in a deeply hierarchical and patriarchal society, the intentions of participation and self-help have been comprehended in the context of deep and compelling experiences of powerlessness, exclusion and humiliation. Accordingly, community engagement with subjects turns out to be an act of informed politicisation. With their transformation into political subjects, Dalit women have acknowledged the need to recognise the connections between their individual problems and experiences and the social contexts in which they are embedded. This form of conscientisation facilitates praxis and collective action by subjects with a special focus on social justice, equality, rights and access to entitlements (Clay and Schaffer, 1984; Andharia, 2007). The impoverished, illiterate and dispossessed Dalit women, through the embodiment of political subjecthood, have gained confidence to sustain their struggle against all the odds, and thus grassroots empowerment through political processes of mobilisation has taken precedence over state- and NGO-directed top-down community development.

Conclusion

It is interesting and instructive to observe how the state, in its various interventions and responses, has considered community as a governmental category or as a demographic category of governmentality. In this it draws consistently on a legitimising discourse of community development that represents itself as benign while carefully disguising the inherent social and political contradictions in its assessment of the community. The premise that 'community' is comprised of deprived and dispossessed individuals guides and governs state responses, but these responses take the form of service delivery and development programmes which do not seriously engage with structural causes of inequality. Therefore community development itself unfolds as a technique of government. Though the state has attempted to bring communities on board to ensure rights, more often than not their strategies have constructed communities as a conglomeration of private, poor and depoliticised individuals. In this way, the state conveys the message that it is not important to help people make political meanings out of their experiences of powerlessness, and thus it leaves dominant ideological assumptions and belief systems uncontested. But as this chapter has argued, communities are not only collections of individuals; they can claim and reformulate subjecthood through collectivisation, in the process turning themselves into political subjects who reclaim and express their agency. Community subjects thus challenge their 'restricted citizenship' status and demonstrate the art and craft of the politics of the hitherto 'governed'.

Finally, as regards this concept of the 'subject', Foucault (1982: 781) conceives its meaning at two levels: 'subject to someone else by control and dependence; and tied to his own identity by a conscience or self-knowledge. Both of these conceptions suggest a form of power which subjugates and makes subject to'. Elaborating on different struggles against subjugation, he (1982) identifies three broad types: against forms of domination (ethnic, social and religious); against forms of exploitation which separate individuals from what they produce and/or against that which ties individuals to themselves and submits them to others in this way (struggles against subjection, against forms of subjectivity and submission). Dalit women's collectivisation demonstrates the extent of their self-reflexivity and their deep understanding of oppression, oppressive structures and possible responses. There is, arguably, a political subject within every oppressed woman as she has a keen sense of the deprivation and denial she is going through and the process of devising strategies to deal with everyday violence has taught her unique skills to negotiate the spaces to fight back and assert herself. Being able to make claims, assert collective agency and know their rights and entitlements make the process of transformation of community development subjects real and radical. And while there is no denying that Dalit women's assertiveness occurs within the frameworks of community organisations that are in some ways accepted by the state, sometimes the outcomes of their mobilisations are more transformative than could ever be anticipated by either the state or dominant social groups.

Notes

[1] Panchayat Raj Institutions are local self-governance institutions in rural India. They are organised at the level of village and/or a cluster of villages.

[2] The introduction of high-yielding varieties of seeds and the increased use of chemical fertilisers and irrigation are known collectively as the Green Revolution, which provided the increase in production needed to make India self-sufficient in food grains.

[3] Abolish Poverty was a popular slogan of the then Prime Minister Indira Gandhi in 1971. Several anti-poverty programmes were launched in tune with the slogan

[4] SCs and STs are two historically disadvantaged groups in India whose welfare and upliftment were ensured though constitutional provisions. Politically SCs prefer being called Dalit and Adivasis is used for the indigenous ST population.

[5] The 73rd and 74th amendments of the Indian Constitution gave constitutional status to decentralised local governance systems.

6   Covering an area of 93,933 km², Uttar Pradesh is the most populous state of India and about 77.7% of people in the state live in rural areas. According to the 2011 Indian census, Uttar Pradesh has the largest SC population, constituting 21% of the total population of the state.

7   The PACS Programme is an initiative of the UK government's Department for International Development aimed at reducing the gap in well-being status between socially excluded groups in India and the rest of the population

8   NEGRA aims at enhancing the livelihood security of people in rural areas by guaranteeing 100 days' wage employment in a year

9   NRHM is a government programme to address health needs of underserved rural areas of India.

10   MMS is the world's largest school feeding programme reaching out to about 120,000,000 children in over 1,265,000 schools/EGS centres across the country.

11   This Act mandates a timely response to citizen requests for government information.

12   Vision statement of GVS, shared by its chief organiser.

References

Andharia, J. (2007) 'Reconceptualizing community organization in India', *Journal of Community Practice*, 15(1/2): 91–119.

Andharia, J. (2009) 'Critical explorations of community organization in India', *Community Development Journal* 44(3): 276–90.

Bachrach, P. and Baratz, M.S. (1972) *Power and poverty: theory and practice*, New York, NY: Oxford University Press.

Banks, S. and Butcher, H. (2013) 'What is community practice?', in S. Banks, H. Butcher, A. Orton and J. Robertson (eds) *Managing community practice: Principles, policies and programmes*, 2nd edn, Bristol: Policy Press, 7–29.

Banks, S. and Orton, A. (2007) '"The grit in the oyster": community development workers in a modernizing local authority', *Community Development Journal*, 42(1): 97–113.

Bauman, Z. (2001) *Community: Seeking safety in an insecure world*, Cambridge: Polity Press.

Boyte, H.C. (2008) 'Essay 7: civic driven change and developmental democracy', in A.F. Fowler and K. Biekart (eds), *The civic driven change initiative: Citizen's imagination in action*, The Hague: Institute of Social Studies (ISS), 1–11.

Clarke, J. (2009) 'Community, social change and social order', in G. Mooney and S. Neal (eds), *Community: Welfare, crime and society*, Maidenhead: The Open University.

Clay, E.J. and Schaffer, B. (1984) '*Room for manoeuvre: An exploration of public policy planning in agricultural and rural development*, Rutherford, NJ: Fairleigh Dickinson University Press.

Fook, J. (2002) *Social work: Critical theory and practice*, London: SAGE.

Foucault, M. (1982) 'The Subject and Power', *Critical Inquiry*, 8(4): 777–95.

Guru, G. (1995) 'Dalit women talk differently', *Economic and Political Weekly*, 30(41–42): 2548–50.

Ives, P. (2004) *Language and hegemony in Gramsci*, London: Pluto Press.

Jha, M.K. (2009) 'Community organization in split societies', *Community Development Journal*, 44(3): 305–19.

Jha, M.K. (2012) 'State, space and political subjects: a case of special economic zones', *The Indian Journal of Social Work*, 73(2): 157–76.

Jha, M.K., Shajahan, P.K. and Vyas, M. (2013) 'Biopolitics and urban governmentality in Mumbai', in S. Mezzadra, J. Reid and R. Samaddar (eds), *The biopolitics of development: Reading Michel Foucault in the postcolonial present*, New Delhi: Springer.

Jones, J. and Wiggle, I. (1987) 'The concept and politics of "integrated community development"', *Community Development Journal*, 22(2): 107–19.

Kang, J. (2011) 'Understanding non-governmental organizations in community development: strengths, limitations and suggestions', *International Social Work*, 54(2): 223–37.

Kaplan, R.D. (1993) *Balkan ghosts: A journey through history*, New York, NY: Random House.

Lipsky, M. (1968) 'Protest as a political resource', *American Political Science Review*, (62(4): 1144–58.

Mansuri, G. and Rao, V. (2004) 'Community-based and -driven development', *World Bank Research Observer* 19(1): 1–40.

Mayer, M. and Rankin, K.N. (2002) 'Social capital and (community) development: a North/South perspective', *Antipode*, 34(4): 804–08.

Meade, R.R. (2011) 'Government and community development in Ireland: the contested subjects of professionalism and expertise', *Antipode*, 44(3) 889–910.

Moffatt, K., George, P., Alphonse, M., Kanitkar, A., Anand, V. and Chamberlain, J. (2011) 'Community practice at a crossroads: the impact of the global on the local in India. *Community Development Journal*, 46(1): 104–21.

Parada, H. (2007) 'Regional perspectives from Latin America: social work in Latin America. History, challenges and renewal', *International Social Work*, 50(4): 560–9.

Rodrigues, V. (ed) (2007) *The essential writings of B.R. Ambedkar*, New Delhi: Oxford University Press.

Samaddar, R. (2010) *Emergence of the political subject*, New Delhi: Sage Publications.

Shahid, M. and Jha, M.K. (2014) 'Revisiting the client-worker relationship: Biestek through a Gramscian gaze', *Journal of Progressive Human Services*, 25(1): 18–36.

Shaw, M. (2011) 'Stuck in the middle? Community development, community engagement and the dangerous business of learning for democracy', *Community Development Journal*, 46(S2): ii128–ii146.

Sheth, D.L. (2004) 'Globalisation and new politics of micro-movements', *Economic and Political Weekly*, 39(1): 45–8.

Thomson, D.E. (2011) 'Strategic geographic targeting in community development: examining the congruence of political, institutional, and technical factors', *Urban Affairs Review*, 47(4): 564–94.

Westoby, P. and Botes, L. (2013) '"I work with the community, not the parties!" The political and practical dilemmas of South Africa's state-employed community development workers', *British Journal of Social Work*, 43(7): 1294–311.

Yeo, E. and Yeo, S. (1988) 'On the uses of community: from Owenism to the present', in Yeo, S. (ed), *New views of co-operation*, London, New York. NY: Routledge, 231.

PART 2

Practising politics

Identity politics, community participation and the making of new places: examples from Taiwan

Yi-Ling Chen

Introduction

Since the 1990s, a new cultural strategy that emphasises local identities and community participation has resulted in the creation of new urban places in cities in Taiwan. Many of these urban places have become new destinations for tourists and local people, involving the revitalisation of heritage, the reuse of spare space, and mega urban projects. This new cultural strategy is related to political decentralisation and economic transformation, both of which are driven by post-industrial development and new identity politics.

Locality has become an important focal point for mitigating the impacts of globalisation in the majority of industrialised countries. Due to the rise of post-Fordism and deindustrialisation, the economic bases and spatial structures of most places have changed. Global economic change also affects new discourses of urban development. Neoliberalism has reshaped previous urban policies that emphasised redistribution and balanced development, to include principles of competitiveness, privatisation, entrepreneurship, flexibility and decentralisation. This new emphasis has made it necessary for local governments and communities to play increasingly important roles in urban development. Within the terms of neoliberalism, however, community development becomes a double-edged sword. It can mean an increasing burden on community groups in mitigating social problems caused by the retrenchment of the state in providing welfare services. But it also potentially recasts people as 'active subjects in politics' who are able to join together and transform space into meaningful place (Shaw, 2011: 307).

In this chapter, two urban projects are used to explore the political and economic contexts of place-making in Hualien City, a small tourist city on the east coast of Taiwan. It explores the process of economic and political restructuring in Taiwan in the 1990s, the contextual factors informing the cultural strategies of central government, and the processes enacted for making new places in Hualien City. It goes on to argue that the rise of local identities and community participation in Taiwan has led to some degree of community empowerment, but that this is due primarily to a state project to build a Taiwanese identity and a democratic citizenry.

In the 1990s, identity politics stimulated the development of new places, the emergence of community groups, and a new practice of participatory community design that calls for the involvement of community members in the design process of public space or community works. In other words, exogenous global forces driven by capitalist restructuring were not the main factor initially; in fact, it was increasing economic stagnation that caused the original political purposes to be replaced by economic goals. Place-making today is more reliant on profitability, but nonetheless, state-led cultural projects have encouraged the growth of community organisations and their active political involvement in local affairs.

New uneven geography and strategies of redevelopment

Global economic change influences the spatial structure of urban systems and causes new problems in urban development around the world. Sassen (2000) argues that, in developed countries, the importance of a city is influenced by the internationalisation of its economic activities, and a transnational urban system connects cities in a hierarchical relationship. Areas outside the national, state-wide, or global network will become increasingly marginalised (Sassen, 2000: 55–7). The resulting deindustrialisation is a common problem for many industrialised cities because of rising unemployment and urban decline.

In response to urban decline, several cities around the world have successfully transformed themselves into centres of post-Fordist production and consumption, and employment in those cities is typically based on a service and cultural economy (Hamnett and Shoval, 2003). Strategies to accomplish this include the development of cultural industries (Hamnett and Shoval, 2003), the marketing of reinvented cities (Ward, 1998) and attracting the 'creative class' (Florida, 2002) – strategies which target the generation of tourism and the new knowledge-based economy. Some cities are more progressively promoting sustainability and equality (Fitzgerald and Leigh, 2002) and some are enacting place-based programmes of community development corporations. These are nonprofit community-based organisations intent on improving the physical and economic assets in their communities (Vidal and Keating, 2004).

However, the supposed benefits of such development strategies are challenged by some authors. Harvey (1989), for example, points out the dangers of commodification and entrepreneurship of urban governments. Similarly, MacLeod's (2002) study of Glasgow illustrates a city under urban entrepreneurship, in which commercial interests took over the leadership of urban development to the exclusion of marginal groups and other progressive urban policies. Brenner and Theodore (2002) argue that an emphasis on distribution and equilibrium is replaced in neoliberal discourse by an emphasis on local competition and on concentrating industrial clusters in specific regions in order to enhance the importance of the city-region in the international division of labour. Leitner et al (2007) propose alternative ideas to contest neoliberalism: collective welfare; equality, justice, and social welfare; cooperation; consensus decision making; understanding and respecting multiculturalism; and considering the environment. They also suggest that the movements that contest neoliberalism emphasise attachment to local places and incorporate views and practices that centre on the local economy, culture and ecology. These movements focus on grassroots democracy, community and economic development, and the prioritisation of quality of life over profit. Therefore, the strategies initiated at the community level possess the potential to balance the increasingly uneven development led by globalisation.

The importance of local communities

In these development strategies, locality is a key arena for responding to the impacts of globalisation. Local actions are crucial for many reasons. According to Clarke and Gaile (1998: 3), the operation of the new economy is based on a regional scale. They argue that the international competitiveness of an urban region is determined by whether it can create an economic cluster of companies or specialised labour, and so the active roles of cities and local governments are imperative. In other words, local governments are the key political agencies to comprehend the tendencies of globalisation and seek ways to empower their citizens to adapt to the global economy.

Another reason local action has become significant is the decentralisation of governance due to shifts in policy under neoliberal discourses, including privatisation, entrepreneurship, flexibility and the reduction of the role of central government (Brenner and Theodore,

2002). In response to decentralisation, local governments and community organisations play a vital role in leading local development. The increasing responsibilisation of the local can mean a conservative form of governance that supports reductions in welfare, but it also can possess progressive potential, to incorporate local groups in an effort to change the role of the state (Craig et al, 2011).

The word 'local' can refer to a region or a locality that is an embedded community, or a place. Place has certain unique characteristics that are meaningful to the people who interact with them (Coe et al, 2013). Locality has a similar meaning, but it puts more emphasis on the uniqueness of a place (Massey, 1993). The territory of the local is inevitably somewhat vague because its scale and boundaries are uncertain. This ambiguity reflects Swyngedouw's (2004) observation that globalisation is a process of geographical rescaling which emphasises a new politics of scale. Places are experiencing the process of deterritorialisation/reterritorialisation, and their domains are transferrable. Nevertheless, as David Harvey (2009) argues, the local is still an important site of social struggles and emancipation. In this sense locality can be a site of contestation between different actors and interests.

Smith (2001: 1) questions the binary dichotomisation of the global vs. the local, arguing that the local or embedded community is often 'represented as a static, bounded, cultural space of being where personal meanings are produced'. The binary argument wrongly assumes that local people have coherent and stable cultural values and traditional ways of life and that the global dynamism of capitalist (post-) modernity destabilises community-based social organisations. Smith (2001) points out that the social and spatial transformations of a place are not necessarily passive reactions to global changes but can be driven by many forces. In this sense, the local is never simply unitary but comprises a variety of social groups interacting differentially with transnational networks. Community development could therefore be seen as a process of 'place-making' that involves power struggles among different groups, and urban space is constantly in the state of being shaped and reshaped by the spatial practices of different people and groups.

This chapter discusses two places in Hualien City, analysing the interactions of major actors in place-making processes. As mentioned already, global economic change driven by capitalism is not the only force for local transformation. In Taiwan, democratisation and the rise of local identity politics have rearranged political institutions and relations between different governmental agencies and communities.

Since democratisation in the late 1980s, community movements have been especially active and have played crucial roles in place-making. The transformation of local communities as political actors originated not only from bottom-up grassroots movements, but also from a top-down political project to build a new Taiwanese identity. To understand the political and economic context of Hualien's urban development after the 1990s, three major actors are identified: central government, local government and community organisations.

Economic and regional development in Taiwan

In the 1990s Taiwan gradually underwent a process of deindustrialisation. Labour-intensive industries, which had linked Taiwan to the new international division of labour in the 1960s, began to lose their comparative advantage and mostly chose to relocate to China. The economic growth rate in Taiwan subsequently slowed and its industrial structure also changed rapidly. By the mid-1980s, employment in service industries exceeded that in the manufacturing sector and by 2011 only 5% of employees were in agriculture. In terms of regional development, electronic and information industries are based in the northern region of Taiwan. The eastern region, where Hualien is located, is the least industrialised (Ching and Chou, 2007). The economic development of the different regions is reflected in the population distribution: in 2011, 44.6% of the population was in the northern region, and only 2.5% was in the eastern region (CEPD, 2011). The population continues to be concentrated in the northern region because of its high-tech industries and numerous service jobs. In Hualien County, the population has steadily decreased: as of 2011, it was only 338,800. Its major economic base is now the tourism industry (Li, 2005) and average household income is lower than the national average (CEPD, 2011) while its poverty rate ranks third in Taiwan (Department of Social Welfare, Ministry of Interior, 2011). Given this broader context, the chapter will now address some of the key factors which have been significant in framing the parameters and limitations for community participation and community development.

The degree of autonomy of local government

As noted already, local governments play an important role in enabling localities to react to globalisation. However, the existing administration system in Taiwan is essentially a top-down structure in which local governments have limited autonomy due to a number of factors, including a lack of financial resources. Tax law in Taiwan is such that most tax revenue goes to the central government. Therefore, local governments rely on real estate taxes, which have had a relatively slower growth rate than industrial or commercial sector taxes. In less-developed areas, the tax revenue from real estate is especially limited (Wu, 2003). For example, the tax base of Hualien County is among the lowest of the counties of Taiwan (Kou, 2007). This centralised tax system renders local governments unable to guide the restructuring of the city with a more comprehensive view of urban development (Chou, 2002).

The eastern region of Taiwan has been considered a marginal border area since the Ching Dynasty, due to the geographic isolation caused by the high central mountain range (Hsia, 2005). Despite being considered as the least progressive place, the development plans of the Hualien County government in the mid-1990s still aimed to achieve two goals: industrialisation and tourism development (Chi et al, 2005). Whereas, in the 1980s, political and social movements spread across the island, in Hualien, most such movements met with failure. Compared to those of the adjacent county, I-Lan, which is more politically progressive, Hualien's social and environmental movements were less able to prevent the development of polluting industries, for example. One reason was the internal conflicts among Hualien's community groups, but perhaps most significant was the lesser autonomy of its local government (Chi et al, 2005). Unlike the government of I-Lan County, Hualien County did not have sufficiently developed strategies for local development, preferring to follow central government policy. Therefore, while I-Lan has developed a vibrant local identity that makes environmental protection and cultural preservation central concerns for development, Hualien faces much resistance on these issues from local politicians because the pressure exerted by local residents around environmental concerns is not strong enough. However, the policy reform in the 1990s aiming at empowering the local community has gradually changed the situation.

The impact of central government's policies: cultivating local autonomy to build a new nation

Although local government lacks autonomy within Taiwan's present political system, cultivating local autonomy has been one of the goals of the central government since the 1990s. To this end, government has enacted several policies aimed at organising community groups and revitalising local culture, with its motivation primarily political:

to construct a new Taiwanese national identity. The secondary reason is economic: to find ways to utilise local culture to create a cultural economy, or tourism, in order to prevent the decline of places that are not in the growing industrial cluster. However, while the political goal was initially regarded as more important than the economic one, later the importance of the economic purpose increased. A centralised and top-down policy that fosters local autonomy is indeed very contradictory, prompting questions about the context and provenance of such policies and about whether local governments or communities can actually increase their independence under them. As will be explained, three subsequent policies played a key role for Hualien in empowering local communities, by first constructing an identity to connect people with their living areas, redefining as well as rediscovering local history, and then encouraging creative applications of local culture for tourism or cultural commodities.

Community construction policy

At the end of the 1980s, the Kuomingtang (KMT) government was facing political and economic challenges. Domestically, political and social movements were emerging, while internationally, the countries in Southeast Asia and China were rising. The KMT government needed to adopt new economic and cultural strategies to respond to these challenges. Culturally, the government planned to construct a distinct Taiwanese identity in an attempt to differentiate itself from Chinese culture and history. President Lee Teng-Hui initiated the *ben-tu-hua* (indigenisation) policy and directed the Council for Cultural Affairs to carry out a community construction policy, beginning in 1994. This policy, influenced by the ideas of the Japanese community movement, encouraged the formation of community groups to revitalise local culture and establish cultural space by preserving heritage or building new community centres, museums and art centres. This policy served several purposes. Politically, it encouraged involvement in local affairs and shaped the habit of civic democratic participation, which had been prohibited up until the late 1980s. A goal of national policy was, therefore, to activate community consciousness, and nurture a sense of local self-identity, which would in turn transform Taiwanese identity for a new nation. Economically, it attempted to combine local culture and industrial development in order to create a cultural industry to revitalise local economies (Yen, 2007). Community solidarity and identity were thus mobilised in service of the nation and the economy.

Redefining cultural heritage

A second central government policy critical for urban development in Hualien City has been the Culture Assets Preservation Law. Historical preservation is a complicated issue due to Taiwan's uncertain global status. Historical preservation was largely neglected before the 1970s because Taiwan's 300 years of history was unfavourably compared with China's 5,000 years (Yen, 2007). Before the KMT came to power, Taiwan had been a Japanese colony for 50 years, a period of history that the KMT wished to forget. This amnesia continued until the end of the 1970s, when the United Nations recognised the Communist Chinese government and Taiwan began to experience diplomatic isolation. After that, the KMT government could no longer claim its legitimacy as a legal and representative regime for China and its cultural discourse shifted from Chinese-centric to Taiwanese-centric, hence raising the status of historical preservation to state policy.

The Council for Cultural Affairs was established in 1981 and the Culture Assets Preservation Law was enacted in 1982. However, the definition of heritage at that time was based on its relevance to Chinese culture: aboriginal or Japanese colonial buildings were not recognised as heritage sites (Yen, 2007). The recognition of these buildings finally came about in the 1990s, when the state became interested in local culture as a means of building a new Taiwanese identity (Yen, 2007). A wider definition of heritage is important for Hualien City, which was mainly built by the Japanese; under this new definition, many Japanese buildings can now be preserved.

Promotion of culture and creative industry

Cultural heritage policy attempts to accomplish the same political and economic goals as the community construction policy. In 2000 the Democratic Progressive Party (DPP) came into power, and because it was more dedicated to the goal of creating a cultural economy, the stimulation of local economic development became a priority. Facing ongoing economic restructuring in Taiwan, due to more intense global competition and China's magnetic effect, the DPP enacted a national policy in 2002, Challenge 2008 – National Development Plan, which aimed to construct Taiwan as a 'Green Silicon Island'. The plan proposed reforms to the political, financial and fiscal domains and produced ten key plans to invest in manpower, research and development, global logistics, distribution channels and the living environment. This plan demonstrated government efforts to develop a knowledge-based economy by enhancing labour and innovation and, for the first time, cultural and creative industries were incorporated into national policy. In addition to economic development, this plan intended to establish a sustainable living environment by encouraging a bottom-up approach to community development, including training community workers, funding local initiatives, and helping establish more community organisations. Many community workers are actually the funders of community organisations. They have received training in how to write grant proposals and investigate community resources, and organisational skills but their positions are mostly temporary because of the instability of funding. During the KMT's authoritarian regime, community organisations only followed top-down political orders. The new booming communities after the 1990s are more self-organised and bottom-up, creating a greater vibrancy of places.

Among the ten key plans, two have had a vital influence on the urban development of Hualien City. One was the Cultural and Creative Industry Development Plan and the other was the New Home Community Development Plan. The Cultural and Creative Industry Development Plan chose five places in Taiwan to set up cultural and creative parks, among them the former Hualien Winery. It aimed to create a favourable environment for the development of creative industries by providing studios, galleries, performance halls or other conference rooms for artists to promote cultural business. The New Home Community Development Plan was a continuation of the Community Construction Plan from the 1990s. It proposed the establishment of a Museum of Local Culture, to guide local governments and communities in the reuse of empty space to establish various cultural facilities in an attempt to 'enhance local cultural activities, tourism, and business' (Council of Cultural Affairs, 2004).

These centralised policies were intended to transfer some power to local governments and communities so that the locality could enhance its capacity to define its ambitions and adjust itself to the new challenges of globalisation. Lu (2004) found that since the late 1980s, local governments and communities had in fact increased their autonomy and resources through processes of democratisation. His case studies of natural conservation showed that communities, local indigenous tribes and local governments have played more active roles, but their autonomy has varied according to the characteristics of their members; that is, local government, community groups and local businesses. Clearly, the capacity of the community will influence how it utilises the resources from central government. Some communities are better able to seize available opportunities and grow into lively and self-sufficient places. Similar contradictions emerge as recurring issues of community development in other contexts when it is deployed by governments to secure 'national' or centrally-determined goals.

New places in Hualien City

Several kinds of new urban places in Hualien City have emerged since the 1990s. The two 'new places' highlighted in this chapter, Pine Garden and the Hualien Old Winery, are actually newly renovated Japanese buildings. These two places were chosen as pilot sites under national cultural policy and reflect the transformation of cultural policies from a political to an economic orientation.

In the 17th century, Hualien was a base for gold mining for the Dutch and Spanish colonists. The establishment of large settlements began during the Ching Dynasty (1644–1912), but the Ching government did not initiate any major construction in Hualien. In 1895 Taiwan became a Japanese colony. After a rebellion by Ami indigenous tribes, the colonial Japanese government established an administrative office in Hualien (Chu, 2006). The Japanese government started modern city planning based on a grid system for Hualien City and built up its infrastructure, including harbours, railways, airports and manufacturing plants. As a result, almost all of the historical buildings in Hualien City were built in the style of Japanese colonial architecture. Lacking official recognition as cultural heritage sites before the mid-1980s, these Japanese buildings disappeared very quickly. Preservation efforts finally began after the redefinition of cultural heritage in the 1990s. In the two preservation efforts described below, local communities, local government, and central government played different roles. The study of actors in each case helps to examine the meaning of local autonomy and the distinctive forms that community development takes in this city.

Pine Garden

Pine Garden was originally a Japanese military office built in the 1940s. After 1945 it was transformed into a resort for American army personnel. Later, it was managed by different agencies and then gradually abandoned, but the unique history and architectural style still made the building one of the top 100 historical architectural sites in Taiwan. In 1995 the site was identified for conversion into an international hotel. Local community members, comprised of artists, teachers, environmentalists and local representatives, opposed this plan and formed an organisation to preserve the pine trees and the building.

They held meetings and artists' workshops in Pine Garden and lobbied local politicians for support. Their organisation successfully gained support from the Hualien County government, which applied its power in urban planning to change the designated land use from hotel to park and further submitted an application to the central government to designate Pine Garden as a cultural heritage site. In 2001 the Council of Cultural Affairs chose Pine Garden as one of the pilot projects for reusing empty space and provided funding for renovation. With the funding from central government for promoting locally initiated organisations, several community organisations and artists formed a new organisation, the Association of Artistic and Cultural Reform on Hualien's Environment (AACRHE), and hired architects to conduct the renovation (Wang, 2004). Local residents were able to contribute their ideas about its function, spatial arrangement and management according to their needs. It is significant that the process of renovation and design was participatory – an idea which had been gradually introduced to Taiwan's urban planning after democratisation – and Pine Garden was a pioneering case. The AACRHE also played a crucial role in pushing for the renovation of the Hualien Old Winery later. At the end of 2003, Pine Garden was reopened to the public. The space was first managed by the AACRHE, and later subcontracted to a professional artist management company, Art Source Corp. The funding for management was provided partly by a coffee shop in the park, but mostly by the Council of Cultural Affairs.

The policy of reuse of empty space originated from the ideas of urban redevelopment in Europe and North America. Facing the problems of deindustrialisation, cities in those countries renovated abandoned buildings and created new destinations to enhance the economic base. The renovated buildings could be used as offices, housing, public markets, shops and art centres. Policy for the reuse of empty spaces in Taiwan, however, was guided by the cultural agency of the government. Therefore, the function of the new spaces was primarily for cultural purposes. Limitations were placed on commercial use (Yang, 2006: 41), and although this limitation was initially met by doubts, it has turned out in this case to be beneficial to maintaining the quality of this historical building.

Pine Garden is now a very popular public space and tourist destination in Hualien. It has an art gallery and a local museum, primarily promoting local artists, writers and poets. Every year, it hosts the International Pacific Poetry Festival. Although the operation of the renovated building continues to rely on government funding, the Art Source Corp is effective at fund raising and creating art products which sustain operations. In this sense, Pine Garden could be said to represent an exemplary case of a local museum.

The Hualien Old Winery: the cultural and creative park

The Old Winery, a Japanese factory built in 1913, became vacant when the Taiwan Beer Company moved to a new site in 1988. Located at the centre of the city, it has a large footprint (3.3 acres). As in the case of Pine Garden, preservation efforts were started by the AACRHE. In 2001 the Hualien County government changed the designated land use of the winery to a historical park. In 2002 the national development plan chose the location as a creative and cultural park, and since it was a national plan, the Council of Cultural Affairs took charge of the renovation. The county government assisted with the process, along with the participation of community organisations. Management was first turned over to the AACRHE after renovation in 2007, funded mostly by the Council of Cultural Affairs (Chen, 2007). The city centre is a very dense commercial area without much open space. The opening of this park therefore transformed the overall quality of the city centre.

The management of the park was more complicated because it is much larger than the Pine Garden, and it is directly supervised by central government, albeit at arm's length. From June 2007 to December 2009 three different community groups ran the park, but they found that the restrictive regulations allowed for no real autonomy (Chiang, 2010). As an important part of the national plan, the cost for renovation and operation of the Old Winery was quite large, so there was little room for trial-and-error experiments. This lack of flexibility inhibited its growth. This top-down process also excluded local participation and made no provision for communication with local artists (Keng Seng Daily News, 2011). In addition, the charges for exhibitions and performances were unaffordable for most of the local artists, and the lack of enthusiastic local participation in the management after the renovation kept the Old Winery from developing the vibrant atmosphere of the Pine Garden.

The park was intended to function as a centre for culture and tourism, and greater priority was eventually assigned to promoting cultural business. In 2009 the Council of Cultural Affairs enacted *Creative Taiwan: The Action Plan for the Development of Creative and Cultural Industries*. In 2011 the Council signed a 15-year contract with a new management team, comprising five different companies in land development, hotels and art galleries. In other words, the park will be run with a primary focus on profitability. This clearly has implications for local participation.

Examining these two cases

In both cases, renovation has been more or less successful because of the active role of local communities, the support of the county government, and funding from the central government. In addition, both places are located on publicly-owned land and are preserved as historic buildings. In both cases, the major actors that initiated preservation were community organisations, although local government support was important in seeking resources and funding from central government, as well as applying its authority over land use to redefine the space and preserve the two sites. But it is significant that the community here has less autonomy in relation to future development plans, because central government leads the processes of policy making and funding provision. After the renovations, in both cases private organisations took over. Although both places initially relied heavily on funding from central government, such subsidies have gradually been reduced, causing management to gradually change from nonprofit community organisations into profit-oriented private companies. At this moment, Pine Garden seems to be more successful than the Old Winery because it has had smaller-scale, greater community participation from the beginning, and less control from central government. The long-term outcomes of these developments are still unknown, but it is certain that communities have been successfully mobilised around cultural policy – and many more new places have been created since by community members.

Conclusion

In contrast to the situation in many Western industrialised cities, the rise of locality in Hualien was initially due not to exogenous global forces driven by capitalist restructuring, but to endogenous political projects to build a Taiwanese identity and democratic citizenry. These state-led projects encouraged the growth of community organisations and their active political roles in local affairs. The new identity, based on locality, changed the definition of history and heritage, and hence many abandoned spaces could be renovated as new places for the community.

The national policies, which promote local autonomy and local culture, provide opportunities for community groups to be involved in local affairs and become critical actors in local development. The processes of making new places have revitalised their consciousness and connections with the locality by rediscovering the uniqueness of a long-suppressed local history. By the early 2000s community groups had successfully revitalised many historical sites in Taiwan. UNESCO awarded the Asia-Pacific Conservation Award to Taipei's Bao-an Temple in 2003 for its 'invisible value of community mobilization' (Lin and Hsing 2009: 1329–30). Lu (2002) recognises that the empowerment of the community is becoming a new form of governance, one that is reconstructing state–society relationships (Hsu and Huang 2011: 147), in which the nation state reduces its authoritarian status by decentralising power to the community level.

However, the changing management regimes in these new cases also shows the limits to and on community organisation. Economic stagnation after 2000 shifted the focus to economic purposes, and the culture industry was treated as an important strategy for creating new economic bases for urban and rural places. The primary consideration therefore became profitability, and profit-oriented private companies have taken over the management from nonprofit community organisations. These developments must also be considered in the context of the retrenchment of the state from direct involvement in community affairs.

Clearly the mobilisation of the community can be a double-edged sword: the construct of community deployed may be at odds with more progressive versions of Taiwanese identity; or it may represent a hybrid form of neoliberal governance (Hsu and Huang, 2011). National policies lean more and more towards transferring responsibility from 'government to the individual households and local communities' in order to emphasise community care and financial independence (Hsu and Huang, 2011: 147). But it is a hybrid form because central government still dominates funding and policy making.

Nevertheless, the birth of these new places has involved increasing participation by local communities and facilitated the formation of self-identity. Such empowerment has the potential to turn people within those communities into active citizens, to change the ways of local governance, and influence the direction of future development. Although the economic benefits are still being examined, cultural strategies have enhanced the self-identity not only of the people in those communities affected, but also people all over Taiwan. It is now popular to set new tourism objectives, such as visiting all 319 villages in Taiwan, taking bicycle tours around the island, and making ecotourism visits to indigenous tribes. These activities demonstrate a new taste for and appreciation of local culture that scarcely existed before.

References

Brenner, N. and Theodore, N. (2002) 'Cities and the geographies of actually existing neoliberalism', in N. Brenner and N. Theodore (eds) *Spaces of neoliberalism*, Malden, MA and Oxford: Blackwell, 2–32.

Chen, M.Y. (2007) *The research of Hualien Old Winery Creative and Cultural Park*, Masters Thesis, Graduate Institute of Local Studies, National Hualien University of Education (in Chinese).

Chi, J.J., Shen, J.L. and Lin, S.L. (2005) 'Maixiang difang zichu de defang fazhang: Ilan yu hualien de huanjing yu fazhang keti' [Towards local autonomy and development: I-Lan and Hualien's environment and development], *East Taiwan Studies*, 7: 31–56 (in Chinese).

Chiang, C.Y. (2010) *Hualien jiou jiou chang chuang yi wenhua yuanqu weiwai guangli zi yangjiou* [*The study of outsourcing management for the Hualien Creative and Cultural Park*], Masters Thesis, Graduate Institute of Public Administration, National Dong-Hwa University, Taiwan (in Chinese).

Ching, J.H. and Chou, T.L. (2007) 'Differentiations in Taiwan's regional industrial clusters: the impacts of China effects', *Journal of Geographical Science*, 49: 55–79 (in Chinese).

Chou, J.L. (2002) 'Quanqiou hua guotu ce lue yu Taiwan dushi xitong bian qian' [Globalization, national strategies of land use, and the changing urban system in Taiwan], *City and Planning* 29(4): 491–512 (in Chinese).

Chu, J.P. (2006) 'Hualien xian defang zhili de zhuan xing yu ji yu' [The opportunities and transformation of local governance in Hualien County], paper presented at the first conference of Hualien Studies, Hualien, Taiwan (in Chinese).

Clarke, S.E. and Gaile, G.L. (1998) *The work of cities, globalization and community/Volume 1*, Minneapolis, MN: University of Minnesota Press.

Coe, N., Kelly, P. and Yeung, H.Y.C. (2013) *Economic geography: A contemporary introduction*, 2nd edn, Oxford: Wiley-Blackwell.

Council for Economic Planning and Development (CEPD) (2011) *Urban and regional development statistics, Taiwan*, http://statistic.ngis. org.tw/index.aspx?topic=4.

Council of Cultural Affairs (2004) 'Section 2 hardware development of cultural environment. Taiwan', *Challenge 2008: The Six-year National Development Plan*, www.nbic.org.tw/dbpdf/%ACD%BE%D42008R ev-20030106.pdf

Craig, G., Mayo, M., Popple, K., Shaw, M and Taylor, M. (2011) (eds) *The community development reader*, Bristol: Policy Press.

Department of Social Welfare, Ministry of Interior (2011) *Households and persons of low-income families*, sowf.moi.gov.tw/stat/month/m3-01.xls.

Fitzgerald, J. and Leigh, N.G. (2002) *Economic revitalization: Cases and strategies for city and suburb*, London: Sage.

Florida, R. (2002) *The rise of the creative class: And how it's transforming work, leisure, community and everyday life*, New York, NY: Basic Books.

Hamnett, C. and Shoval, N. (2003) 'Museums as flagships of urban development', in L. Hoffman, S. Fainstein and D. Judd (eds) *Cities and visitors: Regulating people, markets and city space*, Malden, MA and Oxford: Blackwell, 217–36.

Harvey, D. (1989) 'From managerialism to entrepreneurialism: the transformation in urban governance', *Geographiska Annaler*, 71(B.1): 3–17.

Harvey, D. (2009) *Cosmopolitanism and the geographies of freedom*, New York, NY: Columbia University Press.

Hsia, L.M. (2005) 'Jieguo yu xingdong zhi jian: bian chuei shehuei ji qi zhuti xing de yu she yu fansi' [Structure and agency: the assumption and reflection on the marginal society and its subjectivity], *East Taiwan Studies*, 7: 3–16 (in Chinese).

Hsu, J.Y. and Huang, L.L. (2011) 'From cultural building, economic revitalization to local partnership? The changing nature of community mobilization in Taiwan', *International Planning Studies*, 16(2): 131–50.

Keng Sheng Daily News (2011) 'Wenchuang yuanqu qian 15 nian changyue' [15 years contract for the cultural creative park], 20 October, www.ksnews. com.tw/newsdetail.php?n_id=0000231856andlevel2_id=101.

Kou, W. J. (2007) 'Hualien xian zhengfu chai zheng gaiguan fenxi' [Financial analysis of Hualien County government], Financial report No. 095-014, 16 November, National Policy Foundation, www.npf. org.tw/post/2/3674 (in Chinese).

Leitner, H., Sheppard, E., Sziarto, K. and Maringanti, A. (2007) 'Contesting urban futures: decentering neoliberalism', in H. Leitner, J. Peck and E. Sheppard (eds) *Contesting neoliberalism: Urban frontier*, New York, NY: Guilford Press, 1–25.

Li, W.D. (2005) 'Bianchuei hualien?' [Marginal Hualien?], *East Taiwan Studies*, 7: 209–36.

Lin, Cheng-Yi and Woan-Chiau, Hsing (2009) 'Culture-led urban regeneration and community mobilization: the case of the Taipei Bao-An Temple area, Taiwan', *Urban Studies*, 46(7): 1317–42.

Lu, H.Y. (2002) *The politics of locality: making a nation of communities in Taiwan*, London: Routledge.

Lu, D.J. (2004) 'Taiwan xiandi baoyu de zhili' [Governance of in situ conservation in Taiwan – A review of alternative cases since 1990], *Journal of Experiential Forest*, 18(1): 13–27 (in Chinese).

MacLeod, G. (2002) 'From urban entrepreneurialism to a "revanchist city"? On the spatial injustices of Glasgow's renaissance', in N. Brenner and N. Theodore (eds) *Spaces of neoliberalism*, Malden, MA and Oxford: Blackwell, 254–76.

Massey, D. (1993) 'Power-geometry and a progressive sense of place', in J. Bird, B. Curtis, T. Putnam, G. Robertson and L. Tickner (eds) *Mapping the futures: Local cultures, global change*, London: Routledge 59–69.

Sassen, S. (2000) *Cities in a world economy*, 2nd edn, Thousand Oaks, CA: Pine Forge Press.

Shaw, M. (2011) 'Community development and the politics of community', in G. Craig, M. Mayo, K. Popple, M. Shaw and M. Taylor (eds) *The community development reader*, Bristol: Policy Press.

Smith, M.P. (2001) *Power in place: retheorizing the local and the global in urban studies*, http://hcd.ucdavis.edu/faculty/webpages/smith/articles/Powerinplace.pdf.

Swyngedouw, E. (2004) 'Globalisation or 'glocalisation'? Networks, territories and re-scaling', *Cambridge Review of International Affairs*, 17(1): 25–48.

Vidal, A.C. and Keating, W.D. (2004) 'Community development: current issues and emerging challenges', *Journal of Urban Affairs*, 26(2): 125–37.

Wang, T.L. (2004) *Xianzhi kong jian zai li yong yu dushi lianjie guanxi zhuan bian* [*Reuse of the lost space and a change of the linkage in the city – a case study of Pine Garden*], Masters Thesis, Graduate Institute of Environmental Policies, National Dong-Hwa University, Taiwan (in Chinese).

Ward, S.V. (1998) *Selling places: The marketing and promotion of towns and cities 1850–2000*, London: E and FN Spon.

Wu, S.C. (2003) *Difang shaizheng zizhu xing zhi yan jiu* [*The financial autonomy of local governments: A case of Hualien County*], Masters Thesis, Graduate Institute of Public Administration, National Dong Hwa University, Taiwan (in Chinese).

Yang, H.C. (2006) *Gongsi xieli yingyong yu xian zhi kongjian zai liyong zhi yan jiu* [*Research of the application of Public-Private Partnerships on reuse of deserted space. A case study of Chihsing Tan Katsuo Museum, Hualien*], Masters Thesis, Graduate Institute of Environmental Policy, National Dong-Hwa University, Taiwan (in Chinese).

Yen, L.Y. (2007) 'Gou zu renting de shikong xian xiang' [Time–space imagination of national identity: the formation and transformation of the conceptions of historic preservation in Taiwan], *Journal of Architecture and Planning*, 33: 91–106 (in Chinese).

SIX

Community development, venture philanthropy and neoliberal governmentality: a case from Ireland

Niamh McCrea

Introduction

The involvement of community development[1] with philanthropy offers an illustrative example of the complexities inherent in community work practice and of the possibilities for and constraints on socially transformative praxis under conditions of neoliberalism. While philanthropic funding can resource community organisations to challenge unjust state policy, philanthropy has also been promoted as a compensatory mechanism for retrenchments in state welfare provision (Daly, 2011; Forum on Philanthropy and Fundraising, 2012). Furthermore, philanthropic foundations have emerged as key 'partners' in the development of social policy, blurring the boundaries between public and private (Ball, 2012) and raising serious questions regarding democratic accountability. Philanthropy is itself a product of unequal capitalist social relations and, by definition, depends on profound inequalities in wealth for its very existence. Finally, philanthropic organisations are key conduits for the normalisation of market and managerial rationalities (Edwards, 2008; Ball, 2012) and their engagements with grantees raise enduring questions concerning organisational independence and the cooption of political agendas (INCITE!, 2007).

While each of these interrelated themes is worthy of detailed scrutiny, this chapter critically examines the impact of philanthropy on community development through an exploration of one key question. It asks whether involvement with philanthropy inevitably moderates community development's political demands, focusing in particular on whether philanthropically-funded community development work can challenge capitalist interests. This chapter understands community development to be a democratic practice concerned with egalitarian social change, involving either paid or unpaid workers and activists. It recognises, however, that this democratic potential is bound up with, and often constrained by, the interests, perspectives and struggles of the multiple social actors – communities, workers, professionals, state institutions, funders – which give it meaning (Meade, 2012). Although the organisational forms which characterise modern philanthropy have become increasingly diverse (Daly, 2011), the main focus in this chapter is on the role of philanthropic foundations. Foundations can be defined as asset-based, private, self-governing and nonprofit-distributing entities which serve a public purpose (Anheier and Daly, 2008). Historically, foundations mainly took the form of operating institutions such as hospitals and schools. In the 19th and 20th centuries, however, a sharper division between operating and grant-making foundations emerged. Today, foundations pursue their objectives exclusively through grant making, or by implementing their own programmes and services, or through a combination of both (Anheier, 2001).

The following discussion briefly contextualises foundation philanthropy in the US, Britain and Ireland since the late 19th century, before turning to an overview of literature on the role of foundations in funding egalitarian social change. It then responds to the chapter's central question by means of a case study of the alliance between the Migrants Rights Centre Ireland (MRCI), a Dublin-based community development organisation which campaigns on workers' rights, and one of its principal funders, the One Foundation (ONE), a philanthropic foundation which espouses a so-called venture philanthropy model of giving. Drawing on this case and on Foucault's concept of governmentality, the chapter demonstrates that community development workers can influence the outcomes of philanthropic investment in very significant ways. Equally, however, it is suggested that community development practice, perhaps unavoidably, remains intertwined with the rationalities and practices of neoliberalism.

Philanthropic foundations in context

The foundation field has been dominated by US philanthropy since the turn of the 20th century when a number of rich industrialists, most famously Andrew Carnegie and John D. Rockefeller, transferred part of their massive wealth into private trusts with a view to 'improv[ing] the general condition of the people' (Carnegie, 1889, cited in McCarthy, 1989: 50). Over the subsequent decades, the largest of these foundations became 'major social institution[s]' (Bulmer, 1995: 275) which eschewed traditional charitable approaches associated with servicing the needy in favour of systematic, long-term problem solving and 'scientific philanthropy'; that is, the advancement of research and the application of scientific knowledge to public policy and social reform (Dowie, 2001). In the early 1960s, US foundations turned their attention towards the social movements which came to the fore at that time. Foundations funded elements of the civil rights, environmental and feminist movements (Jenkins, 2001) and there is evidence of a certain degree of support for worker organising (Kohl-Arenas, 2013). This period also saw the formation of foundations which experimented with democratic forms of organising that involved community activists in funding decisions (Ostrander, 1995). The US foundation field expanded significantly in the 1990s following developments such as the stock market boom and the growth of the technology and media sectors (Toepler, 2008). By 2011, there were 81,777 grant-making foundations with assets totalling $662 billion active in the US. Their donations for the same year amounted to approximately $49 billion (Foundation Center, n.d.). Data compiled by the Foundation Center (2010: 4) indicate that, in 2008, 14.7% of overall grant making was given to social justice causes.

In Europe, the foundation field has had a very different history. The number and influence of foundations during much of the 19th century were strongly linked to the relative strength of emerging nation states and it was only in Britain that 19th-century foundations were allowed to develop with minimal state interference (Anheier, 2001). British foundations established during the Industrial Age funded welfare services, were active in supporting the arts and also supported causes such as anti-slavery (Anheier, 2001). Like their US counterparts, 'scientific philanthropy' underpinned the work of British foundations such as Rowntree, which was established during this time (Bulmer, 1995).

During the 20th century, foundations in Europe were profoundly weakened by the combined upheavals of two World Wars, the Holocaust, economic crises, the workers' movements and the rise of communism. In the 1940s and 1950s, institutionalised philanthropy in Western Europe largely gave way to the welfare state and between the 1950s and 1980s, foundations scarcely appeared on the public agenda (Anheier, 2001). Since the 1980s, however, economic growth together with the crisis of welfare states, the rise of neoliberal ideology and growing uncertainty among governments as to their own roles have led to a 'phenomenal revival of philanthropy' (Daly, 2010, n.p.; Anheier, 2001). This period has been accompanied by shifts in foundations' public role, most notably, their increased involvement in emergent forms of 'networked governance' (Ball, 2012) within which business and civil society stakeholders participate alongside the state in the formulation and delivery of public welfare. Daly (2010) also situates the shifting role of philanthropy in the UK in relation to reconceptualisations of citizenship which have emerged since the 1980s. She points to the growth of the discourse of 'responsible' citizens which, for the wealthy, 'lessened their obligations in terms of paying taxes but increased expectations of the roles they can play as active citizens' (Daly, 2010: n.p.). Unsurprisingly, philanthropy was championed by the Conservative-Liberal Democrat 'Big Society' programme in the mid- to late-2000s as part of its efforts to marshal voluntary action to address the (alleged) failures of 'big government' (Daly, 2011).

In Ireland, the 'Report of the Forum on Philanthropy and Fundraising' (2012), a committee comprising representatives from government departments and philanthropic organisations, is perhaps the strongest statement to date of the Irish state's commitment to fostering a culture of philanthropy, though it builds on nascent efforts since the late 1990s (see Department of Social, Community and Family Affairs, 2000). While the Forum's report is expressed in explicitly neoliberal terms – noting, for example, that 'partnership with philanthropy … ha[s] the potential to reduce government expenditure on social service solutions in the long term' (Forum on Philanthropy and Fundraising, 2012: 20) – the 'responsibilisation' of civil society in Ireland cannot be regarded as wholly new (Meade, 2012). The Catholic Church dominated the provision of education, health and welfare services during the 19th century and its influence remained with the establishment of the Irish Free State in 1922. The self-help principle of subsidiarity was a central tenet of Catholic social doctrine, and limited state involvement in welfare during this era is partly attributable to the widespread acceptance of this ideology (Considine and Dukelow, 2009) – an ideology which also influenced significant strands of Irish community development (Forde, 2009). Moreover, the Irish welfare state evolved in a haphazard manner, and the universalism which characterised the British welfare state in the post-war period was not a feature of the Irish system (Kirby, 2010).

However, the number of foundations in Ireland remains small. According to the European Foundation Centre (EFC), there were 35 'public-benefit foundations' in Ireland in 2014. The same source notes that the total assets of foundations in Ireland in 2010 were €790 million (EFC, n.d., *a*). This compares with 12,400 foundations in the UK in 2013. The largest 300 of these foundations had assets in the same year of €52.8 billion (EFC, n.d., *b*) and a total spend of €2.8 billion.

What is particularly notable about Ireland is the dominance of three foundations. In 2009, 85% of the then €82 million aggregate grant-making budget of foundations derived from just three organisations, one of which was ONE and all of which were limited life (McKinsey & Company, 2009). The largest foundation in Ireland is the Atlantic Philanthropies (Atlantic), which distributed $52.3 million to Irish organisations in 2012 (Atlantic Philanthropies, 2014).

Impact of philanthropic foundations on social movements

In Ireland and the UK, where funding for community development has been dominated by the state, literature on the relationship between community work and philanthropy remains sparse. This section, therefore, draws on critical scholarship on the impact of foundations on the political claims of social movements in the US. Debates within this body of work dovetail with the contiguous literature concerning community development and the politics of state funding. This has highlighted how funding can align workers and communities with state agendas, 'technicise' political claims and widen acceptance of neoliberal logics (see Larner and Craig, 2005; Shaw, 2011).[2]

The impact of philanthropy in the US has been considered from a range of perspectives. Haines (1984), for example, contests the position advanced by McCarthy and Zald (1977) that external patronage is critical to the establishment and success of social movements. Instead, he regards foundation funding as an attempt to 'pacif[y] the black population and ... accommodate certain manageable black demands' (Haines, 1984: 42). Research by Jenkins and Eckert (1986) challenges this view, arguing that many funders responded favourably to protest campaigns. Rather than attempting to control grantees, they contend that foundations 'channel' social movements by selecting moderate groups with a proven track record and familiar organisational forms.

A less benign interpretation of the consequences of philanthropic funding on movement goals is the subject of Roelofs's Gramscian reading of US foundations. For Roelofs (2003: 125), foundations minimise dissent against capitalism and, echoing Haines, view their beneficiaries as 'containment vessels'. As contributors to a more recent collection of critical essays in *The Revolution Will Not Be Funded* (INCITE!, 2007) attest, such dangers continue to exercise radical activists concerned about their own complicity in a system of funding so closely tied to capitalism. Nonetheless, in framing the problem in such a deterministic fashion, Roelofs may negate the prospect that these coopted radicals – or indeed their funders – may occupy complex, shifting and sometimes contradictory subject positions, at times shoring up capitalist interests while at other times opposing them (Death, 2010). Roelofs's analysis also seems to suggest that, were it not for the intervention of funding regimes, movements would be untainted by complicity with the rationalities of capitalism. This neglects the way that activists are already implicated within neoliberal capitalism through a range of social relationships and practices such as consumption or social media (Death, 2010). Moreover, movement organisations often work in an environment in which the political and economic climate, rather than the agenda of foundations alone, inhibits socially transformative claims.

Kohl-Arenas (2011) discusses this problem in her research on philanthropic funding of the Farm Workers Movement and its legacy organisations in California's central valley since the 1960s. In the 1960s, the Rosenberg Foundation purposively sought to effect structural changes to the farm labourer system, and foundation capital played a key role in enabling the emergence of grassroots leaders and organisers that were critical to the movement's early successes. Kohl-Arenas also highlights, nonetheless, the very real limits to the foundation's willingness to compromise capitalist interests when faced with a growers' backlash. Significantly, Kohl-Arenas notes that foundations' failure to challenge the generative causes of farm workers' poverty was mirrored within the movement itself. She describes a 2003 foundation-funded Farm Worker Community Building Initiative (CBI) tasked with designing regional responses to poverty and poor health outcomes:

> [The CBI] proposed solutions that held every stakeholder, except growers, accountable. Workers could improve their own health through education. Housing could be improved by lobbying the state. Health care services could be improved by providing multi-cultural training to health care providers. Aside from the occasional mention of 'a few bad actors' change in the ways in which large-scale industrial farms operate was never mentioned. (Kohl-Arenas, 2011: 819)

This consensus-driven community development was promoted by community organisers, who, faced with a global financial crisis, market competition and the increasingly 'policed status' of undocumented workers, came to regard collaborative approaches as 'the only thinkable strategy for improving the lives of farmworkers' (Kohl-Arenas, 2011: 820).

Analyses such as these disrupt binary oppositions between authentic, transformative social movements, on the one hand, and hegemony-spreading foundations, on the other. They draw attention to the complexity of the relationship between philanthropy, community organising and social change, highlighting how philanthropic programmes are grafted onto existing political arrangements and how micro-techniques of governance deployed by *both* philanthropy and community development produce and proscribe what is 'thinkable' in terms of social transformation (see also Guthman, 2008). Such insights, as Kohl-Arenas argues, are usefully explained with reference to Foucault's idea of governmentality. 'Government', for Foucault, is any rational, calculated activity or programme directed towards the shaping of human conduct (Dean, 1999). According to Dean, 'governmentality' has two broad meanings within the literature. The first refers to the relationship between practices of government and the rationalities or 'mentalities' of rule, that is, the often taken-for-granted 'bodies of knowledge, belief and opinion' (Dean, 1999: 16) which underpin them. For example, regarding philanthropy as a mode of government illuminates how foundations, informed by specific rationalities, animate community development organisations in particular ways. However, governmentality's emphasis on productive power and the many levels at which power operates also draws attention to how philanthropic programmes are created and sustained by the competing and convergent agendas of multiple actors. The second broad usage of the term refers to historically specific regimes of governmentality, for instance, 'neoliberal governmentality'. The latter describes how market-oriented rationalities and practices are shaping institutions, citizens and other objects of governance within advanced liberal democracies (Larner, 2000; Brown, 2003). The following section draws on these two understandings of governmentality in order to frame MRCI's relationship with ONE and with the wider politics of neoliberalism. It demonstrates how MRCI has shaped the outcomes of philanthropic investment in ways which were at odds with ONE's capitalist origins. It also suggests, however, that this cannot be regarded as an out-and-out victory for counter-hegemonic rationalities and points to the narrowing space for resistance outside the parameters of neoliberal governmentality itself.

ONE, MRCI and worker empowerment: challenging neoliberal governmentality?

ONE was a limited-life foundation which operated between 2004 and 2013 with a mission to 'improve the life chances of disadvantaged children and young people in Ireland and Vietnam' (One Foundation, n.d., *a*). During its lifetime, it donated a total of €75 million to organisations working in the areas of children's rights, migrants' rights, youth mental health and social entrepreneurship (O'Carroll, 2013). ONE was founded by Declan Ryan, a former director of Ryanair, and Deirdre Mortell, a former director of fundraising at children's charity Barnardos. ONE's assets derived from Ryan's personal fortune, which was generated through his involvement with Ryanair and other low-cost airlines. ONE espoused a venture philanthropy model, which combined significant levels of financial support, typically involving multi-annual investments to fund organisations' core costs, with non-financial engagement such as strategic planning, management advice and access to its networks. In return, ONE closely monitored organisations' performance, insisting on high levels of upward accountability around mutually agreed objectives.

Venture philanthropy perceives its role to be that of an active agent in the process of social change, rather than a distant benefactor of citizens' action (Ball, 2012). ONE acted, according to its deputy CEO, as 'a critical friend' to grantee organisations; it occupied a seat on some of its grantees' boards of management and helped shape grantee strategic plans and management structures. Underpinning its model was the view that high-capacity, high-performing, expert-driven organisations – or in the case of social entrepreneurship, strong, passionate thought leaders – are required to achieve positive social change. ONE had a profound impact on the sectors with which it was involved. Between 2004 and 2013, ONE donated a total of €2,350,000 to MRCI (One Foundation, n.d., *b*). This investment, together with funding from Atlantic, and smaller amounts from the Columban Missionary Service and state sources, meant that MRCI's staffing levels expanded from one full-time paid position in 2003 to 17 in 2010.

MRCI was established in 2001 to support the increasing number of migrants coming to live in Ireland at that time. The organisation's mission is 'the empowerment and inclusion of those migrant workers and their families at risk of poverty, social exclusion and discrimination' (MRCI, n.d., *a*). Its primary foci are workplace exploitation, trafficking for forced labour and the rights of the undocumented. The appointment of an experienced community development worker to the position of coordinator (subsequently director) in 2003 and the presence of a lecturer in community work on its board of management have meant that community development has been a defining feature of its organisational identity for most of its history. It has published a number of guides which explain and promote community work (MRCI, 2008; MRCI, n.d., *b*) and its board has formally endorsed 'Towards standards for quality community work' (Ad Hoc Group, 2008), a set of benchmarks for the professionalisation of Irish community development. MRCI's commitment to community development manifests most visibly within its strategies to foster the politicisation, participation and leadership of migrant workers in groups such as the Restaurant Workers Action Group (RWAG), Domestic Workers Action Group (DWAG) or the Agricultural Workers Association (AGWA).

MRCI's strategy and its internal management practices have been developed in accordance with its allegiance to democratic values; yet they have also been shaped by and sometimes overlap with the rationalities of ONE. The foundation gave impetus to a shift in the practices and self-understandings of MRCI from flatter to more hierarchical forms of decision making. However, MRCI has maintained a degree of internal political equality, albeit one that resembles liberal rather than participatory democracy. In turn, MRCI has had some influence on the perspectives of its funder. Although working with MRCI has not dislodged the centrality of the 'expert' from ONE's world view, it has led towards a more pluralised understanding within the foundation as to the *role* of the expert, that is, of the professional as an enabler of others' democratic participation. On the other hand, MRCI's support for an academically credentialised community work profession suggests that there is at least some overlap between the two organisations in this regard: both envisage a central role – though, in the case of MRCI, by no means an exclusive one – for the qualified or officially sanctioned professional in animating the process of social change.

ONE frames its work within a liberal egalitarian discourse of rights and in terms of 'problems' to be 'solved'. It has, therefore, supported campaigns on issues ranging from a constitutional amendment on children's rights to the inhumane treatment of asylum seekers. These are critically important social issues that I do not disparage or dismiss in any way. Notably, however, problem-solving theory 'takes[s] as its starting point some fixed assumptions about the framework or parameters within which action takes place' (Kirby, 2010: 111). Thus, ONE's rationalities do not include any significant analysis of power and are silent on the generative role of structural inequalities in relation to the problems it seeks to address. For example, its CEO noted that:

> 'We're extremely aware of the tension between the world of social change, which is what our portfolio lives in and [the world of business]. We think that we're like a bridge between social change and business. We know there are lots of bad practices and principles in business but we bring the best of what they bring, together with the best of what social change is and can be and we try and create a kind of electric mix that's very special.'

Here it can be noted that 'business' and 'social change' are conceived as separate; the need for the latter is framed as unconnected to the logic of the former. 'Business' is also assumed to proceed untouched by 'the world of social change'.

By contrast, MRCI has publicly aligned itself with community development's more radical traditions, describing it as a practice concerned with 'creat[ing] spaces for action ... to change structures and systems of oppression' (MRCI, 2008: 24). That said, there is evidence of some variability within the organisation as to its staff and board's stance vis-à-vis the capitalist system. While its publications frame its work with reference to Paulo Freire or Margaret Ledwith, a British proponent of radical community development, the agents of migrant disempowerment are rarely explicitly named. For its director, however, community work represents a potential alternative, or part of an alternative, to dominant ideologies including that of neoliberal capitalism:

> '[Our commitment to community work] come[s] from a commitment to a different type of society. And I know that [sounds] kind of wishy washy ... but it's less wishy washy now because we can so clearly see that capitalism in its current form has failed. So *other ideologies* are now not [seen as] so defunct in relation to [capitalism in its current form]' [emphasis added].

MRCI has increasingly adopted a strategy of worker organising as a central pillar of its efforts to advance migrants' workplace rights. This is evident in the establishment of the aforementioned action groups and in its progressively strong links with trade unions. The organisation operates, as one community development worker put it, 'in a very kind of grey area between unions and community work'. Among the measures outlined in its 2009 workplan, for example, were: 'lobby SIPTU [the Services, Industrial, Professional and Technical Union] and UNITE (the Union) to focus resources on organising/campaigning in agriculture with potential formal association with AGWA'; 'lobby SIPTU to dedicate more resources on organising/campaigning with domestic workers' and a commitment to 'negotiate with SIPTU to gain a seat on two Catering Joint Labour Committees'.[3] At a meeting of the RWAG which I observed in 2009, one of the main issues discussed by the 15 workers in attendance was whether or not to explore the possibility of formal affiliation with SIPTU. Despite members' mixed experiences of union engagement, the group unanimously decided to proceed.

Following the onset of the financial crisis in 2008, MRCI joined forces with trade unions and other community and voluntary allies to resist attempts by the state and private sector to attack the minimum wage under the guise of 'competitiveness'. Furthermore, union support was seen by MRCI as a critical factor in achieving a successful outcome to its 2009 campaign to reverse regressive changes to the work permit system. As part of MRCI's campaign on workplace mobility, its director secured a one-off grant of €15,000 from ONE in 2010 to fund advertisements in three national newspapers, which highlighted that work permit holders did not have the right to change employer. The publication date was chosen to coincide with a large union rally taking place in Dublin. Although neither MRCI nor ONE was mentioned in the advertisement, on the bottom of the notices was written: 'This ad was funded by an employer concerned with the rights of migrant workers.'

Just because MRCI's action groups mobilise in campaigns to reform the work permit system does not mean that they fundamentally contradict the logic of neoliberal capitalism. Economic 'competitiveness' is repeatedly linked to the presence of a flexible, multi-skilled migrant labour force (Gray, 2006). However, MRCI's promotion of unionisation among hitherto non-organised workers must be regarded as more challenging to the neoliberal project than the absence of such organisation. Moreover, ONE's sponsoring of a form of class-based activism is particularly noteworthy, given Ryanair's notorious hostility to labour organising, and its heavy reliance on complex contractual arrangements, which evade employment law and minimise social protection obligations (O'Sullivan and Gunnigle, 2009). This irony was not lost on the foundation itself. Its CEO observed in an email that:

'[I've been] struck by the power of how MRCI and One have been able to work together on a common goal when we do not agree philosophically on many things but if we keep it practical it is a powerful working relationship that we have both benefited and learned from. One and MRCI would not be natural allies (One = business links, Ryanair/ non union associations etc) but we have managed to forge an alliance anyway.'

ONE's support for worker solidarity points to MRCI's success in demonstrating the efficacy of this strategy for achieving their mutually agreed objectives. But it also suggests that the ONE staff members are not unremitting agents of neoliberalism; their liberal egalitarian concern with improving the lot of migrant families has meant that, in this instance, ONE has operated against the anti-union rationality that has been a standard feature of neoliberal restructuring in many parts of the world. Though not necessarily referring to its union work, an email from ONE's CEO contained an implicit acknowledgement of the grantee's productive power when she noted that her involvement with MRCI had resulted in a "re-invention of how I see the role of 'solidarity' [from outdated to a new relevance]".

This development should, however, be placed in the context of the complicated relationship between trade unionism and neoliberalism in Ireland and, in particular, trade union participation in social partnership. Social partnership is a process whereby government, employers, trade unions, farmers and, latterly, the community and voluntary sector devise economic and social agreements (Kirby, 2010). Despite the involvement of trade unions and community organisations, social partnership came to be seen as a process primarily concerned with national competitiveness and the flexibilisation of labour (Kirby, 2010; Meade, 2012). Kitchin et al (2012: 1308) argue that: 'The relentless focus on the paradigmatic case of neoliberalism's assault on and dismantling of Fordist Keynesian ... infrastructures ... has arguably effaced the recognition that in some cases neoliberalism actually finds itself in harmony with, rather than in opposition to, prior institutional histories'. Irish neoliberalism was not, they suggest, 'an ideologically informed project' (2012: 1304) of the type associated with Thatcher and Reagan. Rather, it was a pragmatic, 'emergent piling up of market-oriented policies, strategies and instruments framed within its localist, clientelist political culture and system that operates across modes and scales of governance' (2012: 1321). In fact, 'rather than pitting the state against the trade unions' (2012: 1307), unions were among the interest groups with whom the state 'brokered' neoliberal reforms. Kitchin et al therefore suggest that union involvement in governance was not a counterweight to Irish neoliberalism but partly *constitutive* of it.

In relation to the alignment between ONE and MRCI, this suggests two things. On the one hand, MRCI has succeeded in shaping the outcomes of its relationship with ONE in a manner which is incompatible with neoliberal rationality. On the other hand, the claim that this represented a triumph of counter-hegemonic rationalities may not be as significant as it might first appear, given the incorporation of Irish unions into the neoliberal project just described. Focusing on the first of these points, the alliance can be explained by a contradiction between ONE's funding practices in this instance and its neoliberal capitalist origins. However, the second point brings MRCI a little closer to the rationalities of its funder given that, in an Irish context, union organising is less likely to threaten neoliberal capitalist interests than might be the case in other jurisdictions. In making this point, the suggestion is not that this was a misguided strategy on the part of MRCI. Rather, it is to contend that framing the relationship between MRCI and ONE – or between either organisation and neoliberalism – in either/or terms offers an inadequate basis for understanding the complexities of the relationship between philanthropy and community work or the complicated and variegated implementation of the neoliberal political project itself (Brenner et al, 2010).

Conclusion

This chapter has demonstrated that philanthropic capital has provided MRCI with significant freedom to challenge a range of injustices faced by migrant workers, a freedom which is particularly important in an Irish context, where state funding regimes have proven hostile to dissent (Crowley, 2010; Meade, 2012). It has also refuted the hypothesis that philanthropic funding inevitably entails a moderation of grantees' objectives. Rather, it has shown that MRCI has unsettled the rationalities of neoliberal capitalism but that its resistance, intertwined as it is with the performance management frameworks of venture philanthropy and with the complicated history of Irish trade unionism, does not – arguably cannot – exist outside the parameters of neoliberal governmentality. This is in keeping with the Foucauldian analysis of power and empowerment, which emphasises that 'protest and government are mutually constitutive ... [F]orms of resistance have the potential to reinforce and bolster, as well as *and at the same time as*, undermining and challenging dominant forms of global governance' (Death, 2010: 236, emphasis in original). This framing of the philanthropic relationship offers greater scope for understanding the complexities of community development praxis in a time of neoliberal governmentality than the binary analyses contained within the cooption or channelling theories previously discussed.

Notes

[1] This chapter uses the terms 'community development' and 'community work' interchangeably as is common practice in Ireland (Ad Hoc Group, 2008).

[2] Relevant here too is literature on the professionalisation, institutionalisation and neoliberalisation of social action in the Global South, which interrogates the funding practices of Northern NGOs and international financial institutions (see Alvarez, 1999; Feldman, 2003; Mueller-Hirth, 2012).

[3] Joint Labour Committees (JLCs) were established to regulate conditions of employment and set minimum rates of pay for workers in certain sectors of employment. They were independent bodies comprising equal numbers of employer and worker representatives appointed by the Labour Court. In 2011 the High Court ruled that the legislation delegating powers concerning pay and conditions to JLCs was unconstitutional. The JLC system has since been reformed and the number of JLCs reduced (Citizens Information, 2015).

References

Ad Hoc Group (2008) *Towards standards for quality community work: An all-Ireland statement of values, principles and work standards*, Galway: Community Workers Co-operative.

Alvarez, S.E. (1999) 'Advocating feminism: the Latin American feminist NGO "boom"', *International Feminist Journal of Politics*, 1(2): 181–209.

Atlantic Philanthropies (2014) *2012 Grantmaking*, www.atlanticphilanthropies.org/2012-grantmaking.

Anheier, H.K. (2001) 'Foundations in Europe: a comparative perspective', *Civil society working paper series*, London: The Centre for Civil Society, London School of Economics and Political Science.

Anheier, H.K. and Daly, S. (2008) 'Philanthropic foundations in modern society', in H.K. Anheier and S. Daly (eds) *The politics of foundations: A comparative analysis*. London: Routledge.

Ball, S. (2012) *Global education Inc.: New policy networks and the neo-liberal imaginary*, Oxford: Routledge.

Brenner, N., Peck, J. and Theodore, N.I.K. (2010) 'Variegated neoliberalization: geographies, modalities, pathways', *Global Networks*, 10(2): 182–222.

Brown, W. (2003) 'Neo-liberalism and the end of liberal democracy', *Theory and Event*, 7(1): 1–18.

Bulmer, M. (1995) 'Some observations on the history of large philanthropic foundations in Britain and the United States', *Voluntas: International Journal of Voluntary and Nonprofit Organizations*, 6(3): 275–91.

Citizens Information (2015) *Joint Labour Committees*, www.citizensinformation.ie/en/employment/employment_rights_and_conditions/industrial_relations_and_trade_unions/joint_labour_committees.html.

Considine, M. and Dukelow, F. (2009) *Irish social policy: A critical introduction*, Dublin: Gill and Macmillan.

Crowley, N. (2010) *Empty promises: Bringing the Equality Authority to heel*, Dublin: A&A Farmer.

Daly, S. (2010) 'Taking stock of "philanthropy studies" in the UK', *NCVO/VSSN Researching the Voluntary Sector Conference 2010*. London: National Council for Voluntary Organizations.

Daly, S. (2011) 'Philanthropy, the Big Society and emerging philanthropic relationships in the UK', *Public Management Review*, 13(8): 1077–94.

Dean, M. (1999) *Governmentality: Power and rule in modern society*, London: Sage.

Death, C. (2010) 'Counter-conducts: a Foucauldian analytics of protest', *Social Movement Studies: Journal of Social, Cultural and Political Protest*, 9(3): 235–51.

Department of Social, Community and Family Affairs (2000) *A White Paper on a framework for supporting voluntary activity and for developing the relationship between the state and the community and voluntary sector*, Dublin: Stationery Office.

Dowie, M. (2001) *American foundations: An investigative history*, Cambridge, MA: MIT Press.

Edwards, M. (2008) *Small change: Why business won't save the world*, San Francisco, CA: Berrett-Koehler Publishers and Demos.

European Foundation Centre (n.d., *a*) 'Ireland country profile', www.efc.be/country_profile/ireland/.

European Foundation Centre (n.d., *b*) 'United Kingdom country profile', www.efc.be/country_profile/united-kingdom/.

Feldman, S. (2003) 'Paradoxes of institutionalisation: the depoliticisation of Bangladeshi NGOs', *Development in Practice*, 13(1): 5–26.

Forde, C. (2009) 'The politics of community development: relationship with the state', in C. Forde, E. Kiely and R. Meade (eds) *Youth and community work in Ireland: Critical perspectives*, Dublin: Blackhall Publishing, 127–50.

Forum on Philanthropy and Fundraising (2012) *Report of the forum on philanthropy and fundraising*, Dublin: Forum on Philanthropy and Fundraising.

Foundation Center (2010) *Key facts on social justice grantmaking*, New York, NY: Foundation Center.

Foundation Center (n.d.) 'Foundation stats', http://data. foundationcenter.org/about.html.

Gray, B. (2006) 'Redefining the nation through economic growth and migration: changing rationalities of governance in the Republic of Ireland?' *Mobilities*, 1(3): 353–72.

Guthman, J. (2008) 'Thinking inside the neoliberal box: the micropolitics of agro-food philanthropy', *Geoforum*, 39(3): 1241–53.

Haines, H.H. (1984) 'Black radicalization and the funding of civil rights', *Social Problems*, 32(1): 31–43.

INCITE! Women of Color Against Violence, (2007) *The revolution will not be funded: Beyond the non-profit industrial complex*, Cambridge, MA: INCITE! and South End Press Collective.

Jenkins, J.C. (2001) 'Social movement philanthropy and the growth of nonprofit political advocacy: scope, legitimacy and impact', in E.J. Reid and M.D. Montilla (eds) *Nonprofit advocacy and the policy process seminar series*, Washington, DC: The Urban Institute, 51–66.

Jenkins, J.C. and Eckert, C.M. (1986) 'Channeling Black insurgency: elite patronage and professional social movement organizations in the development of the Black movement', *American Sociological Review*, 51(6): 812–29.

Kirby, P. (2010) *Celtic Tiger in collapse: Explaining the weaknesses of the Irish model*, 2nd edn, Basingstoke: Palgrave Macmillan.

Kitchin, R., O'Callaghan, C., Boyle, M., Gleeson, J. and Keaveney, K. (2012) 'Placing neoliberalism: the rise and fall of Ireland's Celtic Tiger', *Environment and Planning Part A*, 44(6): 1302–26.

Kohl-Arenas, E. (2011) 'Governing poverty amidst plenty: participatory development and private philanthropy', *Geography Compass*, 5(11): 811–24.

Kohl-Arenas, E. (2013) 'Will the revolution be funded? Resource mobilization and the California farm worker movement', *Social Movement Studies* (advanced online access) DOI: 10.1080/14742837.2013.86372.

Larner, W. (2000) 'Neoliberalism: policy, ideology, governmentality', *Studies in Political Economy*, 63 (Autumn): 5–25.

Larner, W. and Craig, D. (2005) 'After neoliberalism? Community activism and local partnerships in Aotearoa New Zealand', *Antipode*, 37(3): 402–24.

McCarthy, K.A. (1989) 'The gospel of wealth: American giving in theory and practice', in R. Magat (ed) *Philanthropic giving: Studies in varieties and goals*, New York, NY: Oxford University Press, 46–62.

McCarthy, J. and Zald, M. (1977) 'Resource mobilization and social movements', *American Journal of Sociology*, 82(6): 1212–41.

McKinsey and Company (2009) *Philanthropy in the Republic of Ireland: An assessment of the current state and future potential of philanthropic giving in the Republic of Ireland*, Dublin: McKinsey and Company.

Meade, R.R. (2012) 'Government and community development in Ireland: the contested subjects of professionalism and expertise', *Antipode*, 44(3): 889–910.

Migrant Rights Centre Ireland (2008) *Tools for social change: A resource guide for community work with migrant workers and their families in Ireland*, Dublin: MRCI.

Migrant Rights Centre Ireland (n.d., *a*) 'Background', www.mrci.ie/background/.

Migrant Rights Centre Ireland (n.d., *b*) *Mobilising for social justice: Migrant Rights Centre Ireland's community work model*, Dublin: MRCI.

Mueller-Hirth, N. (2012) 'If you don't count, you don't count: monitoring and evaluation in South African NGOs', *Development and Change*, 43(3): 649–70.

O'Carroll, Í. (2013) *Daring voices: Evaluation of the One Foundation's support of advocacy in children's rights, immigrant rights and mental health reform in Ireland*, Dublin: One Foundation.

One Foundation (n.d., *a*) 'Welcome to the One Foundation', www.onefoundation.ie/.

One Foundation (n.d., *b*) 'Migrants Rights Centre Ireland', www.onefoundation.ie/index.php/portfolio/migrant-rights-centre-ireland/.

Ostrander, S. (1995) *Money for change: Social movement philanthropy at the Haymarket People's Fund*, Philadelphia, PA: Temple University Press.

O'Sullivan, M. and Gunnigle, P. (2009) '"Bearing all the hallmarks of oppression": Union avoidance in Europe's largest low-cost airline', *Labor Studies Journal*, 34(2): 252–70.

Roelofs, J. (2003) *Foundations and public policy: The mask of pluralism*, Albany, NY: State University of New York Press.

Shaw, M. (2011) 'Stuck in the middle? Community development, community engagement and the dangerous business of learning for democracy', *Community Development Journal*, 46(S2): ii128–46.

Toepler, S. (2008) 'Foundations roles and visions in the USA', in H.K. Anheier and S. Daly (eds) *The politics of foundations: A comparative analysis*, London: Routledge.

SEVEN

A shifting paradigm: engendering the politics of community engagement in India

Martha Farrell and Rajesh Tandon

Introduction

Community development, as a distinctive approach to socioeconomic development, began to be official practice in India in the early 1950s. Although such approaches have, in different ways, addressed women's experiences of discrimination in society, the specificity of women's needs and their gendered identities have largely been ignored. As a result, the agency of women has not, historically, been given sufficient attention within the dominant community development paradigm. It is only since the 1990s that specific structures for women's participation have been included in development programmes, although these were originally limited to participation in those 'invited' political spaces (Cornwall, 2002) created and mediated by powerful interests which were not necessarily committed to women's empowerment. In the mid-1990s, when the affirmative policy statutorily reserved places for women in local government institutions, their presence in public spheres did increase to some extent, but, similarly, this did not necessarily ensure that their voices were heard or their contributions recognised.

Participatory Research in Asia (PRIA) was set up as an educational support institution for the empowerment of the excluded in 1982. Its founding inspiration was the theory and practice of participatory research, and its belief in the capacity of ordinary citizens to transform their lives and societies. As we discuss in this chapter, PRIA's experiences of building the collective capacities of elected women leaders has shown that an alternative pedagogy and methodology for addressing gender discrimination is both required and possible. However, this approach has had to challenge embedded inequalities within the institutions of governance and elsewhere, while at the same time addressing power issues within families and communities.

This chapter attempts to analyse the evolution of community development thinking and programming in India using a gender lens. It brings into focus the complex politics and practices of gender discrimination that persist within the structures and institutions of development. Consequently, it also argues that development must be 'engendered', in the sense that it must demonstrate a critical understanding of, and commitment to, the political empowerment of women. Engendering development entails prioritising the special needs and interests of women as equal partners in and active agents of development, not merely as passive beneficiaries (Farrell, 2014). This is necessary in order to transform community development itself, and to ensure real participation and engagement by women in governance, local democracy and development.

Mapping the origins of community development in India

The strategy of development, as a formal process of intervention by various governments, was initiated after the Second World War (in the late 1940s) largely as a means of aiding the reconstruction of war-destroyed Europe. In the context of the emergence of the post-colonial world, early programmes focused on a process of growth, change and transformation, through reconstruction and 'development' in newly formed and independent nations (Rist, 1997). The first milestone in this development paradigm was economic growth, reflected in agricultural modernisation and industrialisation. It was only later that development also came to entail working towards the somewhat more abstract concepts of empowerment, social justice, equity and inclusion.

At this time, particularly in countries with large rural populations, governments embarked on programmes of 'community development' which emphasised the importance of raising the standard of living in rural areas. Alongside this immediate aim, there was also a longer-term goal of creating an infrastructure for future industrial growth. Though agriculture was the primary concern, community development in its more holistic conceptualisation also took into account issues linked to governance, roads, transport, irrigation, education, health and housing. Such planned and government-led processes of development started in India in 1951, after its independence from Britain, with the formulation of the First Five Year Plan for national development. In this Plan, the government emphasised the self-reliance of villages, which would be facilitated through the concept of community development. The characteristics of the first community development projects in India are well summarised in Thorner's description of the Etawah Pilot Project as follows:

> The Etawah pilot project was initiated in India by Albert Mayer, an American civil engineer who had focused on stimulating economic and social progress by the creation of 'model' villages ... In this project, major emphasis was given to increasing agricultural production by the use of green manure, improved seeds, agricultural implements, fertilizers and saline soil reactivation. The process was initiated through adult education programmes led by the Village Level Worker. (Thorner, 1981: 117)

In other words, the focus of the Etawah pilot project was to demonstrate an approach to village development through the collective efforts of the villagers themselves, with some support from government.

Shifting meanings of community development

Following the Etawah model and, as emphasised in its first Five Year Plan, the government of India understood community development primarily as the holistic development of the village community, on the initiative of the villagers themselves. The method that evolved in practice was typically described as 'rural extension', a methodology of providing knowledge of new agricultural practices to farmers. It was facilitated by community development workers who were appointed by the government. However, while the village community was encouraged to work towards the development of their village, in reality the resources provided were more or less controlled by the government extension workers.

In this general approach to community development, the focus was entirely and exclusively on the village itself. There was no attempt to relate their development requirements to the larger context of the district or nearby cities around them. Significantly, the Second Five Year Plan (1956) adopted a different approach, by extending attention to administrative and democratic structures at the district level (districts were often comprised of several hundred villages). In this elaboration of community development, the roles of officials at district level were enhanced to ensure greater cohesiveness, synergy and sustainability of development plans.

By the time of the Third Five Year Plan (1961) the concept and method of rural extension had become more closely integrated with the operations of local elected governments, and local leaders began to work with district-level government officials to implement community development programmes. As this approach began to be applied, the planning and monitoring responsibilities for community development eventually shifted entirely to government officials at district level (Govt. of India, 1962).

This brief review of the government of India's shifting approaches during the period of the 1950s and 1960s is revealing in the way it demonstrates that the meanings of community development can and do change over time. In its first conceptualisation, community development was seen as an approach to village development by the collective efforts of the villagers themselves; the role of the government was merely that of a facilitator. This formulation was premised on the assumption that a village community knows what is best for its development, and the government should simply support local decision making. As government expanded the public funding of community development, however, its official machinery became more extensive, and with it came the realisation of the need to focus beyond the village, to the district. At the outset, the local priorities and initiatives of village communities were to be solicited and orchestrated by government functionaries, called community development workers. However, the collective focus of the village came to be regarded as somewhat unwieldy and government functionaries began working through elected village leaders, in the name of convenience and efficiency.

As can be seen, in this journey the role of villagers themselves in development processes gradually declined, while that of government functionaries, and a few selected leaders, increased substantially. In this sense, community development became virtually an intervention on behalf of the district administration rather than an initiative of the village community on its own behalf (Jain et al, 1985; Maheshwari, 1995).

Fractured communities

In light of some of these tensions surrounding ownership and representation, public reviews of the wider impact of community development programmes of the 1950s began to raise critical questions about the efficacy of this model. First, community development programmes, as implemented by the government of India, tended to treat the village as a unified entity, and made implicit assumptions about the homogeneous and harmonious nature of village life. In reality, Indian village society, despite its geographical and temporal contiguity, was highly heterogeneous, with profound internal differences based on caste and class relations. By ignoring internal hierarchies of status, wealth and power, the community development approach had, inadvertently, enabled village elites to capture most of the benefits accrued through development programmes. Furthermore, by ignoring unequal power relations within the village, community development approaches frequently ended up simply reinforcing the power of existing elites. According to Jain et al (1985), such elite power was commonly based on control over land, higher-caste status and external political connections with district-level officials. As a result, under community development programmes, provision of drinking water, for example, remained largely restricted to upper-caste households, and rarely reached those scheduled-caste households who lived apart. Likewise, primary schools were located in higher-caste neighbourhoods. In general terms, decision-making processes at the village level remained concentrated in the hands of a few upper-caste, financially better-off families, on whom community development workers often seemed content to focus their attention and energies (Jain et al, 1985).

As the scale of community development became more district focused, and as larger numbers of government functionaries began to work with smaller numbers of selected village leaders, this pattern of exclusion and marginalisation of poorer households was further accentuated. Consequently, large numbers of rural households, typically small/marginal farmers or landless labourers, benefitted little if at all from community development programmes until the mid-1960s (Maheshwari, 1995). Indeed, with growing public criticism of this pattern of community development, national planners had quietly dropped this approach by the late 1960s. In any case, a number of wider factors, including the growing economic crisis arising from oil cartels and the Bangladesh liberation struggle on India's borders, meant that resources for village-led bottom-up development began to dry up.

It is important to emphasise that, during this era of community development, the question of gender divisions and discrimination against women was barely considered. There was little or no analysis of gender-based discrimination in village society and in the family. Even when critiques of community development began to emerge, they focused most forcefully on class- and caste-based exclusions (Maheshwari, 1995). It was assumed that men and women within particular classes and castes enjoyed broadly similar status, benefits and access to services.

In the late 1970s the invisibility of women in grassroots development programmes began to be challenged by feminist critics. According to Agarwal (1988), for example, a simplistic approach that ignored gender inequality and discrimination in the family and village society needed to be challenged. As a start, national planners should be sensitised to the structures and processes of gender-based discrimination that were prevailing in the wider society, public institutions, villages and family life.

A new trajectory for community development

The national planning framework in India began to revisit the theme of community development in the Ninth Five Year Plan (1997–2002). Following the severe financial crisis of the late 1980s, the Indian government, like many others, adopted an economic liberalisation approach to development. The earlier, broadly socialist, model of a planned economy gradually gave way to more market-oriented economic policies and reforms. However, it was also during this period that planners really began to come to terms with India's changing demographic patterns. In so doing, they began to recognise troubling issues related to the declining female–male sex ratio in several parts of the country, as expressed in the following quotation: 'There is a serious decline of sex ratio ... It is well recognized that adverse sex ratio is a reflection of gender disparity ... There has been speculation whether female foeticide, sex determination and selective female infanticide are part responsible for this ... Intensive community education efforts are under way' (Govt. of India, 1997: ch 3.8).

The Ninth Plan also acknowledged that those sectors of the population that were underserved in respect of basic needs such as health, education and water, would be growing rapidly in the 21st century, with young women comprising the largest single group. It accepted that decentralised community-based planning had to be scaled up in order to make delivery of services more locally relevant and accountable. As a consequence, national development programmes in respect of primary education, basic healthcare and potable drinking water began to incorporate efforts at community-driven planning, implementation and monitoring of these services. Notably, previous Plans, especially after 1985, had already started to focus on creating structures for community participation and engagement at village level. Catalysed through pioneering NGO efforts and incentivised by international development organisations (including the World Bank), government's primary education, healthcare and drinking water programmes had thus begun to establish user committees at the village and/or hamlet level. These committees were mandated to guide and oversee effective delivery of those services by government functionaries. By the beginning of the Ninth Plan in 1997, all such committees had also begun to reflect a proportionate representation of women, with a view to bringing gender mainstreaming into service delivery mechanisms (Long, 2001). These structures of participation were essentially 'invited' spaces, directly and functionally linked to that specific development programme.

In practice, however, these new participatory structures remained largely tokenistic in respect of gender. By placing women in participatory structures, it had been naively assumed that gender-sensitive delivery of basic services would follow. Insufficient attention was given to the fact that most of the women concerned had no previous experience of the work of committees. Indeed many of them were illiterate, and had absolutely no knowledge of or access to information regarding the issues that they were required to deal with. It appeared, then, that they had been set up for failure, and for power to remain in the hands of men in the community. Several field experiences began to show the inadequacy of women's participation in such formalised participation spaces. One particular critique sums it up well as follows:

> It is all too obvious that women are recruited to the watershed committee to meet procedural requirements. It seems ironic to talk about 'choice', since most women members are not even aware that they have membership of the committee. Both the project bureaucracy and male members know that women will merely be decorative members, leaving men the prerogative to rule the committee. Thus from the very beginning, the stage is set for keeping women outside and excluded from the committee. Women, too, get this sense; hence during the course of the project when meetings take place in their absence and they are sent papers to sign, endorsing decisions taken by male members, they do not resist (Mohanty, 2007: 85).

Therefore, even though a new and ostensibly more nuanced conception of community development began to emerge in this era, some concerns still remained. Clearly there was an acknowledgement of the importance of creating structured spaces for participation of villagers as primary stakeholders. Although the resulting structures deliberately and consciously included representatives of the scheduled caste and women, in the absence of any collective voice, women largely remained a token presence. Furthermore, this new paradigm was no longer about community development as it had been previously understood, but was now more directly focused on community participation. This had the effect of formalising the participation of women in 'invited spaces', even if, in many cases, it did not ultimately make much of a difference in practice. Arguably, within this new model of development, the functions of government workers and their control over decisions only increased.

Statutory mandates and local government reform

In a landmark amendment to the Indian Constitution in 1992, democratically elected local government institutions in rural and urban India became a reality. Known as *Panchayati Raj* Institutions (PRIs) in rural areas (and Municipalities in urban areas), these statutory bodies were expected to transform the practice of socioeconomic development. However, the statutory structures of community participation created through the constitution of PRIs took some time to develop and were still not fully operational even five years later. According to the Constitution, the PRIs would have a three-tier structure: a *Village Panchayat*, a block-level *Panchayat* Committee and a district-level *Zila Parishad*. Membership of all three tiers of committees would be elected every five years, and one-third of places at all three levels would be reserved for women. In several states, the proportion of reservation has since been increased to 50% (Rai et al, 2001). As a consequence of these affirmative measures, at any given point in time there are nearly one million elected women representatives in these PRIs.

Following this constitutional amendment, each tier had certain standing committees for oversight of the different social and economic functions of PRIs. Though named differently in different states, these committees, which oversee education, health and water, existed all over the country. Women not only headed up PRIs at all levels in several places, they also led several of these committees as well. It could be said that the constitutional amendment had created the necessary conditions for gender mainstreaming of those institutions which were mandated to deliver basic services to the marginalised communities in the country. In theory, then, these new structures had certainly created greater space for women's participation in local decision making. In practice, however, the pre-existing structures of community participation that had been constructed in line with various development programmes continued to function. By the beginning of 2000, there were serious contradictions, in operational terms on the ground, between the committees of PRIs with elected women representatives and those appointed by government (PRIA, 2001). The new local governance system created statutorily defined subcommittees for various aspects of development at village level. In effect, these subcommittees as 'statutory spaces' of PRIs came into conflict with the previously structured 'invited spaces' of community participation, set up by different development programmes. For example, a study undertaken into the implementation of primary education programmes illuminates some of the associated contradictions and confusion:

> The PRIs have the advantage of being constitutionally (formally) recognized ... level of government. Their membership is based on direct election from the territorial constituency, thus creating opportunities for true representation of the community. Further specified five year term of function, mandatory provisions for re-election and one third reservations for women ensures greater representativeness and community ownership of these bodies. As compared to the project committees their existence is not dependent on the project or programme duration (the project or programme could be government or non-government project). (PRIA, 1998: 3)

It was only during the Tenth and Eleventh Five Year Plans (2002–12) that the national government began to integrate the two sets of structures of community participation at the local level. Even though formal integration had been achieved at the national level by 2005 (during the Tenth Plan), it was not implemented on the ground until the end of the Eleventh Plan (2012). In any case, neither set of structures, despite claiming to support women's participation in and contribution to the development of their own communities, actually confronted the realities of discrimination against girls and women in the family and the village. As a result, the efforts towards gender mainstreaming in institutions, structures, services and community life remained, at best, half-hearted.

Women's agency

As the above account shows, in the initial history of Indian community development, women's exclusion and involvement was generally ignored. With the later shift to community participation, women were formally invited to participate, but largely constructed as passive beneficiaries, rather than as active agents of change. Structural barriers and patriarchal constraints faced by women at home and in society were taken for granted and consequently remained unchallenged. No concerted effort was made to transform gender relations and unequal power at home, in the village or in the larger society.

The Eleventh Plan framed a new approach to women's participation in development which at last began to articulate a concept of women's agency: 'In the Eleventh Plan (2007–11), for the first time, women are recognized not just as equal citizens, but as agents of social and economic growth. The approach to gender equity is based on the recognition that interventions in favour of women must be multi-pronged' (Govt of India, 2008: 184). This Plan also included a focus on entitlements, representation and prevention of all forms of violence against women. The National Policy on Women in 2001 had already laid the basis for this shift by providing a strong framework of new entitlements which included the right to information, an employment guarantee, forest rights and the right to education. With these rights in place from 2008, it seemed that the wider goal of gender mainstreaming of the institutions and mechanisms of community participation/development might eventually be realised.

However, continued discrimination and recurring incidents of violence, including rape against girls and women, had the effect of reinforcing the societal and institutional status quo. This raises several important questions: Why is it that women's agency is not able to influence the gender dynamics of basic service delivery in favour and support of women? Why is it that statutory and administrative structures that promote women's participation in decision making in local development programmes do not enable gender-fair development outcomes? Why does India's ranking on the global gender inequality index today remain stagnant at around 135 (out of 170 countries) after more than a decade of rapid economic growth? (World Economic Forum, 2014). These are the questions that our work in PRIA sets out to address.

We would argue that gender is a fundamental organising principle in society and, as such, it is a primary way of signifying relations of power and constructing hierarchies. Gendered forms of subjugation and oppression are themselves intersecting and interlocking systems that cut across class, caste and even racial hierarchies (Kabeer and Subrahmanian, 1999). Though the first milestone of development was envisaged as economic growth, its major social, economic and political processes were almost entirely in the hands of men. Since development theorists, planners and practitioners were also invariably men, they tended to value the contribution of men over that of women. Women's contributions to the economic processes were considered to be of little significance and were therefore not included in either the planning processes or impact analysis of development. Furthermore, it was assumed that the targets of all growth and prosperity were poor people (for which read 'men') and that if poor men benefitted, then automatically the benefits would 'trickle down' to their 'poor wives or other women in the family'.

In the Indian context, the cross-cutting themes of class, caste, race, disability and gender are simultaneously experienced by women. For example, as a Dalit (the lowest category in the caste hierarchy), a woman may experience oppression in terms of social exclusion and she may also face oppression from being poor, and be further oppressed by men from within her own family and community. These multiple layers and levels of gendered complexity all act to work against women, and deny them equality in terms of autonomy, power, and access to and control of resources. They therefore need to be considered in a holistic manner, when considering the inclusion and participation of women in all social, economic and political processes.

So, the central question in this thinking is about women's agency. Do women have agency? Can they exercise their agency? Do they have the necessary capabilities to exercise agency for community development? Do women have agency to provide leadership to such socioeconomic development programmes? Under what circumstances do women overcome various structural constraints to exercise their agency and leadership?

Women's political leadership

The move towards the political representation of women at all levels of local government could be said to have been effective in so far as it created a space for women to exercise leadership and develop their potential to challenge their structural position from a place of greater authority and strength. Although the process was fraught with difficulties from the outset, it nonetheless gave women a degree of legitimacy and authority 'to influence others and provide cohesive and coherent direction to accomplish particular missions and tasks ... and inclusive governance through redistribution of power, resources and opportunities in favour of women' (Farrell and Pant, 2009: 44). However, it should also be noted that the statutory nature of the constitutional mandate to enhance women's representation in governance, has meant that in many instances it was implemented with little enthusiasm. This response is hardly surprising for, while women were nominated onto various bodies and committees in order to fulfil the 'one-third participation' quota, they continued to face multiple challenges. In most cases, they had no previous exposure to governance mechanisms and processes and, in any case, there were no female role models for them to emulate. In addition, while the andragogical strategies for building women's capacities to assume their new leadership roles included providing information on their responsibilities as elected representatives, specific administrative functions, and the necessary strategies for influencing service delivery systems, they failed to tackle the need 'to address the history of exclusion, marginalisation and invisibility of women's voices, which prevents the actual exercise of power' (Farrell and Pant, 2009: 53). In too many cases, women representatives were expected to be physically present but not to actually participate in any of the discussions nor to articulate their views. Rather, it was assumed that they would agree with decisions taken, even where those decisions related to matters such as sanitation, water supply or healthcare where women were most directly affected. To put it another way, the issues which could be considered to be most critical in effectively addressing the question of ensuring women's political empowerment and leadership were never even considered. These included the following:

(a) Gendered identities and practices that constricted their participation in political or leadership roles. These included matters such as covering of the face in the presence of village elders and male family members at public events, sitting on the floor while all male members occupied chairs, even if a woman was the *sarpanch* (elected head of local village-level government); making and serving tea to the male members, and never going to meetings unaccompanied, even in the fulfilment of important public roles.

(b) Persistent institutional inadequacies that deter women's access to power. The effective participation of women leaders depends on a number of factors, including 'access to resources of and opportunities for development, strong capabilities built through education, information, skills and the freedom to exercise choice and action' (Farrell and Pant, 2009: 54). No efforts were made to assess the existing abilities of women, to understand the gaps in their knowledge base and make efforts to build their capacities in order to help them understand their roles, act upon their responsibilities and make demands on the system for effective delivery of services.

In other words, the most critical gender dynamic, the public–private divide which so profoundly hinders women's participation in, and negotiation of, the public domain, was not sufficiently recognised as an impediment to political progress. Traditionally, the private domain is associated with household, reproductive work and femininity, whereas the public domain is associated with political authority, public decision making, productive work and masculinity. More often than not those women in leadership positions were either criticised for their inadequacies in fulfilling both of these obligations, or patronised by men for not having the ability to do both (Farrell et al, 2008). Consequently it was difficult for them to break out of the 'gendered trap' of structures and processes that had been intricately woven by patriarchal mindsets. As a result, women were treated (and sometimes behaved) as 'dummy' candidates, while various men within their families and community wielded the real political power (PRIA, 1999a). This case shows that the gendered division of power is reflected in deep-rooted social and cultural practices that cannot be resolved simply through legal measures and institutional structures (McGregor et al, 2009).

An alternative methodology

PRIA's approach to the promotion of women's empowerment and engendered development is grounded in its values of justice and equality. It promotes valuing of women's knowledge such that they can acquire new capacities, and its theory of change entails collectivisation of women, using their knowledge and voice for changing relations of power. Its primary role is to facilitate learning as a collective social praxis by women. Therefore, in order to support women political leaders in their attempts to take up the responsibilities of public office and to encourage other women who were emerging as citizen leaders, PRIA developed and implemented several initiatives across the country, aimed at the enhancement of women's leadership. This section briefly describes this alternative methodology to engage women as active political subjects.

The first of these initiatives was a wide-scale national campaign – the Pre-Election Voters Awareness Campaign (PEVAC) – to support women in exercising their right to contest the election to local *Panchayats*. As a result, many women were elected to public office. Initially, there was substantial reluctance from some sections of the community to accept women as political leaders. Strongly entrenched patriarchy implies that men alone are capable of, and entitled to, hold public office. In several cases, men in the family (husbands, fathers, fathers-in-law, brothers) would assume the role of elected public leaders, while the women actually elected to these offices remained invisible. Reluctance and resentment of men towards women elected leaders made it difficult for these women to perform their leadership roles effectively (Farrell and Pant, 2009).

Therefore, the second stage was even more critical, in order to maintain the motivation of the women involved, and to ensure that men did not wield power in their names. PRIA had been undertaking field-level capacity-building programmes for *Panchayats* in 16 states of the country since 1996. In this phase, PRIA conducted capacity-building efforts especially for women elected leaders, focusing on a range of necessary skills and knowledge:

- rapid literacy (for illiterate women)
- awareness of the roles and responsibilities of governance
- gender sensitisation
- planning for local development programmes
- financial Planning, including budgeting
- conduct of official meetings
- documentation and keeping minutes
- conflict resolution and peace building

Group dynamics, leadership skills, setting of norms and procedures, decision making, conflict resolution, and maintenance of accounts and other documentation were others lessons that had to be learned. Effectively fulfilling their roles and aspirations involved women elected leaders moving beyond the confines of their homes, meeting with officials, participating in skill-building programmes and breaking social norms designed to maintain women's powerlessness.

Soon women were beginning to redefine the very essence of leadership and taking up issues which were critical to their understanding of development, though it took a whole term (five years) to do so. The results were reflected in women attending *Panchayat* meetings regularly, speaking their minds in such meetings, and ultimately influencing the development agenda. In this way, planning took on an engendered lens, with greater attention given to issues of children's education, water facilities, women's health and family planning, electricity, metalled roads and a focus on domestic violence and alcoholism.

Simultaneously, the 'Women's Political Empowerment and Leadership' (WPEL) programme (PRIA, 2009b) was launched, targeting subsequent groups of women who could take up leadership roles within their communities and contest the next rounds of local *Panchayat* elections. It was intended that the challenges faced by the earlier batch of elected leaders would not be repeated the next time. Hence, a programme aimed at supporting women leaders to learn the competencies required to become successful, elected *Panchayat* leaders was undertaken by PRIA. This time round, the first step by PRIA was to identify those women who had the greatest potential for political leadership. Criteria such as confidence in public speaking, the domestic flexibility to stay overnight in residential programmes, support in taking care of young children or other reproductive roles were all considered in the selection of women for political leadership. The learning content was based on the articulated needs of women leaders and on the basis of the earlier curriculum for capacity-building programmes. The entire WPEL programme, from its inception to conduct of training needs analysis, orientation programmes and capacity-building workshops, was conceptualised, coordinated and organised by PRIA team members, based on field interactions undertaken over the preceding several years. Many civil society organisations supported this process of selection of leaders.

The programme of WPEL has reflected PRIA's commitment to gender mainstreaming since its very inception, and has brought out very clearly the key issues and challenges that women face in private and public spheres and that inhibit their participation in, and contribution to, community development processes. These insights have been critical to PRIA's methodology of building the capacities of women as citizen leaders and political representatives.

The approach has consistently focused on women developing an awareness of the various gendered identities and practices that limit their capacities and prevent them from exercising personal and political agency. The starting point is developing an awareness of gender discrimination within households, including a common preference for male children, stereotypical notions of roles based on gender, and a lack of educational opportunities for women. From here, awareness raising moves towards an analysis of systemic discrimination and deeply embedded patriarchal values which exist within institutions of family and governance and in those mechanisms that deny them participation and engagement in community processes.

Concluding remarks

Three critical conclusions can be drawn from the above. First, the initial approach of the Indian government to community development ignored issues relating to gender discrimination and the resultant inequality that exists both within the family and the larger society. As a result, the benefits of the programmes served to reinforce and perpetuate existing patriarchal and gendered power relations.

Second, the paradigm shift in policy towards women's empowerment through affirmative action, particularly the representation of women in institutions of local governance, had a significant impact in improving the priority given to women's agendas. Yet these changes were neither effective nor sustainable because they overlooked the structural constraints and obstacles that women faced. In reality, women's leadership in the institutions of governance was ultimately tokenistic because it was displaced by male vested interests, both within the family and community, and including male political leaders.

Third, effective participation and leadership by women requires attention to their individual and collective learning as an integral part of development projects. PRIA's experience, briefly described in this chapter, demonstrates some practical steps that need to be taken if women's empowerment and leadership potential is to be realised through community development efforts.

Finally, community development needs to be reconceptualised as a political and transformative methodology that enhances the collective capacities of the excluded, particularly women, to engage with the institutions and processes of development. Without this explicit emphasis on the politics of development (and underdevelopment) in gender relations, community development is unlikely to achieve its promise, as conceived nearly seven decades ago.

References

Agarwal, B. (1988) *Structures of patrichiarchy: State, community and household in modernising Asia*, New Delhi: Kali for Women.

Cornwall, A. (2002) *Making Spaces, changing places: situating participation in development*, IDS Working Paper 170.

Farrell, M. (2014) *Engendering the workplace: Gender discrimination and prevention of sexual harassment in organisations*, New Delhi: Uppal Publishing House.

Farrell, M. and Pant, M. (2009) 'Women's political empowerment and leadership: pedagogical challenges', *Participaton and Governance*, 2(2): 42–56.

Farrell, M., Saxena, T., Thekkudan, J. and Pathak, P. (2008) *Engendering workplaces: Framework for a gender policy*, New Delhi: PRIA.

Govt. of India (1962) *Third five-year plan*, New Delhi: Planning Commission.

Govt. of India (1997) *Ninth five-year plan*, New Delhi: Planning Commission.

Govt. of India (2008) *Eleventh five year plan*, New Delhi: Planning Commission.

Jain, L.C., Krishnamurthy, B.V. and Tripathi, P.M. (1985) *Grass without roots – Rural development under government auspices*, New Delhi: Sage Publications.

Kabeer, N. and Subrahmanian, R. (1999) *Institutions, relations and outcomes: A framework and case studies for gender-aware planning*, New Delhi: Kali for Women.

Long, C. (2001) *Participation of the poor in development initiatives: Taking their rightful place*, London and Sterling, VA: Earthscan.

Maheshwari, S. (1995) *Rural development in India: A public policy approach*, 2nd edn, New Delhi: Sage Publications India Pvt. Ltd.

McGregor, C., Clover, D., Farrell, M. and Bhattacharya, S. (2009) 'Women's political education: developing political leadership in Canada and India', *Calumet*, 8(1): 5.

Mohanty, R. (2007) 'Gendered subjects, the state and participatory spaces: the politics of domesticating participation in rural India', in A. Cornwall and V.S. Coelho (eds) *Spaces for change?: The politics of citizen participation in new democratic arenas*, London: Zed Books.

PRIA (1998) *Community organisations – Towards better collaboration*, Society for Participatory Research in Asia, New Delhi, www.pria. org/docs/community_organisations_towards_better_collaboration. pdf.

PRIA (1999a) 'Development projects: a step towards women's empowerment', *Participation & Governance*, 3–6.

PRIA (1999b) *Women leadership in Panchayati Raj institutions: An analysis of six states*, New Delhi: PRIA.

PRIA (2001) *Parallel bodies and Panchayati Raj institutions (experiences from the states)*, New Delhi: Samskriti.

Rai, M., Nambiar, M., Paul, S., Singh, S. and Sahni, S. (2001) *The state of Panchayats: A participatory perspective*, New Delhi: Samskriti.

Rist, G. (1997) *The history of development: From Western origins to global earth*, London and New York, NY: Zed Books.

Tandon, R. and Jaitli, N. (1998) *Community organisation: Towards better collaborations*, New Delhi: PRIA.

Thorner, A. (1981) 'Nehru, Albert Mayer and the origins of community projects', *Economic and Political Weekly*, www.epw.in/special-articles/nehru-albert-mayer-and-origins-community-projects.html.

World Economic Forum (WEF) (2014) *The global gender gap report*, www.weforum.org/issues/global-gender-gap.

EIGHT

The politics of diversity in Australia: extending the role of community practice

Helen Meekosha, Alison Wannan and
Russell Shuttleworth

Introduction

This chapter examines the politics of diversity in Australia and critically reflects on the ambivalent legacy of community practice. Following Banks and Butcher (2013: 11), we use the term 'community practice' to refer to engagement in the community which is more inclusive of a variety of professionals than that traditionally associated with community development or community work. With that, we accept that different disciplines and forms of intervention inform community practice itself. Our chapter starts from the recognition that, while the broad commitment to welfare or development articulated by diverse community practitioners may have progressive potential, their work practices have often been experienced as controlling and politically regressive. In fact, we would suggest that, in the contemporary context, community practice may be driven more by neoliberal and market considerations than by commitments to social justice and social change. Rhetorically at least, 'community' places particular emphasis on collectivism, and the value base of much community practice – community development in particular – has advocated greater redistribution of wealth, power and resources. We would contend, however, that this egalitarian promise has already been seriously undermined by the Australian state and its (reversals of) welfare and social policies: while the rhetoric of partnership and social inclusion is adopted at institutional and policy level, the reality has been a transformation of community practice itself. This chapter focuses on the politics of diversity from a disability and social housing perspective,[1] drawing insights from historical and contemporary developments, and using case studies to suggest some grounds for hope in what often appears to be a hostile and reactionary political landscape.

Challenges to a progressive politics of identity

Some recent developments in Australia illustrate the structural and ideological challenges now facing a progressive politics of diversity. In late 2013 the federal government made an extraordinary appointment – at least to those involved in community practice with people who inhabit the margins of society: immigrants, refugees, disabled and homeless people, Aboriginal peoples, and a multitude of other groups. The appointment of Tim Wilson, from the conservative think-tank the Institute of Public Affairs (IPA) as a Human Rights Commissioner with responsibility for freedom of speech, came at a time when the human rights of the marginalised were being systematically curtailed. For example, he and the IPA were key architects of Attorney-General George Brandis's proposal to remove the racial vilification provisions (section 18C) from the Race Discrimination Act. Disputing this dramatic legislative change and the Attorney-General's comments that people had a 'right to be bigots' (Aston, 2014), Rachel Ball (2013), one of the signatories to an open letter signed by more than 150 diverse organisations pleading to save section 18C, countered powerfully with the following:

> Why not mention Lex Wotton, the Aboriginal community leader who is not permitted to attend public meetings without government approval and who is prohibited from speaking to the media? Why not mention Ranjini, a refugee who has spent years in immigration on the basis of a secret security assessment that she can't challenge? Why not mention Andrea Pickett, a mother of 13 who was killed by her estranged husband after being turned away from crisis accommodation? (Open Letter to Attorney-General, 2013)

After vigorous public debate, criticism by ethnic leaders, community protests and in the light of the continuing support for cultural diversity in Australia, the Prime Minister Tony Abbott was forced not to progress these changes to the legislation (Aston, 2014). In this example, we see the somewhat contradictory status of diversity politics in contemporary Australia: on the one hand, a progressive politics of diversity reflected in this committed stance against racism; and, on the other, a renewed attempt to legitimate and institutionalise bigotry. It also suggests that in the neoliberal human rights environment there is actually an increasing transfer of power *away* from the poor and marginalised towards anti-collectivists and those whose interest lies in diminishing human rights. Indeed the Human Rights Watch World Report for 2014 (Human Rights Watch, 2014: 292) concluded that Australia has seriously tarnished its record of protecting civil and political rights by watering down its obligations to asylum seekers. Furthermore, as we were finalising this chapter in May 2014, the position of the Disability Discrimination Commissioner at the Human Rights Commission was abolished in the federal Budget. Thus, we would argue that in order to understand the contemporary politics of diversity, reflection on its contested but changing historical and political context is essential.

The dialectics of community practice: the historical context

Australia is located in the global South and, while a relatively rich country, it is still viewed by global capital as a source of raw materials and holds a peripheral position in global society, culture and economics (Meekosha, 2011: 669). Briefly drawing on its history in the 20th century, we see how the dialectical nature of community practice, including both social work and community work, has been evident through the state's changing approaches to engagement with Aboriginal Australians, migrants and disabled people. Clearly social policy is not static, and diversity politics has, over recent decades, been informed by shifting ideologies that have variously emphasised 'control', 'assimilation' and 'multiculturalism'.

Australia is a colonial settler society with a history of land theft and genocide against the traditional owners of the land: the Aboriginal and Torres Strait Islanders. Human Rights Watch (2014: 294) sums up the situation thus:

> Aboriginal Australians still, on average, live 10–12 years less than non-indigenous Australians, have an infant mortality rate almost two times higher, and continue to die at alarmingly high rates from treatable and preventable conditions such as diabetes and respiratory illness. Although they live in one of the world's wealthiest countries, many indigenous Australians do not have access to adequate healthcare, housing, food, or water.

Aboriginal people have, over time, witnessed the collusion of various community practitioners and related health and welfare workers in racist, even genocidal, practices, most notably in the removal of children from their families and communities (HREOC, 1997). These children, known commonly as 'the Stolen Generation', were taken to reserves, or placed with white families in order to assimilate them into white society. From the very beginnings of colonialism in Australia the politics of diversity as managed by the state can be seen as underpinned by an ideology of control: to ensure that whiteness and the traditions and practices emanating from the global North reigned supreme. Disabled people were similarly 'controlled', by being institutionalised and locked away from mainstream society. Disabled girls and women were sterilised in a eugenics policy preventing those considered inferior from 'breeding'. More enlightened policies of the 1970s and 1980s revolved around 'normalisation' and independent living, but still the aim of health and welfare practitioners was primarily to help 'assimilate' those disabled people who most approximated to the 'norm' (Meekosha and Dowse, 2007).

Following the Second World War, the federal Australian government embarked on a massive nation-building project under the banner of 'White Australia'. Over a million immigrants were brought in from post-war Europe: Australia had to populate or perish. Arthur Calwell, Minister for Immigration and the programme's main architect, was totally committed to assimilationism. The White Australian policy remained intact until 1973 when the Whitlam Labor government decreed that multiculturalism was to become the guiding principle and policy. The cultural diversity that came with waves of migration was now to be celebrated, not denied. Despite warnings from right-wing commentators that incoming Asians would fracture society, by 1983 73,000 refugees from South East Asia had settled in Australia. Many were Vietnamese, following the end of the 'American' War. In the burgeoning multicultural policy context of this period, community practitioners were now constructed as people who could work at the grassroots, 'empowering' emergent community associations and improving community relations between the older established groups and the recent arrivals. For example, the 1980s saw the establishment of Migrant Resource Centres, where community workers were employed to support multiculturalism by providing resources and services to migrants and refugees. Rather than being asked to assimilate to White Australian ways, newcomers were to be empowered to develop their own community organisations and continue their cultural traditions (Review of Post Arrival Programs and Services for Migrants, 1978).

The language of empowerment was subsequently recast in even more challenging ways by the organisations *of* politicised disabled people working *for* disabled people that began to emerge in Australia from the early 1980s. Seeking to turn what were regarded as personal troubles into public issues, these organisations became recognisable as a distinct social movement with 'disability as a motif and symbol of identification' (Meekosha and Jakubowicz, 1999: 396). Through their self-organisation and critiques of professional power, they prompted some community practitioners to rethink the terms of their engagement with disabled communities. Gains continued to be made in the arena of human rights and social policy, and disabled people began to be represented in public and policy forums and thus find their voice in various forms of collective advocacy. However, as a changing politics of diversity began to take shape in Australia from the 1970s onwards, a concern with issues of power, rights and empowerment became more central to the discourses and actions of many community practitioners. They began to see their role as empowering marginalised communities, enabling such communities to draw on their own skills to challenge inequalities and oppression and to take power for themselves.

Although it is clear that community practice has been compromised by its historical collusion with the state's control agenda, it can, as contemporary authors suggest, nonetheless show progressive potential. Aboriginal social workers have advocated community development approaches to working with Aboriginal communities (Menzies and Gilbert, 2013). Briskman (2007: 160) also argues that the tenets of community development in particular can 'disrupt the social control constructs that are still attributed to social work'. This demonstrates the diversity of community practices themselves and the potential for collaboration between Aboriginal and non-Aboriginal community workers in working with Aboriginal communities.

Neoliberalism, reactionary politics and some contemporary limits on community practice

In Australia small community- or area-based programmes have been funded in disadvantaged areas since the 1970s and 1980s (Kenny, 1996; Shelter NSW, 2003; Mowbray, 2005). Today, community practice skills remain complex and diverse, contextual and cultural, and community practitioners are mainly employed through the community or voluntary sector, which is in turn largely funded by the state. Even as the state becomes ever more committed to and compromised by neoliberal values, the trend for a wide range of practitioners to work in community contexts nonetheless continues. Bryson and Mowbray's (1981) concept of community as a 'spray on solution' is a helpful metaphor which still holds true, highlighting the continuing tensions in realising the more progressive values and goals of community practice. Their argument is, essentially, that governments deploy the concept of 'community' to address social problems that were in fact largely caused by the state's underfunding of programmes and services. Revisiting their paper in 2005 Bryson and Mowbray (2005: 100) further challenged the contemporary notion of 'social capital' as simply 'new clothes for old concepts'. We would agree that a form of community 'capacity building' that is not premised on the redistribution of wealth and resources or invocations of social capital that fail to support genuine community organising will do nothing to reverse the devastating impacts of neoliberalism or bring about social justice. The ongoing prospect of cuts in public expenditure, such as have followed the global financial crisis, mean that even these more modestly conceived 'capacity-building' projects are under threat, irrespective if they are, in reality, a continuing reflection of the ethos of personal responsibility and governing through community (Mowbray, 2005).

In the contemporary context, the capacity of community practitioners to organise against injustice has arguably become even more restricted with the rise of a neoliberal frame of reference. Connell (2010: 33) describes neoliberalism as 'a large-scale historical project for the transformation of social structures and practice along market lines'. The particular significance of neoliberalism for community workers lies in the commodification and outsourcing of welfare and social services to the market (see Braedley and Luxton, 2010). The neoliberal agenda in Australia redistributes wealth from the poor to the wealthy, from women to men, and rolls back gains made for women, as illustrated by increasing poverty among sole parents, the vast majority are of whom are women (ACOSS, 2013). It also negatively affects the working conditions of community practitioners themselves. While some gains may have been made in obtaining decent living wages for workers in the Australian community sector (State Government of Victoria, 2012), the majority of those working either as paid workers or unpaid volunteers in the community are women.[2]

In addition, neoliberalism in Australia interacts with a wider political climate that in many ways seems increasingly intolerant of multiculturalism, egalitarianism and human rights. The last two decades have seen new waves of racism and populist nationalism – the most notable being the emergence of One Nation led by Pauline Hanson. During the conservative years of Prime Minister Howard (1996–2007), the dream that Australia might become a republic became more distant and while lip service was paid to cultural diversity, a number of examples demonstrate the limits of this conception in practice. Successive governments have sought to move disabled people off the Disability Support Pension and into work – often in low-paid and dangerous sectors of the economy. Aboriginal land rights are no longer supported (Altman, 2013); land has become a source of profit with the mining boom in wilderness areas compromising Aboriginal people's sustainable ways of living. Australia continues to be in breach of the International Covenant on Civil and Political Rights as a result of its offshore processing of asylum seekers (Human Rights Law Centre, 2012). Private 'armies' such as G4S, a British multinational security company, are contracted to guard refugees for the Australian state, and violence perpetrated against refugees has resulted in at least one death (of an Iranian asylum seeker Reza Barati in Manus Detention Centre in Papua New Guinea on 17 February 2014). The policy of offshore processing and settlement has also meant that opportunities for progressive community practice with refugees have been severely restricted.

On 13 February 2008 then Prime Minister Kevin Rudd formally apologised to Aboriginal Australians for the pain and suffering they and their ancestors had endured and for their continuing social exclusion today. Under the Rudd (and later Julia Gillard) Labor government, Australia promoted a range of measures to support 'social inclusion', however one of the first acts of the incoming Coalition[3] government in September 2013 was to disband the Social Inclusion Unit charged with examining and overcoming disadvantage. For community practitioners who work with historically excluded communities, such policy reversals and reactionary agendas are hugely disheartening. While there is great cause for pessimism, in the following sections we consider what a progressive politics of diversity for community practice might look like, and how it might both acknowledge, yet still seek to move beyond, the defeatism of the current historical moment.

Community practice and the politics of diversity: some reflections

Just as genuine social inclusion celebrates diversity and a myriad of identities, likewise an inclusive politics of diversity would suggest that there is no one right way of doing community practice: people should be able to have a say in determining their own solutions according to their own needs and in concert with their own identities. However, this seems more like an aspiration than reality in many instances. For example, while the increasing residualisation of Australian public housing has led to the 'concentration of seriously disadvantaged households' (Morris, 2013: 1), little attention is given to the diverse needs of many of those who live there: Aboriginal families, disabled people and older people. In this sense, more often than not, assumptions of a homogeneous 'community view' are reflected in housing practice and policy.

Another key trend in Australian policy that contradicts a pluralist conception of diversity, and one that mirrors experiences in the UK (Taylor, 2003), is the privileging of centrally determined definitions of need and performance indicators in community programmes. Consequently, local people have little opportunity to define either what is important or what should happen. As Craig (2010: 43) reminds us, 'behind the rhetoric of social inclusion, empowerment and participation, still at issue is what community means for practice'.

As noted already, a more recent addition to the focus on human diversity is disability. Most societies have deeply embedded cultural and social mores and norms that distinguish people with certain kinds of impairments from 'normal' people. These norms and attitudes often disable and discriminate against such persons so that they are marginalised from the wider social milieu. Social and community work practice remains at heart about social relationships and the power embedded in them. Yet it has recently come under sustained criticism for remaining at the level of the individual and for failing to address the broader structural and human rights aspects of the disabling experience (Meekosha and Dowse, 2007; Soldatic and Meekosha, 2012; Meekosha and Soldatic, 2014). Indeed, the medical dominance over disabled people has often meant that disabled people have been seen as inhabiting the domain of those services and practices which deal with the 'adaptation, adjustment and rehabilitation' of individuals. In consequence, most disabled people remain excluded from mainstream community practice as they are both outside 'normal' communal structures and perceived as having no community of their own.

Recent community practice and community development scholarship has been more inclusive of disability as an identity category, but the assumption still prevails that the grand triumvirate of class, gender and 'race'/ethnicity are more structurally pervasive (for example Ife, 2013). The consequent downplaying of other identity categories such as disability, or indeed sexuality, may inadvertently reinforce a hierarchical view of disadvantage and oppression. This is both counterproductive and divisive. Furthermore, even when diversity is cherished, there is a danger that particularism may flourish, so that we find a multiplicity of approaches to social change that are seen to be in competition rather than in solidarity with each other. In reality, many marginalised groups share universal needs, but a fragmented politics of diversity could lead to a relativist approach, which ignores structural inequalities and is therefore dangerous for politics (Ife, 2013: 77). In this form, community practice is not in opposition to neoliberal thinking, but becomes 'part of the problem'.

In the following sections we use two case studies to illustrate the importance of principles of diversity, empowerment, participation and social justice for community practice. The first explores how community workers have acted as allies of disabled people to campaign against injustice and inequality. The second examines the practice of diversity in a social housing neighbourhood with older people, Aboriginal people and people with psychiatric disability. Both illustrate how community practice can challenge existing power relations and injustice to develop alternate approaches, and we examine how community workers can demonstrate a progressive politics of diversity while working both in neighbourhood contexts and alongside activist groups. We also touch on a key dilemma in community practice – the limitations of localism (Banks and Butcher, 2013: 25) – by looking at how campaigns that are led by disabled people, but work collaboratively with universities, have made vital links between local, national and global contexts. These case studies point to a critical community practice which challenges discrimination, supports people to act and participate on their own terms and promotes social justice (Butcher et al, 2007). But underpinning such progressive approaches to diversity in practice is a critical analysis of power: we argue as others have done (Craig, 2010; Mayo and Robertson, 2013) that the disparities of power between government and communities are central to understanding the politics and potential of community practice.

Case 1. Community practice with disabled people in multiple contexts

Disability is a social, economic, political and cultural issue, resulting from the impact of practices of exclusion on people with a variety of physical, intellectual, cognitive and psychological impairments (Shuttleworth and Kasnitz, 2006). We argue that working with disabled people as allies in the disability rights movement is an important and fruitful arena for community practitioners in Australia. For example, community practitioners working with People with Disability Australia

(PWDA) have, through the 'Shut In' campaign, advocated for disabled people to be released from institutions and nursing homes to live in communities (Shut In, 2014). They are also campaigning to prevent the building of new facilities that are now named 'cluster housing', 'villas' or 'intentional communities' because they are perceived as simply maintaining the control function of institutions, despite the new terminology. To highlight these issues, community events are organised, such as an anniversary reunion of the closure of an institution bringing former residents, staff and advocates together, where the past is not forgotten but the future is celebrated. Social media, in the form of blogs and videos, legitimates the stories of previously institutionalised disabled people: this serves to engage the broader community and to share the sense of connectedness with other disabled people and the membership of PWDA (Shut In, 2014).

Women with Disabilities Australia (WWDA) is a feminist grassroots national organisation that has supported women campaigning against involuntary sterilisation, using advocacy and lobbying at a national and international level to change policy and legislation (Frohmader and Meekosha, 2012). WWDA has also worked tirelessly with women's groups and governments to raise awareness of the endemic violence against disabled women and the lack of accessible refuges and services. A fundamental driving value is reorienting community practice against violence to be more inclusive of disabled women. Too often community practitioners see a disabled woman experiencing violence as being too hard to accommodate – creating pathways to safety for *all* women should be the priority. Strategies pursued by WWDA have included working with women refuge workers on the ground to ensure refuges take account of the needs of the diversity of disabled women. This means more than simply physical access to premises and entails seeking out disabled women to sit on governance and advisory committees and developing accessible formats of manuals and guidelines. For example, practitioners need to allocate more time to communicate and build trust with women with learning difficulties than might usually be the case. Further, emergency procedures need to cater for blind women. All these inclusive developments need to be carried out in consultation with and with participation by disabled women (Dowse et al, 2013).

Located in Melbourne, the Sexuality and Disability Alliance (SDA) is a group of young disabled people that advocates for the sexual rights of disabled people by organising forums and developing other projects to break down the barriers that disabled people confront in achieving sexual well-being. Community practitioners and university allies also work alongside the group's members to publicise and raise the visibility of the issues they face. In this regard SDA and its allies have developed research and progressive policy on the issue of facilitated sex for persons with disability. One successful outcome has been the funding of a small research project by Deakin University to investigate this issue, in collaboration with members of SDA.[4]

Disabled activists working in cross-impairment groups have been fighting for human rights in Australia since the beginning of the 1980s. Ironically, for many disabled people, their first experience of politicised communities occurred in their attempt to break away from the institutional care which was dominant in the 1970s. Many disabled people now find support and a shared sense of common purpose in working in advocacy groups and/or making their issues visible through arts and performance. Community is also built through cultural expression, be it music, drama or creative writing. As they perform themes of struggle, negotiate normativity or celebrate difference, disabled artists make political issues visible in new ways. In these developments, there may be a supportive role for community practitioners who can contribute to the formation and nurturance of disability arts groups, not least in lobbying for funds.

Case 2. Diversity in place: community practice in social housing neighbourhoods

Building on a social justice framework, a recent action research study in social housing neighbourhoods in Sydney[5] developed participatory approaches for working with Aboriginal women, people with psychiatric disability and older people living in social housing in Sydney. Modest community-based projects led to new approaches to Aboriginal tenant participation, the production of a mental health film and local activities for older people, many from culturally diverse backgrounds. Four central issues that emerged for community practice were: the importance of developing projects around diverse lived realties; the key role of community advocates; the importance of stories in creating new spaces of participation; and the vital role of local celebrations and cultural events.

'Starting with where people are at' is regarded by many as a core principle in community practice (Checkoway, 2013; Ife, 2013). However, this can generate divergent understandings of need and competing priorities for action among the diverse communities living in public housing. In this case, the Aboriginal women wanted child-friendly neighbourhoods, culturally appropriate services, and to be heard. The older people wanted age-friendly neighbourhoods, particularly for people with more limited mobility and dementia, as well as educational and social activities. People with psychiatric disability were motivated by their experiences of living daily with discrimination, stigma and exclusion. They wanted jobs, education and meaningful daytime activities. To be heard and treated with respect by services was equally important. Working with people around what is important in their daily lives can lead to active engagement and participation (Ledwith and Springett, 2010; Ife, 2013), and challenges assumptions that local communities are homogeneous. In this project (Working from the Ground Up, 2012), although the needs expressed by residents were very diverse, the gendered nature of community and neighbourhood work was always evident (Grimshaw, 2011). For example, older women wanted local services and support for people with dementia, most of whom were older women living alone; Aboriginal women wanted improvements for their children. In all cases, the absence of neighbourhood services and facilities directly affected the lives of low-income women.

Employing a local Aboriginal woman, as well as people with lived experience of mental health issues and social housing, as advocates was crucial for engaging with participants, building trust and determining what happened next: repeatedly, local people said that they particularly trusted the community advocates. Starting with the experiences and perspectives of local people can support them to speak out in other contexts (Beresford and Hoban, 2005) while research has shown that community development can contribute to improved mental health and inclusion (Rose and Thompson, 2012; Seebohm et al, 2012). Experiential knowledge has been vital for the success and relevance of this project.

Both the process and outcomes of efforts to create new approaches to Aboriginal tenant participation have highlighted that the assumptions and demands of Aboriginal community development may be very different from practice in other contexts (Green and Baldry, 2008). For example, the 'whiteness' of community practice in social housing neighbourhoods can begin to be exposed (Walter et al, 2013). As Aboriginal women 'yarned' about living in social housing (Working from the Ground Up, 2012), new Aboriginal tenant participation approaches evolved from these discussions and stories, demonstrating how innovative approaches can be generated by 'taking guidance from local people and respecting their traditions and perspectives' (Briskman, 2007; Menzies and Gilbert, 2013: 68). In another process, a low-budget film was made – incorporating statements, drawings and spoken excerpts – because people involved in a mental health project said they did not want their lives to be represented in yet another 'boring $2 PowerPoint presentation'. In this way, the project began to develop new participatory spaces (Cornwall, 2008) and to illustrate the centrality of dialogue as a basis for transformative change (Ledwith and Springett, 2010: 127).

Celebrations became particularly significant. While the literature on arts-based community development highlights the role of the arts in social inclusion and neighbourhood renewal (Kay, 2000; Carey and Sutton, 2004), small community-led social events are also important for strengthening and validating neighbourhood diversity. In this case, older people held multicultural celebrations; Aboriginal people organised celebrations of Sorry Day and NAIDOC Week;[6] and the mental health film was publicly launched at a cinema. But of equal significance were local neighbourhood celebrations where diverse groups came together. What was perhaps most important was that these events were based on a sense of belonging and solidarity born of living in public housing: they acknowledged diversity, but also resisted the fragmentation of the neighbourhood into discrete interest groups or categories.

Conclusion: re-envisioning a new politics of diversity for community practice

While the practice approaches outlined in the two case studies did not bring about fundamental transformations in the distribution of income or resources, they nonetheless offered novel and interesting possibilities for change in marginalised communities. As Shaw (2008: 33) argues, a community development approach can 'maintain the status quo and preserve privilege, [but] it can also create an increasingly rare public space for the expression of various forms of common position and collective identity or, indeed, dissent'.

Our experience shows that community practice must become more sensitive to issues of diversity, and incorporate a contemporary, critical understanding of power relations in society. This demands an understanding of how dominant cultures seek to maintain power through practices of oppression and marginalisation. We argue that a progressive politics of inclusion necessarily reinforces the value of a cooperative and coalition politics in which fragmentation is resisted. The commitment is for community practitioners to work towards 'solidarity from the vantage point of ... differences' (Meekosha 1993: 189). Critically, a new politics of inclusion would also insist on material improvements in peoples' lives and guarantee their basic rights, including acceptable standards of housing, clean water, healthcare and income for all marginalised groups.

In their engagement with communities, practitioners must be prepared to combine a critical analysis of power and inequality with openness to the strengths and assets of marginalised communities. The aim here is to move beyond resistance in order to collaborate in processes that can defuse hegemonic power and effect positive change. The struggle against pessimism and demoralisation for community practitioners is ongoing. Nonetheless, we find the enduring ideas of Antonio Gramsci and Paulo Freire (Ledwith, 2001) as relevant for community practice in contemporary neoliberal times as they have been in previous eras. We are reminded, for example, of Gramsci's conception of 'organic intellectuals' when faced with the dangers of speaking 'for' the people, rather than 'with', or alongside, them. Similarly, the community practitioner, operating as a popular educator in a Freirean sense, and despite the persistent challenges of a globalised world, can still retain an important role in helping communities not only to understand the world, but also to take action to bring about social justice.

Notes

[1]   The section on social housing is based on research undertaken as part of the Australian Research Council Linkage Project LP0882776, 'Working from the Ground Up: A participatory approach to community regeneration in public housing neighbourhoods'.

[2]   In 2012 a campaign for equal pay resulted in a decision by Fair Work Australia to award social and community services workers wage increases of between 23% and 45%. This particularly affected low-paid women workers.

[3]   At the time of writing in 2014, the federal government in Australia is known as the Coalition where the Liberal Party holds power with the National Party. The Liberal Party is a classic party of right wing liberalism and a strong supporter of economic rationalism. The National Party traditionally represents rural voters and farmers and is a party of the right.

[4]   Health and Social Development, Deakin University Grant: Facilitated Sex and Disability: Perspectives of Adults with Disability Who Use Support Worker Services (Small Research Grant) (Investigator: Dr Russell Shuttleworth) 2014–15.

⁵ The Working from the Ground Up (WFGU) project trialled and developed a range of community initiatives in two social housing neighbourhoods in Sydney. WFGU (Working from the Ground Up, 2012) was an action research project of the Universities of Sydney and NSW (Investigators: Professor Jude Irwin, Professor Eileen Baldry and Associate Professor Susan Goodwin). The fieldwork on which this section is based is part of doctoral research undertaken by Alison Wannan.

⁶ The annual Sorry Day has been held since 1998 to remember and commemorate the past and present members of the Stolen Generation, Indigenous children who were forcibly removed from their families (AIATSIS, 2015). NAIDOC stands for National Aborigines and Islanders Day Observation Committee. NAIDOC also refers to a week-long celebration held in July each year. The aim is to 'celebrate Aboriginal and Torres Strait Islander history, culture and achievements and is an opportunity to recognise the contributions that Indigenous Australians make to our country and society' (NAIDOC, 2014).

References

ACOSS (2013) *Back to basics: Simplifying Australia's family payments system to tackle child poverty*, Strawberry Hills: ACOSS.

Altman, J. (2013) 'Special issue: arguing the intervention', *Journal of Indigenous Policy*, 14 (September).

Aston, H. (2014) 'Tony Abbott dumps controversial changes to 18C racial discrimination laws', *The Sydney Morning Herald*, 5 August, www.smh.com.au/federal-politics/political-news/tony-abbott-dumps-controversial-changes-to-18c-racial-discrimination-laws-20140805-3d65l.html#ixzz3GwWb8rBN.

Australian Institute of Aboriginal and Torres Strait Islander Studies (AIATSIS) (2015) 'Dates of Significance', http://aiatsis.gov.au/explore/articles/dates-significance.

Ball, R. (2013) 'Who's less free: Andrew Bolt, or children in detention?', *The Guardian*, 19 December, www.theguardian.com/commentisfree/2013/dec/19/whos-less-free-andrew-bolt-or-children-in-detention.

Banks, S. and Butcher, H. (2013) 'What is community practice?', in S. Banks, H. Butcher, A. Orton and J. Robertson (eds), *Managing community practice: Principles, policies and programmes*, 2nd edn, Bristol: Policy Press, 7–29.

Beresford, P. and Hoban, M. (2005) *Participation in anti-poverty and regeneration work and research*, York: Joseph Rowntree Foundation.

Braedley, S. and Luxton, M. (eds) (2010) *Neoliberalism and everyday life*, Montreal: McGill-Queen's University Press.

Briskman, L. (2007) *Social work with Indigenous communities*, Sydney: Federation Press.

Bryson, L. and Mowbray, M. (1981) 'Community: the spray on solution', *Australian Journal of Social Issues*, 16(4): 225–67.

Bryson, L. and Mowbray, M. (2005) 'More spray on solution: community, social capital and evidence based policy', *Australian Journal of Social Issues*, 40(1): 91–106.

Butcher, H., Banks, S. and Henderson, P. with Robertson, J. (2007) *Critical community practice*, Bristol: Policy Press.

Carey, P. and Sutton, S. (2004) 'Community development through participatory arts: lessons learned from a community arts and regeneration project in South Liverpool', *Community Development Journal*, 39(2): 123–34.

Checkoway, B. (2013) 'Social justice approach to community development', *Journal of Community Practice*, 21(4): 472–86.

Connell, R. (2010) 'Understanding neoliberalism', in S. Braedley and M. Luxton (eds), *Neoliberalism and everyday life*, Montreal: McGill-Queen's University Press, 22–36.

Cornwall, A. (2008) 'Unpacking "participation": models, meanings and practices', *Community Development Journal*, 43(3): 269–83.

Craig, G. (2010) 'Community capacity building', in S. Kenny and M. Clarke (eds), *Challenging community capacity building*, London: Palgrave Macmillan, 41–66.

Dowse, L., Soldatic, K., Didi, A., Frohmader, C. and van Toorn, G. (2013) *Stop the violence: Addressing violence against women and girls with disabilities in Australia. Background paper*, Hobart: Women with Disabilities Australia.

Frohmader, C. and Meekosha, H. (2012) 'Recognition, respect and rights: women with disabilities in a globalised world', in D. Goodley, B. Hughes and L. Davis (eds), *Disability and social theory: New developments and directions*, London, Palgrave Macmillan, 287–307.

Green, S. and Baldry, E. (2008) 'Building Indigenous Australian social work', *Australian Social Work*, 61(4): 389–402.

Grimshaw, L. (2011) 'Community work as women's work? The gendering of English neighbourhood partnerships', *Community Development Journal*, 46(3): 327–40.

Human Rights and Equal Opportunity Commission (HREOC) (1997) *Bringing them home: report of the national inquiry into the separation of Aboriginal and Torres Strait Islander children from their families*, Sydney: Human Rights and Equal Opportunity Commission.

Human Rights Law Centre (2012) 'Offshore processing regime breaches fundamental human rights, HRLC tells parliamentary inquiry', Human Rights Law Centre, http://hrlc.org.au/offshore-processing-regime-breaches-fundamental-human-rights-hrlc-tells-parliamentary-inquiry/.

Human Rights Watch (2014) *World Report 2014*, www.hrw.org/sites/default/files/wr2014_web_0.pdf.

Ife, J. (2013) *Community development in an uncertain world*, Melbourne: Cambridge University Press.

Kay, A. (2000) 'Art and community development: the role the arts have in regenerating communities', *Community Development Journal*, 35(4): 414–24.

Kenny, S. (1996) 'Contestations of community development in Australia', *Community Development Journal*, 31(2): 104–13.

Ledwith, M. (2001) 'Community work as critical pedagogy: re-envisioning Freire and Gramsci', *Community Development Journal*, 36(3): 171–82.

Ledwith, M. and Springett, J. (2010) *Participatory practice: Community-based action for transformative change*, Bristol: Policy Press.

Mayo, M. and Robertson, J. (2013) 'The historical and policy context: setting the scene for current debates', in S. Bennett, H. Butcher, A. Orton and J. Robertson (eds), *Managing community practice: Principles, policies and programmes*, 2nd edn, Bristol: Policy Press, 31–46.

Meekosha, H. (1993) 'The bodies politic – equality, difference and community practice', in H. Butcher, A. Glen, P. Henderson and J. Smith (eds), *Community and public policy*, London: Pluto Press, 171–3.

Meekosha, H. (2011) 'Decolonising disability: thinking and acting globally', *Disability and Society*, 26(6): 667–82.

Meekosha, H. and Dowse, L. (2007) 'Integrating critical disability studies into social work education and practice: an Australian perspective', *Practice*, 19(3): 169–83.

Meekosha, H. and Jakubowicz, A. (1999) 'Disability political activism and identity making: a critical feminist perspective on the rise of disability movements in Australia, the USA and the UK', *Disability Studies Quarterly*, 19(4): 393–404.

Meekosha, H. and Soldatic, K. (2014) 'Disability-inclusive social work practice', in L. Beddoe and J. Maidment (eds), *Social work practice for promoting health and well-being: Critical issues*, London: Routledge, 143–55.

Menzies, K. and Gilbert, S. (2013) 'Engaging communities' in B. Bennett, S. Green, S. Gilbert and D. Bessarab (eds), *Our voices: Aboriginal and Torres Strait Islander social work*, South Yarra: Palgrave Macmillan, 50–72.

Morris, A. (2013) 'The residualisation of public housing and its impact on older tenants in inner-city Sydney, Australia', *Journal of Sociology*, DOI: 10.1177/1440783313500856.

Mowbray, M. (2005) 'Community capacity building or state opportunism?', *Community Development Journal*, 40(3): 255–64.

National Aborigines and Islanders Day Observance Committee (NAIDOC) (2014) 'NAIDOC Week 2014: 6–13 July', www.naidoc.org.au/.

Open Letter to Attorney-General (2013) 'Australia must retain strong and effective protections against racial vilification', www.hrlc.org.au/wp-content/uploads/2013/12/Open-Letter-Racial-Vilification-Protections.pdf.

Review of Post Arrival Programs and Services for Migrants (1978) *Migrant services program*, Canberra: Australian Government Publishing Service.

Rose, V. and Thompson, L. (2012) 'Space, place and people: a community development approach to mental health promotion in a disadvantaged community', *Community Development Journal*, 47(4): 604–11.

Seebohm, P., Gilchrist, A. and Morris, D. (2012) 'Bold but balanced: how community development contributes to mental health and inclusion', *Community Development Journal*, 47(4): 473–90.

Shaw, M. (2008) 'Community development and the politics of community', *Community Development Journal*, 43(1): 24–36.

Shelter NSW (2003) *Tenancies, communities, and the (re)development of public housing estates: a background paper*, Sydney: Shelter NSW.

Shut In (2014) 'Shut In campaign to close institutions', www.shutin.org.au.

Shuttleworth, R. and Kasnitz, D. (2006) 'The cultural context of disability', in G. Albrecht (ed), *Encyclopaedia of disability*, Thousand Oaks, CA: Sage, 330–7.

Soldatic, K. and Meekosha, H. (2012) 'Disability and neoliberal state formations', in N. Watson, A. Roulstone and C. Thomas (eds), *Routledge handbook of disability studies*, London: Routledge, 195–206

State Government of Victoria (2012) 'Pay equity implementation', www.dhs.vic.gov.au/funded-agency-channel/spotlight/pay-equity-implementation.

Taylor, M. (2003) *Public policy in the community*, Basingstoke: Palgrave Macmillan.

Walter, M., Taylor, S. and Habibis, D. (2013) 'Australian social work is white', in B. Bennett, S. Green, S. Gilbert and D. Bessarab (eds), *Our voices: Aboriginal and Torres Strait Islander social work*, South Yarra: Palgrave Macmillan, 230–57.

Working from the Ground Up (2012) *Report of phase two: Developing and trialling initiatives*, Sydney: University of Sydney and University of New South Wales.

NINE

The politics of environmental justice: community development in Ecuadorian and Peruvian Amazonia

María Teresa Martínez Domínguez and Eurig Scandrett

Introduction

This chapter addresses community development with indigenous communities in Ecuadorian and Peruvian Amazonia, whose territories have been the site of conflicts with the oil extraction industry. The argument developed in this chapter interconnects community development and environmental justice and is the result of a dialogue between the authors, based on case studies from the experience of one of us, Martínez Domínguez, who worked between 2000 and 2009 as an activist, researcher and community worker with indigenous communities in the oil production areas of the Amazon. The indigenous peoples with whom Martínez Domínguez conducted her work were the Cofán from Dureno, the Kichwa from Sarayaku, both in Ecuador, and the Shipibo-Konibo from Canaán de Cachiyaku in Peru. The case studies include work with these groups as well as with employees of the oil companies and 'intermediaries' in the NGOs, the Church, activists and academics, including many adopting the role of community development practitioner, whether employed to do so or not.

Martínez Domínguez describes the background to this work:

'My original intention was to bring indigenous voices to the forefront of academic debate: to expose the impacts of the unsustainable development promoted by the oil industry and to identify the strategies used by indigenous people to regain control of their own development. From the beginning I thought my main informants would be indigenous people with whom I had built relationships over the years through my work in Amazonian communities.

159

However, people in all the oil-affected communities I worked with considered it necessary to include the points of view and strategies used by the 'powerful' oil companies as well as the indigenous people. Therefore, the decision of researching the 'powerful' in the oil conflict was taken in agreement with my informants. The ethical stance of the research remained politically committed to the interests of the indigenous 'survivor' communities.'

There is a lack of critical research about the powerful in society, and the need to 'study up' (Williams, 1989) has not been fully addressed. This is accentuated by the commodification of research and the barriers which powerful actors erect against researchers who are attempting to scrutinise the state and corporate power (Tombs and Whyte, 2002). The powerful are not exempt from public scrutiny. If they do not provide information when confronted with critical and independent research, they leave researchers with few options but to use deception and selective communication. Martínez Domínguez explains:

'When researching the 'powerful' and their activities in oil-affected areas, I felt at times as a spy, an unintended but necessary role to access information from the oil companies, an exhausting and stressful double-role. One coping mechanism was my work in the indigenous communities. The reason why I embarked on this research was because various communities and friends had asked me to. I had previous experience of working as a community worker and as an activist in oil-affected areas, and was in an ideal position to carry out this type of research. This required spending long periods of time in indigenous communities where I was given various community development roles, from leading workshops to designing project proposals and helping to organise cultural events. On other occasions I found myself in the middle of a protest or a violent situation, and needed to have a standpoint, as my role as an activist and international witness was required.'

In this context, the detached researcher has no place: on the contrary, community development, research and activism may go hand in hand and each can support the other. In that sense, the case material discussed here should be regarded as activist ethnography and action research undertaken by Martínez Domínguez (Reason and Bradbury, 2006).

This chapter constitutes a critical reflection on these experiences in dialogue with Scandrett.

We understand community development to be a *process* through which communities collectively mobilise to defend or enhance their means of livelihood and quality of life and a *practice* by key individuals who consciously facilitate this process, whether through community appointment, political commitment or professional employment. Theorists of community development have recognised the contradictions in its practice. Since the origins of community development in European colonialism and 'development' as a means of building the allegiance of post-independence populations, community workers have been located within communities that have been identified as 'problematic' by outsiders, and tasked with the contradictory role of supporting communities to identify and mobilise in support of their collective interests which may be opposed to the interests of the powerful (Mayo, 2008).

For the purpose of this chapter we have classified the actors in the relationship between community and the oil industry as the 'powerful', the 'survivors' and the 'intermediaries', all of whom have some locus in community work. The 'powerful' includes the state and foreign oil companies, state institutions, public relations (PR) companies, the military and foreign governments. The 'survivors' consist of indigenous people and their local, regional and national organisations. The 'intermediaries' include local, national and international NGOs and aid agencies, the Church, local councils, activists, academics and some governmental institutions that lead with indigenous issues.[1] These categorisations are not intended to be analytical but rather heuristic and it is acknowledged that complex diversity exists within them. However, in interpreting the role which key agents play in the processes that are either explicitly named or may be understood as community development, this categorisation is helpful.

In a region where the presence of the state is minimal, the oil industry has become the main source for community development in indigenous communities through its 'Corporate Social Responsibility' (CSR) programmes in an effort to consolidate its presence in indigenous territory, what Collins (2006) has called 'dispossession through participation'. In many cases these industry-led attempts at community development are in conflict with communities' own development strategies and life projects. Some indigenous groups have evolved and transformed over the centuries into societies that represent a troublesome alternative to the current dominant neoliberal system that is based on concentration of power and accumulation of wealth.

Neoliberal states in Latin America: oil industry expansion and 'Corporate Social Responsibility'

The national and transnational oil industry has been able to act with almost total impunity since the start of its operations in Latin America at the beginning of the last century (Kimerling and FCUNAE, 1993; Varea, 1995; Maldonado, 2001; Sawyer, 2004; Oilwatch, 2005; López, 2007). Four main interrelated factors favoured the unregulated growth of the industry: (1) the dire need of states for quick-fix and resource-based solutions to the economic crises of their countries; (2) the shift in the 1980s from a corporatist to a neoliberal system imported from the US and other Western countries; (3) the lack of regulations on environmental and indigenous rights issues; and (4) expansion of the civilisatory mission of the evangelical group, Summer Institute of Linguistics (now SIL International).[2]

The Ecuadorian case is illustrative of an economy that suffered two major resource crises: the cacao crisis in the 1920s and the banana crisis in the 1960s. As Acosta (2003) points out, in the 1980s Ecuador 'changed from poverty-stricken banana grower to new-rich producer of oil':

> Thanks to the oil bonanza, the GDP increased between 1972 and 1981 at an average annual rate of 8% with spectacular rates in some years (more than 25.3% in 1973), in particular for the industry, which increased by an average of 10% per year; while the product per person increased from $260 in 1970 to $1,668 in 1981.

Although at the beginning of the 1970s the industry was under the control of the state, its remarkable profits in the following years attracted foreign investment. This, together with a favourable international climate for oil investments and the shift from a corporatist to a neoliberal ideology in the government, aided the entry into the country of transnational oil companies (Perreault, 2001; 2003: 66). Neoliberal regimes have also encouraged corporate-led globalisation by promoting free trade, privatisation and deregulation. Oil transnationals operating in Latin America did not have to worry, until recently, about complying with any environmental regulations or national and international laws regarding the individual and collective rights of indigenous people.

While the lengthy absence of environmental laws eased the uncontrolled development of the industry in indigenous territory, the lack of a regulated frame for consultation with and participation of the affected communities has become one of the main complaints of indigenous peoples and organisations (Melo, 2006: 19). The International Labour Organization (ILO) Convention 169 stipulates that indigenous peoples have the right to be consulted regarding any legislative or administrative measure that may affect them, oil developments included. However, in the case of resource exploration, the state is the owner of the subsoil. This means that indigenous peoples do not have integral ownership of their territory, since they own only what is on the surface. The fight for outright ownership of their lands has been the most contested issue during the 20 years of gestation of the United Nations Declaration on the Rights of Indigenous Peoples (UNDRIP). The declaration signals a great advance since it recognises the right of indigenous peoples to self-determination and free, prior and informed consent but it still does not give any veto control to the communities, a matter that is highly contested by governments.

Finally, another important factor for the entry of the oil industry into the Amazon was the previous arrival of the missionaries of the SIL, widely considered to have opened the doors to the extractive industries in the Amazon in the 1960s and 1970s by breaking the social cohesion of the indigenous communities and building airstrips that were later used by the oil companies (Stoll, 1983; Perkins, 2005: 141–3; Yashar, 2005: 146).

During the first years of the oil industry companies did not have to worry about the environmental and social impacts of their operations. Indigenous organisations were in their infancy, and most indigenous communities were unaware of the impacts that the industry might bring. Government planning was beginning to show recognition of environmental and indigenous rights, while social control in indigenous communities was assured by the presence of evangelical and Catholic missionaries. This does not mean that indigenous communities peacefully allowed the entry of the industry. Company representatives, especially those in charge of the seismic phase of the operations, were subject to attacks by various indigenous groups, but overall their paternalist strategy of petty gifts and short-term unskilled jobs for indigenous people kept the resistance at bay.

Although localised indigenous protests had been common since the colonial period, indigenous peoples started to influence national politics by forming or joining class-based organisations. The gradual departure from class ideals was partly due to the influence of the new indigenous intellectuals and the promotion of indigenous culture by the Catholic Church (León, as cited by Van Cott, 2005: 104). Amazonian organisations found it easier to organise around ethnic demands than

Andean organisations. The social relations of production in much of the Andean region of many Latin American countries involved the *hacienda* system of contracted debt, in which Indian labourers (*conciertos*) were virtually owned by the *hacienda* owner. By contrast, in the Amazonian region the *hacienda* system had little impact. In addition, the remoteness of Amazonian communities, the bilingual education programmes promoted by missionaries versus the imposition of Spanish in public schools, and their special concept of territory contributed to the 'indianisation' of the movement. The main claim of Amazonian indigenous organisations was for indigenous territory, as the colonisation and extraction of natural resources promoted by both corporatist and neoliberal governments represented a direct threat to their collective subsistence. This constituted a marked difference from the concept of territory practised by Andean communities, where land was a social and economic production unit. The indigenous mobilisations in the 1990s consolidated the indigenous movements and made them visible and influential on a national and international scale.

The mobilisations carried out by the Amazonian indigenous movement during the last three decades have set an example of indigenous organising through non-violent actions and have marked the beginning of a new power relationship between the state and indigenous peoples whose demands could no longer be ignored. These mobilisations had an impact in the development of international law (ILO Convention 169 and the UNDRIP) and a whole range of international initiatives which have set up non-enforceable guidelines and principles for corporate responsibility, among them the United Nations Global Compact initiative and the Organisation for Economic Co-operation and Development (OECD) Guidelines for Multinational Enterprises.

These initiatives have considerably changed the pattern of relationship between the state, companies and communities. In order to operate in a friendly environment, companies in Latin America use community relations programmes (CRPs) as part of their CSR strategy. Parts of these agreements are compulsory for the companies by law, such as the compensation and reparation payments made for the use of the territory and for environmental contingencies. However, companies also see these programmes as voluntary 'good neighbour agreements' that can be negotiated to minimise conflict.

CRPs are often the only community development strategies in these regions. Oil companies claim these programmes seek to mitigate the social impacts of oil extraction in the communities and to improve access to healthcare and education (Martínez Domínguez, 2008).

There are no binding international or national standards on how these programmes should be implemented (Varea, 1995; Wray, 2000; Narváez, 2004; Shamir, 2004). A common characteristic of all the programmes analysed in these case studies is that they have become a tool for the oil companies to access indigenous communities, promoting division and dependency on the company.

Visions of development

Community development led by the 'powerful': good neighbour agreements, PR strategy and the absence of the state

Wray (2000: 56–60), who carried out fieldwork in the Ecuadorian Amazon and examined the complex relations between the state, the companies and indigenous peoples, explains that the agreements reached during negotiation of a CRP vary depending on three factors: the phase of the oil operation, the level of international awareness about the specific project, and the strength of the indigenous organisation. We would add other factors: the PR strategy used by the company and the state to promote oil activities; the environmental and social record of the company; the size of the company; and whether it is national or transnational. During the seismic phase of the operations the agreement between the companies and the communities tends to be short term, since the company cannot assure the discovery of oil reserves, and if the finding is not economically viable it will cease operations in the area. In the exploration phase the agreements are long term, as this minimises conflict, and companies fund whole projects instead of specific demands. The first contact with the communities normally takes place through the environmental impact assessment (EIA) or, more recently, through the consultation process. Some indigenous organisations complain that companies use the EIA to access the communities and start negotiations and the CRPs to secure their permanence in the communities.

What has happened in practice is illustrated by the case of the indigenous community of Sarayaku in Ecuador and the Argentinean oil company CGC. Although consultation had not taken place, CGC contracted the PR company Daimi Service to help them sign an agreement with the communities of the oil block and start seismic operations in Sarayaku territory. In an interview a representative at Daimi explained:

'This case was especially challenging for us, so I decided to invest my own money and told the company [CGC] that if I did not manage to sign agreements with all the communities in the oil block they would not have to pay me. They had tried before with other consultants and they achieved nothing, but we managed to sign a contract with 26 of the 28 communities.' (David Luján, 15 March 2007)

Luján stated that the practices of his company are based on high levels of transparency, taking into account the perspectives of all the actors and working with the local authorities. This claim contrasts with interviews carried out with indigenous leaders from different areas in Ecuador who accused Daimi of favouring the interests of the oil companies, blackmailing leaders and working under cover.

CGC used an aggressive PR strategy in the Pastaza region because it met with strong resistance in the Sarayaku community. The Sarayaku fought back and organised the *Kapari* (meaning 'shout') campaign to create awareness of the conflict, which was supported internationally. The Sarayaku are an exceptional case, in which a single and isolated community has managed to resist what seemed inevitable, the exploitation of oil in its territory. However, the price paid for this resistance has been high, as the community has lived in a state of alertness and psychological pressure for the last decade, and the damage caused to the social network by the interruption of their cultural traditions, the animosity created with neighbouring communities and the violation of sacred places by CGC will be very difficult to repair.

Many of the oil contracts in the Amazon area were signed 30 years ago, when there was no need for consultation or CRPs. Although consultation rights and environmental regulations are not retroactive, communities that were never compensated for the use of their territory are now starting to claim compensation, as in the dispute between the Shipibo-Konibo people of Canaán in Peru and the Maple company. After various direct actions that brought the conflict to the national level, the community managed to sign a compensation agreement with the company and a long-term CRP. An indigenous leader of the local organisation FECONBU reflects on the struggle of the people of the community of Canaán for compensation and the direct actions – 'fight actions' in his words – that they took:

'Before the fight actions we got only palliatives from the company ... then we carried out three fight actions and we waited a long time for the company ... We proposed that the company should pay us five million soles [approximately 1.6 million dollars] for the use of our territory over the years ... What we have got is 152,000 soles per year [approximately 49,800 dollars] and a community relations programme, but we still do not see results ... The company thought we were asking for too much because they value the territory in a very different way ... but this payment is just for the use of our land, no environmental or health impact assessment of our population has been done yet ... as a federation we all agreed that we are against oil exploitation in our lands ... We have a new company coming, Amerada Hess, they want to exploit oil in all the river basin, but we all agreed to say no ... Now the problem is ... when other communities see that here in Canaán we have got compensation, they may think this is easy to get, they may think oil companies are good for our development, but then what is going to be left for us in the future?' (Arturo Valiente, interview, 17 October 2006)

Valiente's commentary stresses the importance of CRPs as a negotiating tool for both sides, but it also shows that they can be a double-edged sword. On the one hand communities that have not received any sort of compensation from the oil companies for decades are right to demand compensation which takes into consideration the value that indigenous peoples attach to their land. This is often a complex matter, since many of the affected areas have an unmeasurable value for the people. However, if a price for compensation is to be set, the calculations cannot be based only on the price per hectare set by the national government. On the other hand, the prospect of compensation and a long-term CRP can lead the community to engage in a development process over which they do not have control.

For many communities the CRP negotiated with the company, before or after oil exploitation, is the only external support they get, and for them it becomes a matter of survival and an opportunity for development. Many communities see transnational companies as institutions with endless funds which take out all the resources of the country without leaving real benefits for the people; their demands may therefore range from capacity-building training to the construction of a school or a road. Negotiation between an oil transnational and an indigenous community is an uneven process, in which communities often do not have access to the information and legal advice necessary for fair negotiation. Even in the ideal case that a fair process is established, once the company takes on the role of the state a clientelist relationship is created, which is difficult to break.

The case of the state oil company and medium-size companies varies slightly, since they normally do not have the same economic resources to negotiate the CRPs as an oil transnational. The PR strategy of the national oil companies is also less aggressive, although practices such as militarisation of the oilfields and the cooption of indigenous leaders are common.

Companies are aware that they are replacing the state and that they should not be the ones in charge of the development of indigenous communities; however, most of the oil company CEOs and representatives interviewed for this research blame the state for its inability to institutionalise the extraction of resources in the Amazon region, its absence from the negotiation with communities, and the lack of investment in the communities in which oil is extracted.

Although state health and education programmes do not reach many indigenous communities, state presence is not entirely lacking in the Amazon region. For more than two decades, especially since the arrival of the oil industry, the region has gradually developed its administrative structures, and decentralised state institutions are present in every Amazonian province. National representatives of the state may not participate in the negotiations between the companies and the communities, but a multi-stakeholder local or regional board could be created to monitor the transparency and accountability of the oil operations and to decide the best way to distribute the percentage of the oil rent that by law goes to the local and regional governments. Although state institutions in the Amazon region are under-resourced they can still play an important role in institutionalising oil operations in the region.

The state and oil companies, as powerful actors in the oil conflict, are both responsible for this chaotic scenario. The absence of the state in some oil regions of Southern countries does not justify the methods employed by the oil companies to counter resistance and to negotiate with indigenous communities. Among these methods are divisionism, bribery, cooption, psychological pressure, militarisation and legal threats.

In both Ecuador and Peru the principal indigenous organisations and their non-indigenous allies have adopted a clear position against the extractive industries in indigenous territory or have demanded a moratorium on all oil activities until better conditions for indigenous peoples can be guaranteed, but there are other indigenous organisations and voices which see in dialogue and negotiation with the industry the only means of assuring their development and they struggle to achieve a fair negotiation in which respect for indigenous culture is the main priority. The debate around the oil industry is polarised in these two countries. Indigenous peoples may differ in their understanding of how oil-rich territories should be managed and what are the possible alternatives to oil exploitation; however, they converge on vital issues such as the need to preserve their territory, culture and sovereignty. It is on constant dialogue and shared views that their future hangs.

Community development led by the 'survivors': education, cosmovision and political participation

Education seems to be vital for the cultural survival of all indigenous peoples. In those communities whose way of life has been affected by the oil industry, the realisation that education is a long-term survival mechanism is now internalised and has become a priority of development programmes led by the communities themselves.

In order to better respond to external threats such as the oil industry, indigenous people have identified various forms of education and training required. They have also stressed the need for an intercultural model of education which would depart from previous assimilatory policies and would focus instead on identity and diversity. Education of indigenous peoples is a political question, a right in itself linked to the right to self-determination. In Latin America national programmes on Intercultural Bilingual Education (IBE) were started a few decades ago with high expectations had by indigenous organisations that sought the decolonisation of indigenous peoples' education.

It is beyond the scope of this chapter to get into the details of IBE and what it has meant politically for indigenous peoples. However, the main failure of these programmes in Ecuador and Peru has been the control that these states and international institutions have exerted over them, leading to the imposition of the dominant culture and language in indigenous and rural areas, to the detriment of cultural diversity. The effects of this kind of education were described by a Cofán woman:

> 'The western system doesn't respect the ways we think and live, especially through education. That's the biggest threat to indigenous peoples because it's a silent weapon, much more dangerous even than the oil industry because it colonises the hearts and minds of young people, of children, devaluing, and bit by bit it has the effect that the people, the system of [indigenous] peoples, the ancestral structure,

becomes lost. That's the big threat.' (Marta Flores, interview, 12 February 2007)

Some oil-affected communities have decided to take more responsibility for their own education instead of waiting for reforms to materialise. Changes in the school curriculum introduced by the community include the participation of the elders to teach indigenous cosmovision, increasing the time the children spend in nature or in collective communitarian activities, and rescuing the use of the traditional costume instead of expensive state uniforms. These decisions are taken in the general assembly of the community. Meso-American cosmovision is a structured and systemic world view and related belief system that integrates the structure of space and rhythms of time into a unified whole and influences all the aspects of life.

Sarayaku, for example, has received external support to create its own programme for IBE teachers, counting on the help of foreign volunteer teachers who rotate every three months. The training provided in Sarayaku complies with the dispositions of the regional and national IBE programmes, but the community proposes the most relevant topics for the curriculum. For example, 'globalisation and the age of information technology' has become an important subject for the community as they are aware that part of their success against CGC is due to the use of media such as the Internet, radio and filming.

Indigenous people are also aware that education is not limited to the formal sector or the IBE programmes. There are other crucial educational routes if communities want to influence policies and secure representation at various levels of the decision-making process. One of these is the role of the community as cradle for the formation of leaders who may later work for the local and regional federations. Traditionally leaders have worked on a voluntary basis, their election a duty and an honour that could only be avoided with strong justification. Today, leaders from local federations may be paid if the organisation receives funds from NGOs or other institutions. Community members sometimes see leaders as more interested in the salaries offered for these positions than in representing their people. Although envy and mistrust will always exist, leaders and members of communities struggling against the oil industry have worked tirelessly as advocates of indigenous peoples' rights, and some have risked their lives. The oil conflict has brought the leadership of the movement closer to the grassroots and has also served as a springboard to the regional and national levels for those leaders who have been involved in local struggles. The conflict with the oil industry has also created the need to train the youth in rights and advocacy issues, as they will be the future leaders and responsible for organising resistance and developing strategies for survival. The training in advocacy and indigenous and territorial rights has gone hand in hand with community development activities around the revalorisation of traditional culture and the creation of spaces in which the elders and the youth can converge.

A leader of the Cofán community of Dureno explains:

> 'Latterly the whole Cofán people has been worried because the last shamans are now dying, and then what's going to happen? The problem has been lack of confidence, because preparing to be a shaman takes a long time and is difficult. The shamans don't think the young people are interested, and at the same time the young people believe that the shamans don't want to teach them. Also, since the oil companies' arrival the sacred plants have been more difficult to find, and the young people go off to the towns and no longer have time for these teachings ... here an association of young people, AJONCE, has been formed with a double aim, on the one hand that they should know their rights and the threats that the oil industry holds over us, and on the other, to rescue our cosmovision.' (Ernesto Segundo, interview, 11 February 2007)

Since this interview, the community of Dureno has been approached on several occasions by national and foreign oil companies, and AJONCE has had an important role in maintaining the position of the community against oil operations in their territory. AJONCE has received a small amount of funding from Friends of the Earth, but has now managed to become sustainable through a traditional fish farm project and a programme of national and foreign volunteers. Recently AJONCE members built a house of *yajé* (a sacred plant of shamanism) as a centre for learning shamanism and other traditional teachings, but the location of the house at the top of a hill is strategic, as stated by one of the young members:

> 'We decided to build the *yajé* house on the hill because it's a secluded and pleasant place, good for learning shamanism ... but also we were worried by several bids to carry out mining on that hill ... now, with the *yajé* house there, that area can't be used for mining.' (Carlos Flores, interview, 14 January 2007)

Community development led by the 'intermediaries'

The 'intermediaries' also play an important role in the development of oil-affected communities. The roles of intermediary actors are diverse: they may act as supporters of indigenous movements, mediators in the oil conflict, funders of community development projects in oil-affected communities or researchers of the oil conflict. Indigenous peoples and communities coordinate or seek the support of these 'intermediaries' for different purposes, and the participation of the latter in their development can be short term, long term or intermittent. International environmental NGOs such as Amazon Watch, Rainforest Information Network, Oilwatch and their local counterparts are most likely to support indigenous peoples by organising a campaign against a particular oil company and providing information to the communities about the impacts of the industry and their collective rights. Other NGOs such as Oxfam support indigenous communities in such areas as governance and education; Oxfam has been active in evaluating how the ILO Convention 169 principle of prior and informed consent has been implemented in oil-affected communities. Intermediary actors such as political ecologists and the NGOs Acción Ecológica and Friends of the Earth have also helped in unmasking oppression by corporations and states and in recompensing indigenous peoples for past and current environmental and social injustices.

Through such collaboration indigenous peoples and the 'intermediaries' nurture each other and solidarity links are created. Indigenous peoples gain technical and moral support, while NGOs gain the grassroots support of an important actor for their wider agenda against the expansion of extractive industries. However, NGOs and indigenous organisations have admitted in interviews that although they may have a common agenda they still need to work on issues such as representation, capacity building and ownership and that collaboration between them is still a learning process. It seems that there is a new tendency among indigenous organisations to become more selective of the number and quality of the community development projects that they decide to move forward, prioritising the real needs of the community or organisation, its ability to manage funds and its participation in all stages of the project.

Academics, activists, the Ombudsman Office and the Catholic Church have also had an important role as mediators, advisers and human rights monitors in the oil conflict in recent years. Some of them have become prominent as designers of campaigns against the oil industry and community development strategies. At the beginning of the oil industry in the Amazon region, the evangelical organisation SIL, the military and the Catholic Church were the only institutions in the area, and the Church therefore played a prominent role in community development and in opposing the abuses committed by the state and the military at that time. The Church continues to have a strong influence on state officials and society and often uses this power to raise the demands of indigenous peoples. However, the flood of NGOs that has arrived in Amazonia and the increasing involvement of advocacy NGOs in the oil conflict has led to friction with the Church, which is especially critical of the threat to indigenous peoples.

Looking for justice and redress: from environmental justice to ecological debt

The role of a community worker in these contexts is determined by whose interests they are employed to serve. The biggest employers of community workers are the oil corporations whose purpose is to obtain community consent for oil exploration and extraction and to promote a development model compatible with capitalist industry. While indigenous communities have obtained some concessions from negotiating with the powerful companies, including community development goals, this has inevitably been at the expense of loss of their land and environmental resources as well as cultural and spiritual erosion through the imposition of capitalist relations of production. As has been recognised elsewhere, community development is here a tool of neoliberalism, of achieving consent for the dispossession of resources in the interests of corporate capital. Where the state is absent or weak it is unable or unwilling to provide for alternative community development strategies. 'Intermediaries' who engage in community development are faced with the contradiction of falling into line with corporate dispossession or else helping to mobilise against it, in many cases relying on the mixed blessings of international solidarity.

Some networks of NGOs, indigenous organisations and academics have developed discourses that help locate the struggles of communities in wider geopolitical and historical processes, such as environmental justice and ecological debt.

Environmental justice theories challenge dominant views of development by emphasising that the current model is built at the expense of unfair access to the earth's resources and distribution of environmental impacts. Martínez-Alier (2002: 13–14) argues that the environmentalism of the poor, or environmental justice movements constitute a social response to an economic logic based on values incommensurable with those of communities. Community development processes in which the commercial valuation of a community's resources is non-negotiable are flawed from the start. In such processes, alternative values based on indigenous cosmovision are tolerated only so long as they do not impede dispossession. However, environmental justice struggles emerge as part of a rejection of the imposed commercialisation of resources that are culturally valued in non-financial terms. Assessing and analysing the proposed engagement with oil companies' CRPs and financial compensation packages requires a process involving critical community development. It means learning about structures of commercialisation on a scale that is largely alien to indigenous communities, articulating and asserting what is important in indigenous cultures and involving the wider community in negotiation, discernment and mobilising support. There is a strong interrelationship between environmental justice struggles and critical community development processes, whether facilitated by indigenous leaders or outsiders from 'intermediate' groups (Scandrett, 2000).

While principles of environmental justice focus on equity, ecological debt focuses on moral and economic redress. Ecological debt is an economic concept that exposes the legacy of the unfair distribution of resources and the subsequent conflicts this may bring. Neoclassical economics can only make sense of resource depletion, environmental damage, species extinctions or biodiversity loss by attaching a price to the intact resources in order to measure against the marginal price of development which accompanies the damage. However, this consistently undervalues the resources of communities whose poverty, political marginalisation or non-monetised social relations deny them market leverage. As a result, the value in market terms of the legacy of destruction and resource depletion under colonial and post-colonial exploitation is considerable, and far outweighs the financial debt of the countries' governments accumulated through borrowing. Thus, the former colonised countries of the Global South are ecological creditors to varying degrees, while the 'developed' countries owe an ecological debt to the rest of the world.

First ... the exports of raw materials and other products from relatively poor countries are sold at prices which do not include compensation for local or global externalities. Second, rich countries make a disproportionate use of environmental space or services without payment, and even without recognition of other people's entitlements to such services. (Martínez-Alier, 2002: 213)

The Oilwatch network describes various principles which show how the oil industry creates ecological debt: from how oil export prices do not include the costs related to the externalities they produce, to the contribution of the industry to climate change and the extermination of indigenous cultures. Ecological debt does not imply a precise calculation to measure the financial compensation required for repayment – this would be almost impossible to measure and require buying in to the neoclassical logic that ecological models of economics seek to critique. However, as a political and moral tool, the ecological debt concept demonstrates the intrinsic relationship between the exploitation of the resources of the Global South and the wealth of the Global North. The dispossessed indigenous communities of Amazonian Ecuador and Peru are therefore ecological creditors morally, if not legally entitled to recompense. And for community development workers in the Global North, indebted status shifts the terms of engagement with communities in impoverished communities at home. Community development that incorporates an understanding of ecological debt leads to potentially radically new strategies of addressing issues such as housing, fuel poverty, land use planning, anti-pollution campaigns and resource exploitation at home.

The model of environmental justice requires indigenous and outsider community workers to support mobilisation against the oil corporations and their agents, including those who implement CRP. Ecological debt, moreover, is a tool which has been used by community workers across the world to generate international solidarity among all those who are dispossessed by the economic logic of neoliberalism.

Notes

[1] In the research study, all representatives of the oil industry requested anonymity. Permission was granted by most 'intermediaries' and 'survivors' to use their names. Nonetheless, pseudonyms have been used throughout the chapter to protect participants' identities.

[2] SIL International (current name of the former Summer Institute of Linguistics) started in 1934 to train missionaries in basic linguistic, anthropological and translation principles. The group has been denounced for using a scientific name to conceal its religious and capitalist agenda (Bonner, 1999: 20). SIL has been expelled from Brazil, Ecuador, Mexico and Panama, and restricted in Colombia and Peru (Cleary and Steigenga, 2004: 36).

References

Acosta, A. (2003) 'Desde abajo: "Texaco en el banquillo de los acusados"', *Diario Hoy*, 4 June, 15.

Bonner, A. (1999) *We will not be stopped: Evangelical persecution, Catholicism, and Zapatismo in Chiapas, Mexico*, Boca Raton, FL: Universal Publishers.

Cleary, E.L. and Steigenga, T.L. (2004) 'Resurgent voices: Indians, politics, and religion in Latin America', in E.L. Cleary and T.J. Steigenga (eds), *Resurgent voices in Latin America: Indigenous peoples, political mobilization, and religious change*, New Brunswick, NJ: Rutgers University Press, 1–24.

Collins, C. (2006) 'People and place: the Royal Bank of Scotland and "Community Engagement"', *Concept*, 16(2): 9–16.

Kimerling, J. and FCUNAE (1993) *Crudo Amazónico*, Quito: Abya Yala.

López, M.D. (2007) *Pueblos sin derechos: La responsabilidad de repsol en la Amazonía Peruana*, Peru: Intermón-Oxfam.

Maldonado, A. (2001) *La manera occidental de extraer petroïleo*, Quito: Oilwatch.

Martínez Domínguez, M.T. (2008) 'Building bridges: participatory and emancipatory methodologies with indigenous communities affected by the oil industry', *Enquire*, 1(1): 1–17.

Martínez-Alier, J. (2002) *Environmentalism of the poor: A study of ecological conflicts and valuation*, Cheltenham: Edward Elgar.

Mayo, M. (2008) 'Community development, contestations, continuities and change', in G. Craig, K. Popple and M. Shaw (eds) *Community development in theory and practice*, Nottingham: Spokesman, 13–27.

Melo, M. (ed) (2006) *Consulta previa: Ambiente y pétroleo en la Amazonía Ecuatoriana*, Quito: CDES.

Narváez, I. (2004) 'Metodologías de relacionamiento comunitario no ortodoxas: análisis político para abordarlas', in G. Fontaine (ed), *Petróleo y desarrollo sostenible: Las apuestas*, Quito: FLACSO, 75–90.

Oilwatch (2005) 'A civilization based on oil', *Resistance Bulletin*, 56, http://redamazon.files.wordpress.com/2007/11/oil-based-civilizationbol.pdf.

Perkins, J. (2005) *Confessions of an economic hit man*, London: Ebury Press.

Perreault, T. (2001) 'Developing identities: indigenous mobilization, rural livelihoods, and resource access in Ecuadorian Amazonia', *Cultural Geographies*, 8(4), 381–413.

Perreault, T. (2003) 'Changing places: transnational networks, ethnic politics, and community development in the Ecuadorian Amazon', *Political Geography*, 22: 61–88.

Reason, P. and Bradbury, H. (2006) 'Introduction: inquiry and participation in search of a world worthy of human aspiration' in P. Reason and H. Bradbury (eds) *Handbook of action research*, London: Sage, 1–14.

Sawyer, S. (2004) *Crude chronicles: Indigenous politics, multinational oil, and neoliberalism in Ecuador*, Durham, NC: Duke University Press.

Scandrett E. (2000) 'Community work, sustainable development and environmental justice', *Scottish Journal of Community Work and Development*, 6: 7–13

Shamir, R. (2004) 'The de-radicalization of corporate social responsibility', *Critical Sociology*, 30: 669–89.

Stoll, D. (1983) *Fishers of men or founders of empire? The Wycliffe Bible translators in Latin America. A US evangelical mission in the third world*, London: Zed Books.

Tombs, S. and Whyte, D. (2002) 'Unmasking the crimes of the powerful', *Critical Criminology*, 11, 217–36.

Van Cott, D.L. (2005) *From movements to parties in Latin America: The evolution of ethnic politics*, New York, NY: Cambridge University Press.

Varea, A.M. (ed) (1995) *Marea negra en la Amazonía: Conflictos ambientales vinculados a la actividad petrolera en el Ecuador*, Quito: Abya Yala.

Williams, K. (1989) 'Researching the powerful: problems and possibilities of social research', *Crime, Law and Social Change*, 13(4): 253–74.

Wray, N. (2000) *Pueblos lidígenas Amazónicos y actividad petrolera en el Ecuador: Conflictos, estrategias e impactos*, Quito: Ibis Dinamarca.

Yashar, D.J. (2005) *Contesting citizenship in Latin America. The rise of indigenous movements and the postliberal challenge*, Cambridge: Cambridge University Press.

TEN

The politics of democracy and the global institutions: lessons and challenges for community development

Niamh Gaynor

Introduction

One of the great paradoxes of our age is the simultaneous omnipresence and absence of democracy. Wars are fought and justified in its name yet, as global markets and institutions expand their reach and influence, the power of nation states and their communities is diminished. Democracy is all at once everywhere and nowhere, as market imperatives facilitated by global institutions, but not communities and their representatives, determine national and local policy. In this chapter I explore the mechanisms through which global institutions generate broad social support for their policies. Focusing in particular on the most influential institutions, the World Bank, the International Monetary Fund (IMF) and the World Trade Organization (WTO),[1] I argue that these seek to construct not just national policy, but communities themselves, effecting their disciplined inclusion into the globalised, market-driven development project.

I begin the chapter by examining the rise of the World Bank, the IMF and the WTO. I highlight the principal policies of these institutions, together with their now well-documented social and political impacts. I then go on to explore how, in the face of increasing challenges to their legitimacy, these institutions have sought to engage civil society groups and their constituent communities as 'partners' in managing and mitigating the social fallout accruing from their policies. Drawing on the global institutions' own discourses, I next demonstrate how this 'third way' for the 'Third World'[2] depoliticises civic engagement and community practice as it necessarily obfuscates the links between local issues and macro-level policies by embarking on an ambitious project of social engineering which seeks to redefine civil society and its agency. Drawing on some of my own experiences and conversations with civic groups and activists, I finally demonstrate the limits to this social engineering approach as communities, angry at their marginalisation and exploitation, either resist engagement in the global development project or, by maximising the opportunities provided by its new policy institutions, demand more effective representation from their civic leaders within it. I conclude with some lessons and challenges for community development in this regard.

Towards the Washington Consensus: the rise of the World Bank, the IMF and the WTO

The World Bank and the IMF were established by the Allies towards the end of the Second World War at Bretton Woods in the US with the aim of preventing a repeat of the economic collapse of the 1930s, which had constituted one of the principal drivers of the war. Although constitutionally part of the United Nations (UN) system, the Bretton Woods Institutions (BWIs), as they are also known, operated in a significantly different manner from the start. While decisions are made in the UN system on a one-country, one-vote basis,[3] decision-making power within the BWIs is based on financial contributions. Thus, the US holds the greatest share of voting power, followed up by a number of European countries.[4] The IMF was to provide short-term loans, thereby supporting an orderly international monetary system, while the World Bank was devised to provide long-term loans for reconstruction after the war. At first, the BWIs' activities were confined to Europe and they provided loans to Denmark, France and the Netherlands in the aftermath of the Second World War. However, the breakdown in the early 1970s of the system of fixed exchange rates followed by the global debt crisis in the early 1980s resulted in a sudden and significant increase in their remit globally (Helleiner, 2011).

The forerunner to the WTO, the General Agreement on Tariffs and Trade (GATT) was also set up after the Second World War, again in part to avoid a return to the 1930s-style trade wars between the major powers, which triggered the depression. However, as time evolved, the GATT developed increasing levels of rules and regulations, which marginalised poorer member states within the global trading system. The upgrading of GATT to the WTO in 1995 brought to public attention a number of these issues, with the Seattle ministerial meeting in 1999 collapsing amid public protests. Multiple rounds of negotiations and talks since that time have ended in deadlock as wealthy countries refuse to capitulate to Southern states' demands for fairness. According to Green (2012: 260–3), four key issues mitigate against fair trade within the WTO today. First, trade rules allow wealthy states to use tariff and non-tariff barriers to keep Southern states' exports out of lucrative markets. Second, the WTO continues to support agricultural trade subsidies in Northern countries, thus making it harder for poor producers to compete. Third, trade rules oblige some Southern countries to reduce tariffs, removing a key source of government revenue and protection of fledgling indigenous industry. And fourth, patenting laws under the WTO restrict Southern countries from accessing new technologies and innovations, as well as from developing indigenous industries. Thus, while the WTO claims that the institution 'provides a forum for negotiating agreements aimed at reducing obstacles to international trade and ensuring a level playing field for all' (WTO, 2014: n.p.), in practice these agreements tilt the playing field heavily in favour of its wealthy member states and their interests.

While attempts to inject some degree of fairness into the rules and regulations of the WTO appear to have been caught in a stalemate since the mid-1990s, its ideological sisters – the World Bank and the IMF – have gone from strength to strength over recent decades. Their big break came with the debt crisis of the 1980s. Caught in a vicious trap of escalating interest rates combined with collapsing commodity prices due to the global recession, countries in Africa, Latin America and Asia, having borrowed heavily during the petrodollar boom of the 1970s, found themselves increasingly unable to service the considerable debts they held with Northern commercial banks. With Mexico's threat of default in 1982 threatening to destroy these banks and bring down the global financial system, the IMF and World Bank stepped in. The loans of the large commercial banks were transferred over to the BWIs, which then set about a joint process of rescheduling and further lending to ensure debtor countries maintained liquidity, thereby maintaining repayments and stabilising the global financial system. In return, the two institutions demanded far-reaching economic reforms in debtor countries, packaged in the form of structural adjustment policies.

Designed to a common template within the BWI offices in Washington (and therefore dubbed the 'Washington Consensus') and steeped in the anti-statist, free-market ideology of the time, structural adjustment policies aimed at stabilising economies and attracting inward investment by – in line with WTO rulings – removing controls on investment and barriers to trade; boosting foreign exchange earnings by promoting exports; and reducing government deficits by severe cuts in public expenditure (Phillips, 2011). As we now know, the results were extremely damaging – economically, but most particularly socially and politically. One of the largest reviews – carried out by a group of academics, trade unions and non-governmental organisations (NGOs) across 12 countries (SAPRIN, 2002[5]) – uncovered the following results:

- *Trade liberalisation* led to growing trade deficits. Transnational corporations were typically the principal benefactors.
- *Financial sector liberalisation* resulted in financing going to large (and generally urban) firms run by a small number of local business elites.
- *Labour market reforms* resulted in more lax labour regulations and increased unemployment.
- *The privatisation of public services* resulted in poorer-quality and higher-priced services, effectively driving them out of the reach of the poor.
- *Public expenditure cuts*, including widespread redundancies within the public sector, together with the removal of subsidies on basic foodstuffs and staples led to widespread hunger and poverty, in many cases culminating in angry and violent 'food riots' on the streets.

In short, the results were devastating. As the Executive Director of the United Nations Children's Fund noted in his Foreword to the agency's landmark critique, *Adjustment with a Human Face*, at the time: 'As is too often the case during times of economic recession, a disproportionate share of suffering was borne by those least equipped to combat the effects of poverty – the most vulnerable of the poor, including children and women' (UNICEF, 1987: 3). If all of this sounds familiar, it is perhaps because, notwithstanding widespread criticism from academics, development agencies and civic groups alike, little of the overall economic policy framework of the Washington Consensus has changed since that time. What has changed, however, is the strategy for its dissemination with, as the following section outlines, civic actors now accorded a central role in this strategy.

From Washington to Post-Washington Consensus: a third way for the 'Third World'?

As noted above, the hegemonic position of the Washington Consensus had begun to run into serious trouble by the beginning of the 1990s, as empirical evidence mounted which illustrated the failures – in social and political, but also in economic terms – of the market-based reforms espoused. One of its most vocal, and arguably influential opponents at the time was the World Bank's former Chief Economist and Nobel prize winner, Joseph Stiglitz. Stiglitz (2008) argued that the intellectual doctrine of the Washington Consensus was too simplistic, being based on simple accounting frameworks and just a few economic indicators which were administered by technocratic economists with no regard to the context specificities of individual countries. He was strongly of the view that development policies should no longer be drawn up in the BWI offices in Washington, but that countries themselves should be the authors of their own policies.

In a series of high-profile addresses and presentations throughout the late 1990s and early 2000s, Stiglitz proposed a range of reforms to the Washington Consensus policy framework. These reforms formed the basis of what became known as the Post-Washington Consensus (PWC) – although, as we will see, the degree to which these represent a step forward or simply more of the same remains questionable. Stiglitz (2008: 53–4) identified the key tenets of this PWC as follows:

- the need for country- and context-specific development policies given that the 'one size fits all' models as advocated by the BWIs have failed;
- the involvement of developing countries themselves in the elaboration of these development plans, rather than drawing these up in Washington;
- some flexibility around the requirement for rapid liberalisation as there is no consensus that this, most particularly in countries with high unemployment, leads to faster economic growth;
- the inclusion of distributional issues and measures to reduce poverty in development planning.

In principle therefore, it seemed as though the PWC represented a significant shift away from the neoliberal tenets of the Washington Consensus, affording countries the space to formulate their own policies while paying heed to issues of distribution and poverty reduction. In practice, however, it soon became apparent that what the BWIs had in mind were the same macro-economic prescriptions, with two additional add-ons. The first was a policy add-on in the form of social safety nets which, taking various forms but generally involving externally funded projects and programmes, aimed at protecting the most vulnerable from the harshest impacts of the market-driven policies. The second, mirroring the popular 'third way' (Giddens, 2000) in Northern (particularly Anglophone) countries, involved determined efforts to foster close working relations with new 'partners' in development, community and civil society organisations (CSOs), nurturing these and building their 'capacity' to effectively manage and mitigate the social and political fallout of market-driven policies, while in the process diffusing conflict and rebuilding popular legitimacy and support for the globalised development project.

Unsurprisingly therefore, and once again reflecting the outdatedness and analytical redundancy of the pernicious dichotomies of 'the West and the Rest' or 'Us and Them' or 'First World/Third World', criticisms of both the PWC and 'third way governance' resonate strongly with each other. Reflecting on the policy content of the new PWC dispensation, Öniş and Şensis (2005) argue that it fails to provide a sufficiently broad framework for dealing with key development issues such as income distribution, poverty and self-sustained growth. Lesay (2011) concurs, arguing that despite its harsh critique of prevalent economic policies and the model of economic development, the PWC still steers clear of proposing any fundamental alternative to the old capitalist model. Such 'policy conservatism' also underpins critiques of UK and US models of 'third way governance' (see, for example, Campbell and Rockman, 2001: 46). As Wetherly (2001: 150) notes, 'the modern world is one in which there are no alternatives to capitalism', therefore the 'third way governance' and welfare reforms (social safety nets in PWC parlance) it espouses fail to adequately address the problems created by the very system they seek to support.

In short, therefore, the principal function of what we might term the 'third way Post-Washington Consensus approach' has been to build popular legitimacy for the ongoing globalised capitalist project, despite its inherently inequitable outcomes. Key and necessary allies in this endeavour have been a range of civic associations representing a reconfigured civil society, engineered and 'capacitated' to partner with global institutions and their interests in effecting the disciplined inclusion and participation of communities in this global capitalist project. In the following section I take a closer look at the discursive and institutional mechanisms through which this engineering takes place.

Politics out, capacity building in: reconfiguring and engineering civil society

From the 1990s forward, this newly branded (post-)Washington Consensus has been carefully and strategically promoted both discursively and institutionally by the BWIs. Discursively, it has been promoted in three ways. The first has involved the rediscovery of and a renewed interest in poverty. Thus, following a distinct market bias in the thematic foci of the influential World Bank annual World

Development Reports (WDRs) throughout the 1980s,[6] the 1990 WDR focused on poverty. However, poverty was framed in this and subsequent reports as a function of internal, domestic factors and policies rather than externally imposed policies[7] (see World Bank, 1989: chapter 2). The second discursive feature of the PWC lies in the World Bank's construction of the poor as somewhat helpless victims in a harsh world of poor internal governance, state ineptitude and corruption. Ignoring the overtly political, structuralist analyses of underdevelopment of the 1960s and 1970s (see, for example, Gunder Frank, 1967) and neatly glossing over the critiques of the Washington Consensus, poor communities are constructed as requiring help and assistance. This construction is particularly apparent in the influential millennial WDR, *Attacking Poverty*, which, focusing on the capacities, opportunities and security of the poor, argues that 'poor people are active agents in their lives, but are often powerless to influence the social and economic factors that determine their well-being' (World Bank, 2001: 3). With a continued emphasis on the primacy of markets for poverty reduction (see chapter 8) one of the central themes of this report is that the poor need help – in both participating in markets (2001: 61) and in mitigating the effects of market-induced shocks.

More recently, following the events of 9/11 in the US in 2001 and the attendant rise of the 'failed state' discourse as a justification for international intervention,[8] poor communities are now also constructed as having a propensity to violence, therefore representing a security threat to more affluent Northern states and societies. As the World Bank states, 'grievances can escalate into acute demands for change – and the risks of violent conflict – in countries where political, social, or economic change lags behind expectations' (World Bank, 2011: 5). Such constructions are not just demeaning and insulting to Southern communities,[9] they are also dangerous and divisive in that, in failing to provide the structural context for grievances and conflict, they induce prejudice and racism among the Northern media and general public. With poor communities now constructed as victims of inept governance with worrisome propensities for violence, the ground is set for the third frame through which the PWC is promoted – paternalistic 'partnerships' with community representatives and CSOs infused with discourses of empowerment, support and the ubiquitous 'capacity building'. Within this discourse, the rich corpus of theorisation on civil society – from Hegel through to Gramsci and beyond – as a site of political contestation between different interest groups is ignored; development problems are now reframed as technical inadequacies rather than the outcome of differential power relations and interest politics; and civil society is reconfigured or engineered as the new 'magic bullet' within this apolitical developmental dispensation.

This reconfiguration assumes three aspects. First, CSOs are reconfigured as apolitical 'partners' in the global market-driven development project, complementing rather than questioning or opposing the efforts of other mainstream actors. This is reflected in the Busan declaration of 2011,[10] which defines CSOs as 'independent development actors in their own right, whose efforts complement those of public authorities and the private sector'. Second, their new political PR (public relations) role is to build public support and legitimacy for BWI reforms and policies. The IMF, for example, which since the 1990s has sought to engage CSOs in dialogue, views CSO engagement as a way of 'strengthening country ownership of policies, which is essential to successful stabilisation and reform. *Constructive dialogue* with CSOs can help build *mutual understanding and increase support for reform*' (IMF, 2013: n.p., emphasis added). The important role CSOs can play in building support for the Fund's work is reflected in the Managing Director's decision, in 2003, to publish and distribute to all staff a *Guide for Staff Relations with Civil Society Organisations*. Within this guide, staff are warned that 'Some CSOs harbour considerable suspicion about the IMF and blame the institution for many ills'. Staff are thus advised that 'It is usually better to focus discussions on finding and consolidating common ground rather than emphasising clashing interpretations and prescriptions'. Staff are further reminded that IMF policies are not open to influence from these CSO groups: 'CSOs may have unrealistic expectations regarding the degree that contacts with Fund staff will influence policy. The fact that staff are open to discussions with CSOs should not be misconstrued to mean that the IMF will necessarily adopt their positions' (IMF, 2003: n.p.).

Third, CSOs are expected to draw communities into the globalised development project through a form of disciplined inclusion which promotes communities' own responsibilities for plugging the gaps and managing the social fallout of this project. This role is heavily promoted by both the World Bank and the European Union – the latter now one of the major global institutions in international development.[11] In the Foreword to its 2003 WDR, which focuses on service provision, the World Bank confidently declares: 'Services work when they include all people, *when girls are encouraged* to go to school, when pupils *and parents participate* in the schooling process, *when communities take charge of their own sanitation*' (World Bank, 2003: xiv, emphasis added). The reason for poor service provision, according to the report, is nothing to do with skewed priorities, but rather internal governance issues.

Community groups therefore have a key role to play in the monitoring and oversight of service provision – employing 'technical' instruments such as budget monitoring, report cards, service delivery satisfaction surveys and so on – all of which necessitate 'capacity building' training. With communities and civic groups thus mobilised in the delivery and oversight of social services, the way is clear for the Bank to focus on the broader macro picture – as reflected in the report of the following year – *Improving the Climate for Investment*. Since 2002, the Bank has developed 'Community Driven Development' (CDD) programmes, which support community management of safety net projects in a range of areas such as 'water supply and sewerage rehabilitation, school and health facilities construction, nutrition programs for mothers and infants, rural access roads, and support for livelihoods and microenterprises' (World Bank, 2014).

In recent years, through the European Commission (EC), the EU has developed what it calls 'an enhanced and more strategic approach in its engagement with local CSOs' (EC, 2012: 4). Echoing the PWC construction of CSOs, the EC (2012: 3) notes that 'While states carry the primary responsibility for development and democratic governance, synergies between states and CSOs can help overcome challenges of poverty, widening inequalities, social exclusion and unsustainable development'. Mirroring World Bank discourse, the EC envisages a key role for CSOs in fostering 'good governance' through oversight on public spending and service delivery. Once again, therefore, through support to select 'partner' CSOs, the active inclusion of communities in the global, market-driven development project is the central focus of EU support. And, once again, this necessitates a depoliticisation of civic engagement, obfuscating the links between local issues and macro-level politics and redefining civic activism in purely technocratic terms.

Such an ambitious engineering of both CSOs and, through these, communities themselves, has both a material and an ideological dimension. Materially, as we have seen, the reconfiguration and engineering is attained through select funding for particular service or safety net projects – as with the World Bank's CDD above or EC funding. At an ideological level, two principal instruments are used. The first comes in the form of the ubiquitous 'capacity building' training workshops organised by donors for CSOs and, in turn, by CSOs for communities. This is justified, as we have seen above, by privileging technical, managerial capacities over analytical capacities. As the EC notes, 'In order to increase their impact, local CSOs must overcome capacity constraints ranging from limitations in technical management and leadership skills, fundraising, to results management and issues of internal governance' (EC, 2012: 10). The second instrument is the range of new 'participatory' policy institutions at national and local levels which, as we will see, offer both constraints and opportunities to civic agency.

The two most widespread PWC policy institutions are the national-level Poverty Reduction Strategy (PRS) processes and local-level decentralisation structures. Developed in the late 1990s, PRS institutions were the PWC institutional mechanism whereby development policy formulation ostensibly moved from Washington to host countries themselves. Moreover, with their 'poverty focus' and emphasis on 'broad-based participation' (see World Bank, 2000), they were hailed as opening the political space to national governments and civic associations for dialogue and deliberation on alternatives to the Washington Consensus. Empirical studies reveal the results of PRS processes to be far more mixed, however, with, in many cases, the same policies and politics emerging as before (see, for example, Weber, 2006; Zack-Williams and Mohan, 2006, for whom the PRS functions as an institutional framework for the inclusion of civic actors within the unchanged and unchanging neoliberal, development project). At more local levels, decentralised institutions, providing the same opportunities for local CSOs and communities to become involved in local policy deliberations and implementation, have also been heavily promoted since the 1990s. As with the PRS, although normatively hailed as opening up a policy space at local levels, empirical studies reveal them to be highly susceptible to elite capture (Chanie, 2007; Crawford and Hartmann, 2008).

While discourse proves a powerful tool of social engineering (due to its relative invisibility), institutions are arguably more malleable. The issue is therefore perhaps not so much how and in whose interests such PWC policy institutions perform, but why they do so and, more normatively, how they might be transformed to challenge the political and economic status quo. Clearly, a non-reflexive, uncritical engagement can result in cooption and the disciplined inclusion of both CSOs and the communities they purport to represent as highlighted above. By contrast, as we see below, a more critical engagement, informed by mediation with communities and constituents, highlights the limitations of this institutional and, ultimately, discursive PWC social engineering approach.

Limits to social engineering: colonising spaces, demanding representation, resisting 'participation'

The global institutions' plans for their new civic 'partners' is flawed in one major respect. Rather unsurprisingly perhaps for undemocratic institutions, the BWIs have neglected the one key element central to the democratic legitimacy of civic organisations – representation. In its reconfiguration of civil society, the BWI project is premised on hierarchical, top-down relations within civil society, with civic leaders exercising control and influence over their constituents, thereby effecting their inclusion in the macro development project. Yet, as we know, civic and community leaders derive their legitimacy from their skills and abilities to mediate with and represent their constituents and communities, and not the BWIs. And so, while examples of the negative effects of the global PWC approach within community practice abound – paternalistic, technocratic approaches emphasising local responsibility and action divorced from the macro-policy environment and the motivations and actions of elite actors – a closer examination of its impact over time reveals more complex dynamics and outcomes.

A few examples from my own research over the years illustrate this. In Malawi, for example, the technical and 'capacity' exigencies of participation in the country's first PRS process in the early 2000s resulted in an increasing professionalisation of civic actors engaged in the process. Having internalised the technocratic, problem-solving discourse dominant within PRS institutions, the principal CSO participating in the process attracted significant levels of international funding, which moved it away from community mobilisation and onto the PWC activities of budget monitoring and safety net provision. While prospering financially from this move, the CSO became increasingly divorced from its constituents. As this gap widened, constituents began to question, via local media and radio, the motivations and level of engagement of their leaders. A crisis of legitimacy for civic leaders ensued as they were charged with turning into yet another elite, urban-based CSO pandering to the exigencies of international donors. Faced with growing criticism across the media and within the Malawian public sphere more broadly, PRS civic actors were forced to redirect their energy and focus, and to develop and consolidate links with community groups across the country. The confluence of three factors – community groups demanding representation through their CSO at a national level; the fact that the CSO's reputation and future now depended on this; and the fact that the BWIs' own somewhat shaky legitimacy rested on claims of 'national ownership' and 'broad-based civic participation' – resulted in, for a short time at least, a reopening and retransformation of Malawi's PRS institutions (see Gaynor, 2010; 2011).

Somewhat analogously, in Burundi local civic and community groups have identified decentralised institutions as a strategic site for contesting the political marginalisation and exploitation of communities by donors and government alike. Having reappropriated the core concepts of accountability (downward, not upward) and participation (as voice, not cost-sharing through voluntary labour), they are working with local communities to prise open the political spaces created locally through decentralised structures and institutions (see Gaynor, 2014a; 2014b). In Rwanda, where rapid economic development depends on a strong, highly authoritarian, top-down system of decentralised governance, community resistance to the increasing costs of state-sponsored programmes, as articulated in community meetings and in confidential research interviews, is apparent, and the legitimacy of local political and coopted civic leaders is once more called into question (see Gaynor, 2015).

The ultimate outcome of each of these cases remains unknown and unknowable. Each represents an ongoing journey – of cooption and contestation – in the context of hegemonic development frameworks privileging elite, market-based interests over those of local communities. They highlight two fundamental points. First, that power relations are not static, but constantly changing – between different groups and within different institutions. It falls to civic representatives to strategically maximise the opportunities available and seize the power where and when they can. And second, that civic actors and community representatives are not passively coopted into these engineered spaces, as we are sometimes led to believe. By losing sight of the reasons they entered these spaces in the first place and losing touch with their constituents, they often allow themselves to be coopted, or, alternatively, remaining loyal to their roots, they resist and sometimes transform these spaces. With all our focus on the power, discourses and frameworks of global and national elites, we sometimes lose sight of the agency of the marginalised, in the process negating or ignoring this, and ultimately reproducing the stereotypes and caricatures of the victimised that are constructed and promulgated by the global institutions.

Towards a conclusion: lessons and challenges for community development

In this chapter I have attempted to demonstrate that the current 'third way for the "Third World"' promoted by the global institutions means little in terms of policy change, but everything in terms of democracy. Necessitating and actively promoting a fundamental reconfiguration of civic agency – from oppositional force to apolitical partner, it represents a highly ambitious project of social engineering, with potentially significant political repercussions. On the one hand, it risks further undermining democracy by coopting and reconfiguring key actors within the public sphere. On the other, both the discourses and institutions it has introduced potentially offer new opportunities for critically engaged groups and individuals to widen and transform the political space, challenging the very basis on which these institutions were founded.

Three issues are worth highlighting in this regard. First, language and discourse matter. A somewhat lazy, uncritical acceptance of the PWC's depoliticised versions of the core concepts – 'democracy' (measured now in numbers rather than substance); 'participation' (active engagement in mitigating local problems arising from the global development project rather than critically interrogating their causes); 'partnership' (on whose terms?); and 'capacity' (whose? To do what?) – leads to a somewhat lazy, uncritical acceptance of a dominant, yet socially dislocating global development framework. Second, institutions matter. Again, a somewhat lazy, uncritical engagement in any of the range of institutions on offer within the PWC framework may initially prove comfortable and financially lucrative to civic groups, but it may ultimately prove their Achilles heel as CSO legitimacy and capacity to represent their constituents comes increasingly into question. And third, neither institutions nor discourses are static. Both are a function of the power relations that circulate within and around them. In a global political economy which seeks to consolidate a hegemonic consensus for an elitist, market-driven development project, it falls to community and civic leaders to reconnect with their roots and, working with their communities, to step outside the globally dominant norms, institutions and frameworks to envision, imagine and articulate alternative social and political projects and futures.

Notes

[1]   While the range of global institutions is vast and constantly expanding, I am focusing on these three institutions as, arguably, they have proven most influential over the past five decades.

[2]   I am using the term 'Third World' disparagingly as, rooted in modernist thinking, it implies a linear pathway to development while ignoring the structural causes of poverty and wealth. I also use other terms, such as Global South and North, with caution as they carry geographically specific connotations which ignore the coexistence of wealth and poverty within individual nations and regions.

[3]   With the exception of the UN Security Council.

[4]   See IMF (2015) for financial contributions of all IMF members.

[5]   The lengthy delay in the production of this report is an interesting story in itself. The report was commissioned by the World Bank in 1997. However the Bank, unhappy with the findings, sought to block publication. By the time the report was finally published (2002), the damage wreaked by these policies was widely known.

[6]   WDRs, which have been published annually since 1978, are the Bank's flagship publication. Each year, the WDR focuses on a particular theme, outlining the Bank's policy and thinking in this area. Given the Bank's influence and resources, WDRs are highly influential in setting donor policy and agendas more broadly.

[7]   While chapter 8 of the WDR 1990 acknowledges the significance of international policy in the areas of trade, aid and debt, it stresses that these can only work in poorer countries' favour when they liberalise their trade and adopt conditions associated with debt relief and aid.

[8]   This discourse is deeply problematic in the case of African states where the Western norm of strong Weberian states (which took centuries to develop in Europe) has never existed and where innovative experiments in state building are ongoing.

[9]   While the links between poverty and conflict are now well established, the popular 'failed state' index (The World Fund for Peace, 2013) is purely descriptive and makes no attempt to analyse the causes of marginalisation and/or grievance.

[10]   The Busan declaration emerged from the 4th High Level Global Forum on Aid Effectiveness held from 29 November to 1 December 2011 in Busan, South Korea. The Forum brought together all major multilateral and bilateral donors and the

declaration is thus reflective of the global consensus on aid issues, including the role of CSOs. See www.oecd.org/development/effectiveness/49650173.pdf.

[11] EU aid overseas now accounts for one and a half times that provided by the World Bank (Hout, 2010: 3).

References

Campbell, C. and Rockman, B.A. (2001) 'Third Way leadership, old way government: Blair, Clinton and the power to govern', *British Journal of Politics and International Relations*, 3(1): 36–48.

Chanie, P. (2007) 'Clientelism and Ethiopia's post-1991 decentralisation', *Journal of Modern African Studies*, 45(3): 355–84.

Crawford, G. and Hartmann, C. (eds) (2008) *Decentralisation in Africa: A pathway out of poverty and conflict?*, Amsterdam: Amsterdam University Press.

European Commission (2012) *The roots of democracy and sustainable development: Europe's engagement with civil society in external relations*, Brussels, http://eurlex.europa.eu/LexUriServ/LexUriServ.do?uri= COM:2012:0492:FIN:EN:PDF.

Gaynor, N. (2010) 'Between citizenship and clientship': the politics of participatory governance in Malawi', *Journal of Southern African Studies*, 36(4): 801–16.

Gaynor, N. (2011) 'The global development project contested: the local politics of the PRSP process in Malawi', *Globalizations*, 8(1): 17–30.

Gaynor, N. (2014a) 'The tyranny of participation revisited: international support to local governance in Burundi', *Community Development Journal*, 49(2): 295–310.

Gaynor, N. (2014b) 'Supporting decentralisation in fragile states: a view from Burundi', *Development Policy Review*, 32(2): 203–18.

Gaynor, N. (2015) '"A nation in a hurry": the costs of local governance reforms in Rwanda', *Review of African Political Economy*, 41(143) Supplement 1: 49–63.

Giddens, A. (2000) *The third way and its critics*, Cambridge: Polity Press.

Green, D. (2012) *From poverty to power*, 2nd edn, Rugby: Practical Action Publishing.

Gunder Frank, A. (1967) *Capitalism and underdevelopment in Latin America*, New York, NY: Monthly Review Press.

Helleiner, E. (2011) 'The evolution of the international monetary and financial system', in J. Ravenhill (ed), *Global Political Economy*, 3rd edn, Oxford: Oxford University Press, 213–43.

Hout, W. (2010) 'Governance and development: changing EU policies', *Third World Quarterly*, 31(1): 1–12.

IMF (2003) *Guide for staff relations with civil society organisations*, www.imf.org/external/np/cso/eng/2003/101003.htm#III.

IMF (2013) *The IMF and civil society organisations*, IMF Fact Sheet, Washington, DC: IMF Communications Department, www.imf.org/external/np/exr/facts/civ.htm.

IMF (2015) *IMF members' quotas and voting power, and IMF Board of Governors*, www.imf.org/external/np/sec/memdir/members.aspx.

Lesay, I. (2011) 'How "post" is the Post-Washington Consensus?', *Journal of Third World Studies*, 23(2): 183–98.

Öniş, Z. and Şensis, F. (2005) 'Rethinking the emerging Post-Washington Consensus', *Development and Change*, 36(2): 263–390.

Phillips, N. (2011) 'Globalisation and development', in J. Ravenhill (ed), *Global Political Economy*, 3rd edn, Oxford: Oxford University Press, 416–49.

SAPRIN (2002) *The policy roots of economic crisis and poverty: A multi-country participatory assessment of structural adjustment*, www.saprin.org/SAPRI_Findings.pdf.

Stiglitz, J.E. (2008) 'Is there a post-Washington consensus consensus?', in J.E. Stiglitz and N. Serra (eds) *The Washington Consensus Reconsidered*, Oxford: Oxford University Press, 41–56.

The World Fund for Peace (2013) 'The Failed States Index 2013', http://library.fundforpeace.org/fsi13.

UNICEF (1987) *Adjustment with a human face: Human development report 1987*, New York, NY: UNICEF.

Weber, H. (2006) 'A political analysis of the PRSP initiative: social struggles and the organisation of persistent relations of inequality', *Globalizations*, 3(2), 187–206.

Wetherly, P. (2001) 'The reform of welfare and the way we live now: a critique of Giddens and the Third Way', *Contemporary Politics*, 7(2): 149–70.

World Bank (1989) *Poverty: World development report 1990*, Washington, DC: World Bank.

World Bank (2000) *PRSP sourcebook*, Washington, DC: World Bank.

World Bank (2001) *Attacking poverty: World development report 2000/2001*, Washington, DC: World Bank.

World Bank (2003) *Making services work for poor people: World development report 2004*, Washington, DC: World Bank.

World Bank (2011) *Conflict, security and development: World development report 2011*, Washington, DC: World Bank.

World Bank (2014) 'Community-driven development overview', www.worldbank.org/en/topic/communitydrivendevelopment/overview.

World Trade Organization (2014) 'About the WTO – A statement by former Director-General Pascal Lamy', www.wto.org/english/thewto_e/whatis_e/wto_dg_stat_e.htm.

Zack-Williams, T. and Mohan, G. (2006) 'Africa from SAPs to PRSP: plus ça change plus c'est la même chose', *Review of African Political Economy*, 32(106): 501–3.

PART 3

Politicising the future

ELEVEN

Disability arts: the building of critical community politics and identity

Colin Cameron

Introduction

In this chapter I discuss the disability arts movement in Great Britain as an example of a self-organised, critically conscious community established with political aims. I consider the role of disability arts in forging individual and collective identities grounded in a re-evaluation of the meaning of disability. I explore ways in which disability arts have challenged dominant representations of disabled people, illustrating my discussion by reflecting on poems by Sue Napolitano. Finally, I introduce the affirmation model, a theoretical development expressing the distinct social critique emerging from disability arts, and conclude by summarising the significance of this analysis for community development approaches.

Two views

I was talking a couple of months ago with a PhD student at Northumbria University about an event he had recently attended during the early stages of his research. This was a non-disabled research student with no previous experience of disability arts, who is developing research into community arts more broadly. The event he had attended had been held by a local disability organisation and had involved, among other 'turns', a woman with learning difficulties performing the Judy Garland song 'Somewhere Over the Rainbow' from the 1939 Hollywood film *The Wizard of Oz*.

The performance had been, I was told, greeted with wild applause and admiration. Not having been at the event I can't say for sure, but having been at plenty of events like this one I feel fairly confident in suggesting that much of the admiration would have been mingled with appraisals such as "Isn't it marvellous what she can do *in spite of her disabilities ...*".

In my mind I contrasted this event with another, held in the same local authority area in North East England in 1994, by a theatre group of young disabled people, some of whom had learning difficulties and others who had various physical and sensory impairments. In front of local councillors this group had performed a number of self-written comedy sketches highlighting and satirising the council's recently published community care plan, the near non-existence of accessible public toilet facilities, the pointless and mind-numbing activities provided at the local day centre, and the woefully inadequate provision of local accessible public transport. Leaving the stage at the end of the performance, one of the young disabled people turned to the assembled councillors and proclaimed, "You're all a bunch of tossers!" This abusive line was unscripted, but nicely expressed the sentiments that had been conveyed in the sketches. I recall that the show was met with constrained rather than wild applause.

There are two pictures here of disabled people involved with local community groups, both involving performance and the arts. One of these involves disability arts and the other does not. As Barnes and Mercer (2010: 207) have expressed it, there is a crucial distinction between 'disabled people doing art' and the more overtly political 'disability arts'. In Masefield's (2006: 72) terms: 'Disability arts are art forms, art works and arts productions created by disabled people to be shared with, and to inform other disabled people, by focusing on the truth of disability experience.' The truth of disability experience depicted by the young disabled people's theatre group, described above, involved being regarded primarily as passive recipients of care; as people who, by and large, wouldn't be accessing public spaces and therefore didn't require accessible toilet facilities; as people for whom attendance at the local day centre would fill up a sizable part of their adult lives; and as people who didn't require access via public transport to the places everyone else goes to because they had 'special' buses instead.

It is important here to make it clear what is meant by 'disability experience' because this is key to the development of our understanding. My intention is that the experience of being disabled should be understood as different to the experience of being impaired. This requires a consideration of the meanings of these terms within the conflicting individual and social models.

While there are some differences in wording, both the individual and social models identify impairment as a relatively long-term physical, sensory, emotional or cognitive characteristic (Cameron, 2014a; 2014b) that can be either congenital or acquired. It is in their definitions of disability, however, that the models diverge. Within dominant (individual or medical model) discourse disability is identified as 'something wrong' with the bodies of disabled people (Oliver, 1996). The World Health Organization (WHO), for example, has identified disability as 'any restriction or lack (resulting from impairment) of ability to perform an activity in the manner or within the range considered normal for a human being' (WHO, 1980, in Cameron, 2014a: 99) and as 'an umbrella term, covering impairments, activity limitations, and participation restrictions' (WHO, 2012, in Mallett and Slater, 2014: 92). In other words, disability is identified as an individual problem to do with some people's bodies, regarded in terms of personal deficit and abnormality; as something to be cured, endured or overcome.

The social model, developed initially by the Union of the Physically Impaired Against Segregation (UPIAS), challenges this dominant view by identifying disability as an unequal social relationship. Within the social model disability is 'the disadvantage or restriction of activity caused by a contemporary social organisation which takes little or no account of people who have physical impairments and thus excludes them from the mainstream of social activities' (UPIAS 1976: 14). This definition was broadened by Disabled People's International in 1981 (in Barnes, 1994: 2) to include people with sensory, emotional and cognitive impairments. Here, disability is 'the loss or limitation of opportunities to take part in the normal life of the community on an equal level with others due to physical and social barriers'.

From a social model viewpoint, disability is not something people *have* (we are not people *with* disabilities), but is something *done to* people with impairments. People with impairments are disabled by poor or non-existent access to the public places where ordinary life happens, and by the condescending or unwelcoming responses of those who occupy these places. 'Disability is something imposed on top of our impairments by the way we are unnecessarily isolated and excluded from full participation in society' (UPIAS, 1976: 14).

The sketches performed by the young disabled people described above did not attempt to ignore or shy away from talking about disability issues, but confronted them head on, challenging mainstream assumptions around what disability was all about. In expressing their dissatisfaction with the state of things in their own local authority, this group was part of a wider movement of disabled people collectively organising to bring about social change and to gain control over their own lives.

The disabled people's movement

> I don't think disability arts would have happened without disability politics coming first … Our politics teach us that we are oppressed, not inferior … Our politics have given us self-esteem. They have taught us, not simply to value ourselves, but to value ourselves as disabled people. (Sutherland, 1989: 159)

Sutherland's comment here describes the close relationship between disability arts and the wider disabled people's movement. The relationship between the different parts of the movement can be described as symbiotic, for each gives meaning to the others, and has enabled the others to grow and develop. In Campbell's words 'The movement is a jigsaw – each piece is vital for the true picture to emerge' (Campbell and Oliver, 1996: 199).

During the late 1960s disabled people were beginning to collectively question the legitimacy of large charities to speak on behalf of, and organise the lives of, people with impairments. Such charities began to be identified as part of the problem of disability rather than as part of the solution. The work of disabled activists like Paul Hunt, an inmate at a 'care' home run by the Leonard Cheshire Foundation, led to the formation of UPIAS. UPIAS was established as a forum for debate about disability issues by disabled people living in residential homes, and rejected the idea that organisations *for* disabled people – led by non-disabled people – were able to comprehend or promote the best interests of disabled people. While UPIAS's key aim was the eradication of all segregated homes perhaps its most important and lasting contribution to the development of the disabled people's movement was the establishment in 1976 of definitions of impairment and disability that would become known as the social model (Barnes, 2014). This framework for understanding became established as the big idea underpinning the emergence of new organisations *of* disabled people during the 1980s and 1990s: local coalitions of disabled people campaigning about issues including access, housing, transport, employment, information, leisure; centres for independent living campaigning for, and later delivering, direct payments so that disabled people could employ their own personal assistants and take control of their lives; organisations campaigning for the closure of segregated 'special' schools and demanding inclusive education; and networks of disabled people conversing nationally under the umbrella of the British Council of Organisations of Disabled People (Cameron, 2014c). It is against this background and within this context that the emergence of disability arts needs to be considered.

Disability arts, community and identity

Community development can be understood as being centrally concerned with building and sustaining active and participatory forms of 'community'. Day (2006) has suggested that, rather than being thought of as something 'natural', 'real' and 'out there' to be discovered and analysed, community can be regarded as a construct which is the outcome of human reflection and agency:

> If they are not to be treated as taken-for-granted facts within the social landscape, then communities have to be seen as resulting from some form of creative process, through which they are built and maintained. This implies that they have a history and trajectory of development, and that there will be continuing processes through which their existence is reproduced. (Day, 2006: 156)

Talking about the disabled community provides a good opportunity to consider this understanding of the term. Prior to the establishment of the disabled people's movement – in itself an elusive description beyond the organisations by which it is constituted (Campbell and Oliver, 1996) – it could easily be disputed whether such a thing as 'the disabled community' existed. Certainly the establishment of a community of self-identifying disabled people, organising and coming together to collectively campaign for equality, faced considerable challenges. Perhaps the most important of these had to do with conventional views regarding disability as a 'discreditable' identity that few would willingly own (Goffman, 1990; Cameron, 2014d).

Pressures to discourage people with impairments from identifying collectively are embedded within everyday life practices, not least by the representation by large charities – organisations *for* rather than *of* disabled people – of disability issues as impairment specific. While the organisations of the disability industry relied for income generation on the identification in the public mind of disabled people as pathetic cases in need of charity, each impairment – cerebral palsy, Down's syndrome, blindness, deafness, MS, epilepsy, and so on – was depicted in terms of its awfulness and its devastating impact on the lives of those so 'afflicted'. There was little reason for people with different impairments to seek association, and many reasons for avoiding each other. The requirement to play roles as passive, grateful recipients of others' kindness led many disabled people to be hostile towards the idea of identifying as disabled and to shun contact with other disabled people for fear of contamination by association. While, as other chapters in this volume explore, community development discourse centres around ideas of collectivity, self- and mutual determination, the role of charities in preventing the development of such a politicised disabled community and identity is clear. Those who identified disability as a social justice issue and campaigned for rights not charity were labelled as 'complainers ... who cannot deal with the problems related to their disabilities' (Murphy, 2005: 161). As is often the case when marginalised groups begin to identify oppression within existing social arrangements, powerful groups with vested interests in maintaining these structures find it easy to ignore or dismiss these claims as unrealistic and misguided.

From its appearance in the early 1980s through the work of companies and agencies such as Strathcona, Graeae and Shape, disability arts took an oppositional stance to these dominant representations. The London Disability Arts Forum (LDAF) was established in 1986 as a space in which disabled artists could engage creatively and communally in re-creating cultural meanings around disability, rewriting stories around disability, and producing new and challenging images of disability. Through the work of LDAF and other disability arts organisations which came into being in the following years – for example the Northern Disability Arts Forum, the National Disability Arts Forum, the Southwest and Northwest Disability Arts Forums – disabled people became involved in forging new individual and social identities based on pride and the celebration of difference.

Cabarets, such as LDAF's The Workhouse, were ground breaking in providing accessible spaces where disabled people could come to enjoy performances by other disabled people. Through music and song, theatre, dance, visual arts, photography, creative writing, film and sculpture, disabled people explored the experience of living with impairment in a disabling society. Disabled artists used anger, passion, humour and satire to reveal the oppressive nature of disability as a social relationship, to expose the oppressive behaviours and assumptions of non-disabled people and to shed light on the way that disabling relationships were constructed in everyday interactions. Morrison and Finkelstein (1994: 127) noted that attendance at a disability arts event could be a radicalising experience: 'Having someone on stage communicating ideas and feelings that an isolated disabled person never suspected were shared by others can be a turning point for many.'

The cabaret events organised by the DAFs became a key focus for community development, consciousness raising, and the development of collective, as opposed to individualised, identity. Disabled people came together to learn from each other and began to understand that the disadvantage they experienced was not the natural consequence of impairment, but was created by a world which rejected impairment. For many this meant emancipation from internalised oppression experienced in a culture where previously they had only ever seen themselves represented as undesirable and abnormal (Reeve, 2014). A process of 'coming out' as disabled meant becoming able to affirm self and to name society rather than self as being where struggle was required (Swain and Cameron, 1999).

Day (2006: 154) has noted that 'communities are brought into being through the interpretive activities of their members, and registered among the concepts which they use in their everyday talk and interaction'. In this sense, it is legitimate to talk about a disabled community having been intentionally created through the activity of disability arts. When, through the development of new narratives, people with a range of impairments collectively identify as disabled on the basis of having been excluded from active participation within ordinary life, a sense of belonging and relationship emerges, as well as the suggestion of a collective response and activity:

> By modifying the frame from one of innate deviance to one of oppression, individuals may come to feel angry not only because the system is unjust but because they have been made to feel ashamed ... The activated feeling of anger propels stigmatized individuals into public space to behave collectively, and feelings of pride emerge (Britt and Heise, 2000: 257).

Disability pride was the principle underlying the increased visibility of disabled people who demanded access to the social mainstream and an end to discrimination. From the early 1990s disabled people organised non-violent demonstrations which led, for example, to the end of ITV's annual Telethon charity fund-raising event; to the provision of allocated spaces for wheelchair-users on buses and trains; and to the establishment of anti-discrimination legislation. This is an example of community development involving commitment to an ongoing struggle for equality and demonstrating the possibility of making gains.

In Day's (2006: 154) terms, community plays a key role in how people think about themselves, their personal and social identities, and their subjectivity. As Brown (2003: 38) has remarked, 'Social change, though serious and vital, can also be uplifting'. For individuals with impairments, strength is found in being part of a community which rejects mainstream requirements to hide impairment and instead affirms and unashamedly flaunts impairment. What emerges is the recognition of the right to active participation in society's institutions without having to pretend to be something that you're not.

Ferguson (2009: 67) has stated that: 'All identities are simply conventional ways of seeing things, of describing and arranging things and of behaving in relation to them. All identities are, ultimately, arbitrary and reside wholly in the attitude of a community for whom such an identity is taken to be "real".' To identify positively as disabled involves collective identification with other disabled people on the basis of being people with impairments who share a certain way of knowing and relating to the world. It involves an affirmation of self and an acknowledgement of the processes and barriers through which disability is reproduced in everyday life, as well as a commitment to challenge these in everyday life practices.

Poetry as politics: Sue Napolitano

Sue Napolitano (1948–1996), a disabled writer and performer in cabarets organised by The Greater Manchester Coalition of Disabled People in the UK in the early 1990s, used performance poetry to explore experiences of self, embodiment, and disability. Her poem *Hump* (Napolitano, 1993a) begins with a series of statements in which she makes her audience aware of her own knowledge of, and hurt at, having spent her life as the butt of other people's jokes. As the poem progresses, however, she becomes defiant: 'This body is where I live my life.' It is a statement of affirmation which finishes by throwing out a challenge: 'Don't make me a symbol for things you don't want to face.' The final verse anticipates Shakespeare's (1997) description of disabled people as 'dustbins for disavowal', onto whom are projected the anxieties of non-disabled people, perpetually anxious to deny their own mortality and physicality.

> *Hump*
> I hear you snigger when I say
> HUMP
> Do you think I hadn't noticed
> The shape of my own back?
> Do you think I didn't wince

When as a child they said
"She's got the hump"?

Do you think I didn't hide in the deep silence
Of unspoken thoughts?
Do you think I didn't learn fast
That in England
To be straight is to be good?

Did you want me to carry on the pretence?
Like a child disowning its mother
Distance myself and claim
"It's nothing to do with me
Must belong to someone else
Don't know why it keeps tagging along behind me."
Are you annoyed that I've broken the silence?

Do you know how long it took me
To say HUMP in public?

But let me tell you
This body has been reclaimed
From the cold stares of strangers
And the eyes of doctors
In cream coloured rooms.
Been loved with kisses and caresses;
Given back to me whole.

This body is where I live my life.

So don't make me a symbol
For things you don't want to face,
Your passions,
Your fears,
The messy bits of life.
Find a way to accept the unacceptable in yourself,
And let my body be.

Napolitano's poem is startling, audacious and transgressive because it
flies in the face of non-disabled assumptions about the way disabled
people feel about their bodies. This is a voice which refuses any longer
to be oppressed or to collude in its own oppression. As poetry, it works

as a politics in its own right in that it both makes political demands and seeks to mobilise community into being, urging activity.

In *Let's Demonstrate*, Napolitano (1993b) outlines a list of expectations about disabled people, who are meant 'to be aware of ourselves as disabled in the same way that (the non-disabled) are about us, and to have the same attitude to it' (Morris, 1991: 19). Napolitano is here speaking from experience, and about things that will resonate with other disabled people. Disabled people are meant to experience their lives as burdens and to have a keen sense of their lives as tragic. They are meant to passively accept their lot and to put up with second-rate lives on the margins of what is going on, rather than being actively engaged as participants. Importantly, they are not supposed to understand disability as oppression: *You're not supposed to know that you've been short-changed* or to *gather with other disabled people*. For it is when disabled people begin to come together on their own terms that they begin to single out elements from their 'background awareness', reflecting on these, making them objects of consideration and objects of action and cognition (Freire, 1974: 56). This kind of activity leads to an altered subjectivity and ends up in what Linton (1998) has termed 'claiming disability'.

Let's Demonstrate

You're not supposed to be happy
Just cheerful all the time.
You're not supposed to have a proper job
But packing screws for peanuts is O.K.
You're not supposed to have friends who like you for
    yourself,
You're not supposed to have lovers,
Just carers who get paid to care.
You're not supposed to have children
How could you, it would be so unfair on them,
And anyway, you're not supposed to have sex.
You're not supposed to go where you want, when you
    want
With whom you want, to do what you want.

You are supposed to be miserable
But putting a brave face on it.
You are supposed to be resigned to your fate.
You're supposed to be shut out, shut in
Isolated, lonely, dependent,
And, if at all possible, pathetic.

You're not supposed to be angry, pissed off, make
    demands.
You're not supposed to know that you've been short-
    changed
For centuries.
You're not supposed to gather with other disabled
    people
To show that you've had enough of not enough.
You're not supposed to be strong.

But we know different, don't we?

In the poem's last line *But we know different, don't we?* Napolitano becomes confidential. She is addressing other disabled people directly. She is telling it like it is and giving voice to thoughts till now unspoken. The title *Let's Demonstrate* suggests what needs to be done. Disabled people must refuse what they are supposed to be.

In *Disabled Apartheid* Napolitano (1993c) draws attention to the way that barriers in the built environment exclude disabled people from participation as equals in ordinary life. Her thinking here is similar to that of Young (1990: 41), who described oppression as 'the disadvantage and injustice some people suffer not because a tyrannical power coerces them, but because of the everyday practices of a well-intentioned liberal society'. When Napolitano writes, *Not that it was deliberate, you understand / They were far too nice for that*, she draws attention to the way in which injustice is masked as sympathy so that its perpetrators cannot recognise it for what it is. She identifies the meddling do-gooding and professional interference of the non-disabled towards disabled people as misguided and unwanted, when what is really needed is environmental and structural change to remove disabling barriers.

Disabled Apartheid

The municipal might of Victorian architecture-
No need for a sign saying
CRIPPLES KEEP OUT
When triumphal stone flights
Of stairs
Smugly bar the way to
The art gallery
The library
The committee meeting.

Not that it was deliberate you understand, They were
far too nice for that,
They simply forgot
To think that we might want to
Get in
Take our share
Play our part
Claim some space
Perhaps they had in mind
That our place
Was outside
With begging bowl in hand.

There is anger in these lines at the discrimination experienced by disabled people who have experienced segregation in a world of day centres, care homes, hostels, sheltered workshops, clubs for 'the disabled' – and told that there is something wrong with *them* – while being denied access to public spaces. Napolitano offers a critique of what may pass for community development – although perhaps more appropriately conceived as community-based services – on the edges of the mainstream, based on top-down, paternalistic assumptions about what disabled people need.

Napolitano's writing needs to be recognised as part of a body of work by disabled artists collectively engaged in shifting disability discourse. While a comprehensive survey of disability artists is impossible here, I want to highlight the work of a number of other UK artists to demonstrate a line of continuity and committed purpose. Simon Brisenden's (1987) poem *Scars* addresses medical paternalism, sexism, normalisation and power inequalities (Sutherland, 2008). Blues singer Johnny Crescendo's *I Love My Body* (1989) makes the point "It's the only one I've got," as a retort to those who expect disabled people to view themselves as tragic cases (Holdsworth, 1989). Folk singer Ian Stanton's (1989) *Chip On Yer Shoulder* pokes fun at various representatives of non-disabled petty officialdom and questions the ability of the non-disabled to see beyond stereotypes (Cameron, 2009). Sculptor Tony Heaton, in his 1991 work *Shaken Not Stirred*, created an emphatic response to the charity industry when he brought a 7-foot-high pyramid of 1,760 charity collecting cans crashing to the ground by throwing an artificial leg at it (Sutherland, 2008). The Fugertivs were a disabled punk band who accompanied Direct Action Network demonstrations with raucous songs including *Let's Riot* (1999) and *The Bus Driver (Abused Me)* (1999) (Cameron, 2009). *The Best Fake*

Charity Collection Buckets (Clark, 2007) shows footage of stand-up comedian Laurence Clark on a busy London shopping street. A series of increasingly bizarre statements are printed on the charity collection bucket he is holding: 'Pay off my mortgage'; 'Please don't put money in here, I will get a criminal record if you do'; 'Sucker! This is a scam!'; 'I am not a charity case'; 'Kill the puppies'. The humour lies in watching the number and variety of passers-by who, in spite of Clark's protests, insist on putting money into his bucket; also in being able to observe the unwillingness of the non-disabled to actually listen to what disabled people have to say (Cameron, 2014e). Aaron Williamson's (2009) *Barrierman* shows Williamson, dressed in a high-visibility health and safety jacket, placing security tape and traffic cones across rights of way in a busy Liverpool shopping area in order to highlight the inconvenience caused by unnecessary and random barriers to public access. Katherine Araniello's *Meet the Superhuman Part 2* (Araniello, 2012) satirises the tautological triumph-over-tragedy drivel spouted by disabled athletes during the 2012 London Paralympics and their endorsement of individual model views of disability (Cameron, 2014e).

The affirmation model

A critical politics has always been at the core of disability arts, in that a demand for access to the mainstream has been central to what they have been all about. An additional, and perhaps unintended outcome, however, has been the development of a disabled aesthetic and a realisation of how bland a place the mainstream actually is. The mainstream requires conformity and standardisation, which is why it has marginalised difference. Disabled people, having owned impairment, have spoken about the value their lives have gained through the experience of impairment, of an enhanced understanding of life. A perception has emerged that it is not they who need to change in order to fit the mainstream but the mainstream which needs to broaden and become less confining in order to include them. These insights have led to the development of an affirmation model (Swain and French, 2000; 2008; Cameron, 2011; 2014f) and definitions which express the distinctive social critique generated within disability arts:

> Impairment: physical, sensory, emotional and cognitive difference to be expected and respected on its own terms in a diverse society
>   Disability: a personal and social role which simultaneously invalidates the subject position of people with impairments

and validates the subject position of those identified as normal (Cameron, 2014f: 28).

In defining impairment as difference, the affirmation model avoids negative evaluative judgements in terms of 'loss', 'abnormality' or 'limitation'. This is not to say that impairment doesn't sometimes, often even, involve pain or discomfort, but is to make the point that this isn't all it signifies. The affirmation model identifies impairment as an important part of people's identities, to be owned as part of who they are, and not as something to be hidden or regarded as a source of shame. Community development practice needs to find ways of ensuring that impairment is regarded as an ordinary part of human experience and acknowledged and included on that basis; rather than as something to be pitied, avoided, overlooked, tolerated or condescended to.

The affirmation model enables us to think about disability in productive terms. It is not just about what people with impairments supposedly cannot do and be, or are prevented from doing and being, but about what society requires them to do and be instead. Where this involves taking on roles as passive recipients of others' benevolence or demonstrations of the unimportance of impairment, it negates the lived experience of difference and signifies the desirability of normality. Disability is a role which requires that people with impairments are unable to relate other than negatively towards their impairments, in order that the advantages of conformity are evident to both disabled and non-disabled people. It allows no room for the radical position which regards impairment as an ordinary part of life. The affirmation model provides a tool to be used in recognising and making sense of disabling assumptions, encounters and practices in everyday life.

Conclusion

The line of continuity identified above might give the impression that disability arts is flourishing. While there still exist some excellent examples of organisations up and down the country – for example Disability Arts Online, Shape London, Dadafest – disability arts has always had to contend with the difficulties involved in taking up a position opposed to views unquestioningly accepted by the majority. Masefield (2008) proclaimed the death knell for disability arts when the Arts Council of England announced the termination of its grant to LDAF and five other disability arts organisations. This meant the closure of the UK's only national disability arts magazine – *Art Disability Culture* – and an end to the country's only disability film festival. The shift of focus from promoting equality to diversity as a funding category, along with the continued entrenchment of neoliberal thinking, has meant that overtly leftist arts have become unfashionable.

Apart from this, the weight of individual model thinking has meant that the establishment of disability arts as a politicised cultural activity was always going to be a struggle. Bowditch, a disabled dance artist, for example, has recently commented on her performance piece *Falling in Love With Frida*, 'It's not about disability, it's about art' (InVisible Difference, 2014). In seeking to disassociate her work from disability, Bowditch is expressing a predictable, if naive, aspiration. We are returned to 'Over the Rainbow' and to Barnes and Mercer's (2010: 207) description of 'disabled people doing art'. While there is no criticism to be made of disabled people – like anyone else – just 'doing art', the potential of politically naive cultural activity to bring about social progress is negligible. Its danger lies in its potential to reinforce reactionary social relations and to play a part in sustaining inequality.

While the values of community development involve commitment to principles of social justice, the limitations of its practice are highlighted by considering ways in which – in spite of intentions – it may unconsciously entrench oppressive social structures. The social model analysis developed by the disabled people's movement and the affirmation model analysis emerging from the disability arts movement have importance in this context in offering critical perspectives for reflection on the potential of community development practice to be emancipatory.

Acknowledgement

I would like to thank Jo Somerset and Greater Manchester Coalition of Disabled People for permission to reproduce Sue Napolitano's work in this chapter.

References

Araniello, K. (2012) *Meet the superhuman part 2* (subtitled), www.youtube.com/watch?v=KjRaN3iahyM.

Barnes, C. (1994) *Disabled people and discrimination: A case for anti-discrimination legislation*, London: Hurst and Co. In association with BCODP.

Barnes, C. (2014) 'Reflections on doing emancipatory disability research', in J. Swain, S. French, C. Barnes, C. Thomas (eds) *Disabling barriers: Enabling environments*, 3rd edn, London: Sage, 37–44.

Barnes, C. and Mercer, G. (2010) *Exploring disability*, Cambridge: Polity.

Britt, L. and Heise, D. (2000) 'From shame to pride in identity politics', in S. Stryker, T.J. Owens and R.W. White (eds) *Self, identity and social movements*, Minneapolis, MN: University of Minnesota Press, 252–68.

Brown, S.E. (2003) *Movie stars and sensuous scars: Essays on the journey from disability shame to disability pride*, Lincoln, NE: Universe.

Cameron, C. (2009) 'Tragic but brave or just crips with chips? Songs and their lyrics in the Disability Arts Movement in Britain', *Popular Music*, 28(3): 381–96.

Cameron, C. (2011) 'Disability arts: from the social model to the affirmative model', *Parallel Lines*, 1(1): www.parallellinesjournal.com/.

Cameron, C. (2014a) 'The medical model', in C. Cameron (ed) *Disability studies: A student's guide*, London: Sage, 98–101.

Cameron, C. (2014b) 'The social model', in C. Cameron (ed) *Disability studies: A student's guide*, London: Sage, 137–40.

Cameron, C. (2014c) 'The disabled people's movement', in C. Cameron (ed) *Disability studies: A student's guide*, London: Sage 40–43.

Cameron, C. (2014d) 'Identity', in C. Cameron (ed) *Disability studies: A student's guide*, London: Sage, 72–5.

Cameron, C. (2014e) 'Humour', in C. Cameron (ed) *Disability studies: A student's guide*, London: Sage, 68–72.

Cameron, C. (2014f) 'Developing an affirmation model of impairment and disability', in J. Swain, S. French, C. Barnes, and C. Thomas (eds) *Disabling barriers: Enabling environments*, 3rd edn, London: Sage, 24–30.

Campbell, J. and Oliver, M. (1996) *Disability politics: Understanding our past, changing our future*, London: Routledge.

Clark, L. (2007) *The best fake charity collection buckets*, www.youtube.com/watch?v=_U_byvTzW4w.

Day, G. (2006) *Community and everyday life*, London: Routledge.

Ferguson, H. (2009) *Self-identity and everyday life*, London: Routledge.

Freire, P. (1974) *Pedagogy of the oppressed*, London: Penguin.

Goffman, E. (1990) *Stigma: notes on the management of a spoiled identity*, London: Penguin.

Holdsworth, A. (1989) *Johnny Crescendo revealed*, London: self-published.

InVisible Difference (2014) Newsletter, http://dancehe.org.uk/archives/1261.

Linton, S. (1998) *Claiming disability*, New York, NY: New York University Press.

Mallett, R. and Slater, J. (2014) 'Language', in C. Cameron (ed) *Disability studies: A student's guide*, London: Sage, 91–94.

Masefield, P. (2006) *Strength: Broadsides from disability on the arts*, Stoke-on-Trent: Trentham.

Masefield, P. (2008) 'Funding cut "sounds death knell" for disability arts', *Disability Now*, www.disabilitynow.org.uk/article/funding-cut-sounds-death-knell-disability-arts.

Morris, J. (1991) *Pride against prejudice: Transforming attitudes to disability*, London: The Women's Press.

Morrison, E. and Finkelstein, V. (1994) 'Broken arts and cultural repair: the role of culture in the empowerment of disabled people', in J. Swain, V. Finkelstein, S. French and M. Oliver (eds) *Disabling barriers – Enabling environments*, London: Sage, 122–8.

Murphy, J.W. (2005) 'Social norms and their implications for disability', in J.W. Murphy and J.T. Pardeck (eds) *Disability issues for social workers and human service professionals in the 21st century*, New York, NY: Haworth, 153–63.

Napolitano, S. (1993a) 'Hump', in *A dangerous woman*, Manchester: Greater Manchester Coalition of Disabled People.

Napolitano, S. (1993b) 'Let's demonstrate', in *A dangerous woman*, Manchester: Greater Manchester Coalition of Disabled People.

Napolitano, S. (1993c) 'Disabled apartheid', in *A dangerous woman*, Manchester: Greater Manchester Coalition of Disabled People.

Oliver, M. (1996) *Understanding disability: From theory to practice*, Basingstoke: Macmillan.

Reeve, D. (2014) 'Psycho-emotional disablism', in C. Cameron (ed) *Disability studies: A student's guide*, London: Sage, 122–5.

Shakespeare, T. (1997) 'Cultural representation of disabled people: dustbins for disavowal', in L. Barton and M. Oliver (eds) *Disability studies: Past, present and future*, Leeds: The Disability Press, 217–36.

Sutherland, A. (1989) 'Disability arts, disability politics', *DAIL Magazine*, September 1989, reprinted in A. Pointon and C. Davies (eds) *Framed: Interrogating disability in the media*, London: BFI, 159.

Sutherland, A. (2008) 'Choices, rights and cabaret', in J. Swain and S. French, *Disability on equal terms*, London: Sage, 79–90.

Swain, J. and Cameron, C. (1999) 'Unless otherwise stated: discourses of labelling and identity in coming out', in M. Corker and S. French (eds) *Disability discourse*, Buckingham: Open University Press, 68–78.

Swain, J. and French, S. (2000) 'Towards an affirmation model', *Disability and Society*, 15(4): 569–82.

Swain, J. and French, S. (2008) *Disability on equal terms*, London: Sage.

Union of the Physically Impaired Against Segregation (UPIAS) (1976) *Fundamental principles of disability*, London: UPIAS.

Williamson, A. (2009) *Barrierman*, www.youtube.com/watch?v=4N2Bu7J4xC8.

Young, I.M. (1990) *Justice and the politics of difference*, Princeton, NJ: Princeton University Press.

TWELVE

Service delivery protests in South Africa: a case for community development?

Lucius Botes

Introduction

> We all need to listen to the messages in the fires and the stones – and not allow ourselves to be deafened by the guns of repression. (Whisson, 2012: 17)

This chapter takes the local community landscape of South Africa as its backdrop, focusing specifically on the rolling service delivery protests that started in 2004, 10 years into the new democracy. It explores whether and how such forms of political action might inform, expand or challenge our vision and expectations of community development. Critiques of the managerial or programmatic turn in community development often point to the associated depoliticisation of its theory and practice. Against that, this chapter focuses on forms of community action, organisation or mobilisation that consciously identify as political. Highlighting the importance of local and everyday contexts for democracy, in this case South Africa's local sphere of government, it considers how communities there have begun to engage with popular protest and resistance strategies. It also considers the resources, interventions and supports that communities may require in order to sustain collective mobilisation.

Using the service delivery protests in South Africa as an illustrative example, this chapter sets out to achieve two aims. First, it seeks to provide a descriptive overview of the current upsurge in community protests in South Africa as a manifestation of civil society's response to service delivery deficiencies and the unaccountability of South Africa's young democracy. Secondly, it explains how a conceptual analysis of power and its interactions with community development could help towards imagining a potential nexus for service delivery protests and community development work.

Service delivery protests: challenging deprivation through political action

A series of local community protests (also commonly referred to as service-related or service delivery protests) erupted in a number of municipalities in South Africa during 2004 and 2005 (Botes et al, 2008a) and continue at the time of writing. Since 2004, progressively more local communities have begun to protest against the government's apparent inability to provide adequate services, including water, electricity, housing, roads and sanitation (Botes et al, 2008b; Marais et al, 2008; Matebesi and Botes, 2011). Protest takes place not only because of the perceived slow pace of service delivery, but often due to the poor quality of services and the practices of patronage and exclusion associated with their delivery. However, Alexander et al (2013), in a study of 2,100 reported protests and drawing on interviews with some 250 key participants, caution against ascribing the root causes of such protests exclusively to 'service delivery' issues. They argue that to do so risks underestimating the importance of protesters' other grievances, relating to concerns about representation, corruption, nepotism, dishonesty, government unresponsiveness, police violence, poverty, jobs and crime. Alexander et al (2013) therefore suggest that the term 'community protests' should be taken to reflect a genuine rebellion by South Africa's poor (see also Alexander and Pfaffe, 2014: 1). In a very recent economic analysis of the microfoundations of direct political action in pre- and post-democratic South Africa, Bedasso (2014: 1, 13–14) indicates that the activist agenda and focus of protest action has shifted from racial–political to economic issues in recent years. Indeed the most consistent pattern in the prediction of direct political action can be summarised as a strong increase in the effects of unfolding and largely economic expectations. For a decade, South Africa has struggled with the problems of legitimacy the service delivery protests create for various tiers of government and participatory governance. In fact, Pieterse and Van Donk (2013: 108), in their contribution to a very reputable *State of the Nation* publication (2012–13), claim that such community protests are one of the leading forces undermining developmental local government in South Africa. And one may even ask whether the service delivery crisis renders South Africa's young democracy virtually ungovernable.

Since 2004 the contours of the protests have been transformed by changes in the tactics used by protesters. The scale of and capacity for violence, devastation and death have escalated to previously unimaginable levels, potentially resulting in huge social and financial costs. There were 2,020 protests between 2011 and 2013 alone while, over the past 10 years, 43 protesters have died because of police action (Van Schie, 2014). Of the 173 service delivery protests recorded in South Africa in 2012, 77.5% were violent, compared with 71.6% of the 155 service delivery protests in 2013 (Van Schie, 2014).

Alexander and Pfaffe (2014) divides social protests into three categories: peaceful, disruptive and violent. A protest is deemed violent when people are injured or property is damaged. Significantly, this research found that by the time protests turned violent, communities had often exhausted peaceful methods of lobbying and claims making. Almost half (46%) of all community protests during July 2012 occurred in informal settlements.[1] This illustrates the desperation experienced by those living on the peripheries of local communities and on the margins of society. A measure of the threat protests pose comes in a *Government Gazette* announcement in 2012 that municipal councillors must be insured against risk, because service delivery protests put their lives and property in danger (Botha, 2012: 1). These developments show that South Africa is moving towards a new phase, where accepted governance channels that facilitate negotiation are either jettisoned or are seen to be failing, with violence-backed demands and protests becoming the accepted mode of bargaining (Cull, 2012). This seems to be borne out in the following quotes from protest leaders, gathered from the fieldwork of sociologist Sethulego Matebesi (2013: n.p.) in the Northern Cape Province of South Africa:

> 'We don't have the luxury of public facilities here ... Our only weapon, as destructive as it may seem to outsiders, was to forcefully shut down schools. You may call it intimidation, but we call it community power' (Leader: Cassel Village Residents' Forum).
>
> 'We never planned any violent strategy. We have exhausted all public spaces of dialogue and they all failed us. The community and not us [leaders] decided to shut down schools. Well, in any case, violence seems to be the only language our government understands' (Leader: Residents' Forum).

It is notable that the continued escalation of service delivery protests occurs despite the fact that there is now a democratic system in South Africa (Matebesi and Botes, 2011) and that the government has an impressive record of service delivery in quantitative terms. A total of 2.8 million starter houses have been built in South Africa over the past 20 years, 87% of all households are connected to the power grid (58.2% in 1994) and 96% of all households have access to piped water (61.7% in 1994) (Sethlatswe, 2014). This is a mammoth achievement for a so-called developmental state. South Africa is also one of the few states in Africa with an extensive social grant system: more than 15 million people receive social grants from the state (child support, foster care, pension, disability, and so on). However, as many other social researchers observe, although there has been progress in alleviating absolute poverty in South Africa, the overall picture is not encouraging. Unemployment has not declined; inequality – as measured by the Gini coefficient[2]– has increased; education, for those who need it most if they are to work their way out of poverty, has declined; many urban areas have not been upgraded; and the housing backlog is still enormous (cf Whisson, 2012: 17; Habib, 2013).

Many commentators in South Africa assert that the root cause of the social service delivery protests in post-apartheid South Africa is not so much poverty but, rather, people's experiences of inequality and relative deprivation (Amtaika, 2013; Habib, 2013; Pillay et al, 2013). In other words, people are dissatisfied when they compare their own quality of life and their economic and social opportunities with those of better-off communities and households. Alongside these alienating experiences of inequality and deprivation the realisation often lingers that the state and its structures do not care at all or do not care enough for people's human dignity. Housing[3] and essential basic services are regularly cited as the key motivations driving protests (see, for example, Karamoko, 2011). Inadequate housing tops the list of grievances (21%), followed by lack of access to clean water and electricity (11% each) and sanitation (9%) (Karamoko, 2011: 32). In addition, corruption, broken promises, unresponsive management at local and provincial level and evidence of incompetence, especially among the leadership of the local sphere of government, feature as a secondary category of key concerns raised by protesters, jointly totalling 17% of grievances (Karamoko, 2011: 31-2; Alexander et al, 2013: 11). Therefore, it is evident that many of the community protests in South Africa are inspired by unmet promises and the limited capacity of its young democracy to deliver on people's hopes and aspirations.

According to Bedasso (2014: 6) economic issues – including jobs and the general state of the economy – overwhelmingly determine the protest agenda. During the high protest years, up to 85% of the protests had economic issues as their underlying factors. Clearly this suggests that class has replaced race as a mobilising force in post-democratic South Africa. Furthermore there are serious deficiencies within the culture of South Africa's public services. According to Habib (2013: 63–8) these are attributable to a combination of blurred boundaries between different spheres of government; the complex and interweaving effects of corruption, affirmative action and cadre deployment of the African National Congress (ANC) government;[4] and dysfunctional public institutions due to inadequate resourcing.

However, an alternative view on service delivery protest is to regard it as emerging from grassroots mobilisations that seek to enhance the accountability of political elites to the country's citizens. In this sense, it could be seen as reflecting communities' efforts to engage with and challenge an unfavourable and inequitable balance of power. In fact Habib (2013: 70–1) depicted protest in this very way during the launch of his book *South Africa's Suspended Revolution*: 'The fundamental deficit in our society is accountability, and unless we build an inclusive society in which poor people are as included as the rich people and the middle class, we are in a real danger of losing the plot.'

In 2009 a similar perspective was articulated by 220 branches of the National Tax Payers Union, which has a presence in towns across 49 different municipalities. Declaring disputes with their respective municipalities, members have withheld their local government tax payment (Mouton, 2013). Here we see that the main issue is not so much about specific services as about whether and how a truly responsive and accountable local government is possible. Clearly, the bridging of interests between distinct and sometimes alienated constituencies is not an easy endeavour, but it is essential for the building of more responsive governments with true civil *servants*, that is bureaucrats, state-employed workers and professionals who seek to serve the people properly. For this to happen, there must also be a fundamental shift in the distribution of wealth in South African society, with a conscious and deliberate commitment that the economy be run in the interests of the poor. Ward councillors are at the centre of a crisis of representation and those power differentials are mirrored by the gaps in earnings between poorer citizens and their putative representatives. For example, part-time councillors in a large municipality now receive a basic salary of R32,712 per month, more than 25 times as much as the older person's grant, a disparity that widens the social gap between councillors and most unemployed residents (Alexander et al, 2013).

Given the local nature of such disputes and their proximity to people's everyday lives and experiences, one could ask what community development workers might contribute towards fostering new relationships between local governments, communities and civil society organisations. Perhaps this building of relations between society, state and market could and should happen if community development workers create spaces for mutual dialogue, what we might refer to as dialogical community development (cf Westoby and Dowling, 2013). In the following section some related issues are explored in more detail.

Service delivery dissatisfaction: a potential space for community development work?

There is to date little evidence to suggest that dissatisfaction with service delivery is viewed as a space within which community development workers might function. In fact, while reviewing all printed newspaper articles in South Africa that referenced the protests – that is, focusing on articles published between January 2012 and April 2014 – the author found very little evidence of the involvement of community development workers in such forms of political action. The author could not detect a single instance, as reported in the newspapers, where 'formal' community development workers participated in the service delivery protests.[5]. This absence confirms the dominance of the assumption that community action and mobilisation are best understood as aspects of the political domain. It also necessarily, but perhaps unintentionally, strengthens the notion that community development and political or mass action are two separate, unrelated and non-integrated fields; a notion that is highly problematic, given the rich history of political, critical and activist-led community work practice both in South Africa and internationally (cf Westoby and Dowling, 2013; Westoby, 2014.)

This absence also raises questions about the proper roles and responsibilities of community development workers in South Africa. Arguably, the nation's more than 4,000 state-employed community development workers find themselves occupying dilemmatic spaces[6] (Westoby and Botes, 2012), where they are at risk of being coopted by the political system. Dilemmas include whether or not they should play a conscientising and/or mobilising role, or whether or not they are mandated only to bring preconceived state- and donor-funded development programmes and projects to the people. It is quite clear that for the majority of state officials in South Africa, community development is reduced merely to service delivery, infrastructural development and economic development (Westoby and Botes, 2012; Marais, 2014: 161). This might at least partly explain why so few community development workers who are employed by the state or NGOs are involved in the organisation of service delivery protests. Indeed one might legitimately question whether community workers *can* participate in such action while they are remunerated by the state and embedded in its structures.

Because service delivery is not happening in terms of pace, process and product in accordance with many communities' expectations, this inevitably forces the different spheres of government to enter into multiple dialogues and engagements with ordinary communities and their leaders. Theoretically at least, this could open up a space for more community development workers to facilitate political action and community mobilisations. However, in practice this does not seem likely. Arguably, because community development is essentially state driven in South Africa (Westoby and Botes, 2012) there is limited scope for the majority of its paid workers to conceptualise and operationalise community development in alternative and more critical ways. In fact, community development in South Africa has largely been viewed and implemented via programmes and projects to bring development *to* the people, who in many cases are regarded as passive recipients of its presumed benefits: it is concerned with how to get people, communities and households to become better off through the implementation of prescribed initiatives. In fact, some people even define development studies as the discipline that uses economic, sociological and political insights to study why certain societies are better off (Marais, 2014). The inverse of this is that developmental work is seen to emanate from a reaction against human poverty, or rather, poverties (cf Max-Neef, 1991).

Analysing community development, politics and power

While, Westoby (2014) acknowledges that many people do not view community activism as a legitimate form of community development, he goes on to warn against the limitations of such a position. He argues that it not only dismisses an entire tradition of community development built around political action, community organising and social mobilisation, but that it also fails to take into account the significant challenges that community development faces within contemporary democratic settings. As Westoby (2014: 108) observes:

[S]ince the launch of neighbourhood-oriented official community development programmes within the UK during the 1950s, there has been a split in community development thinking. More conservative or reformist approaches of community development focussed on social planning and service delivery, while more progressive, or radical approaches have focussed on processes of mobilising, organising, conscientising and politicking.

Echoing, perhaps, these more radical aims and aspirations, protesters in South Africa are demanding their inclusion within all aspects of the socio-political and economic order. Such aspirations are evident in the following quote from a member of the national shack dwellers' social movement, Abahlali baseMjondolo (cited in Matebesi, 2013: n.p.):

'Waiting for "delivery" will not liberate us from our life sentence. Sometimes "delivery" does not come. When "delivery" does come, it often makes things worse by forcing us into government shacks that are worse than the shacks we have built ourselves, and which are in human dumping grounds far outside the cities. "Delivery" can be a way of formalising our exclusion from society. But we have not only been sentenced to permanent physical exclusion from society and its cities, schools, electricity, refuse removal and sewerage systems. Our life sentence has also removed us from the discussions that take place in society. In as much as the government need to deliver services, they cannot do that without engagement or direct engagement ... If people were engaged and consulted about development, then people become a vital tool in their own development and such developments will also be owned at a community level.'

Therefore, given their very real parallels and overlaps, it is necessary to reconnect community development with the discourses and practice of protest politics. Including communities in decisions affecting their livelihood not only brings the material benefits of full inclusion but also honours the right to be taken seriously when thinking and speaking through community organisations (Dugard and Tissington, 2013: 9).

While its purposes may be contested, if one analyses the range of definitions of community participation that are found within the community development landscape, it is clear that the effective devolution of power to local communities, so that they can decide about matters that concern their own welfare and prosperity, stands at the centre of its philosophy and practice. Ultimately, community development is about creating spaces for people to participate in and co-influence decisions impacting on their lives and livelihoods. In the words of Midgley et al (1986: 24): '[it is the] creation of opportunities to enable all members of a community and the larger society to actively contribute to and influence the development process and to share equitably in the fruits of development'. This means, and in contrast to the dominant assumptions of professional community development in South Africa, that community participation or participatory development is by definition *political*, because participation is always about mobilisation and power, as well as the access, control and distribution of resources. This inevitably links community development and participation to the wider contexts of or struggles for political, social and economic change. Furthermore, it means that community development workers and community activists need to think seriously about power; the forms that it takes, the kind of social relationships that it inhabits and the extent to which power can claimed by forms of consensus or conflict politics. In this regard, we can find valuable insights and conceptual resources in the discipline of sociology where power has been variously understood by different theoretical traditions. Sociological engagement creates an opportunity to make explicit some of the assumptions about power that inform community development practice in its various guises. The following paragraphs explore some significant contributions from the field of sociology and how they might inform community development in South Africa.

Functionalist sociologists such as Talcott Parsons (1939) conceptualise power in society as a 'variable sum'. According to this perspective, the amount of power in society is not fixed but variable; power rests with members of society as a whole, and power can increase for the entire society as it pursues collective goals. The logic of such a position is that the empowerment of the powerless can be achieved without any significantly negative effect on the power of the powerful: consensus forms of politics are thus appropriate and adequate for social progress to occur. Because, it is assumed, an increase in the power of one interest group does not necessarily diminish that of another, the powerless can be empowered without the emergence of social conflict and they too can share in the fruits of development, alongside those who have already achieved power. In other words, power is not seen as a scarce commodity, but one that can be enjoyed and shared by all (cf Young, 1993: 163; Checkoway, 1995: 4; Mayo and Craig, 1995: 5). From this perspective, power is also viewed in distributive and generative terms, as a potential resource within every person or community. The implications of this perspective for community development practice are that practitioners should engage with poor and marginalised communities via prescribed interventions; assuming that there is relative harmony and equilibrium in that community; and expecting that stakeholders, even those with very different backgrounds, agendas and expectations, want to share power. A consequence of the Parsonian view of power and social action is that some community development workers may steer communities away from more conflictual tactics or oppositional practices, towards more socially acceptable and institutionally sanctioned forms of engagement.

Alternatively, Max Weber's definition of power is conceptualised in zero-sum terms. It constructs power relationships in more problematic ways, that is, because there is a fixed amount of power in society it generates contests and inequalities (Mayo and Craig, 1995: 5). Empowerment is viewed as a potentially conflict-laden process through which a person or community gives power to, or gets it from, another: the more power one group or individual has, the less others have. Accordingly, the empowerment of the powerless involves gains that, of necessity, have to be achieved at the expense of the powerful. This perspective also acknowledges more negative forms of power in social relationships, including the possibility of dominance or the ability to force one's will onto others. This means that we need to recognise the salience of 'power over', since some people are seen to have control or influence over others. Those who assume power is fixed in volume (that is in Weberian zero-sum terms), see little possibility for cooperative action across hierarchically divided interest groups, and anticipate that existing power holders will resist or coopt any opposing initiative. One implication of this view is that disgruntled communities may resort to alternative and often non-conventional ways of talking to those in powerful positions, including those seen to be responsible for decisions which negatively impact on those communities. In this, some community development workers may also embrace a more adversarial advocacy role, directly challenging those in power.

The Marxist perspective on power (Marx, 1967) raises even more acute issues. According to this perspective, political power cannot ultimately be separated from economic power. Thus, the empowerment of the relatively powerless has inherently limited possibilities under capitalism, and arguably this is even more so within contemporary global market capitalism. Although the poor and the powerless might effectively participate in particular development projects and programmes, gains are necessarily constrained by or confined within the wider requirements of profitability as determined by the global market. Historically, Marxists have also been concerned with the power of ideas, in particular with the setting of ideological agendas and the concept of hegemony (Marx, 1967). A key problem for Marxists is the way that economic and political power relations within capitalism are constructed both as legitimate and as effectively non-contestable. Understanding and challenging this hegemony then become central to the development of alternative struggles for economic, political and social transformation. With respect to the implications of such a perspective on power for making sense of community development and the rolling community protests, protest could be understood by practitioners as localised rebellions of the poor who are, as Habib (2013: 157) puts it, 'driven by concerns around corruption, service delivery and accountability'. This returns us to the discussion, explored earlier in this chapter, of how the protests are driven by people at grassroots level (often marginalised and voiceless), who are demanding improved forms of participatory governance and shouting to be heard.

There are of course many critiques of a predominantly 'negative' interpretation of power. In line with Foucault and Galbraith, Giddens (1991), for example, indicates that power relations can be emancipatory as well as exploitative and dominating. He distinguishes between the 'liberating and productive' and the 'repressive and destructive' aspects of power (cf Robinson, 1996: 13). Nonetheless, taking together the conclusions that might be drawn from this section on sociological theories and their relevance for the relinking of the concepts of power, participation and community development, it is apparent that mainstream community development, as institutionalised in South Africa, may be trapped within a limited view of power, leaving little room for an appreciation of conflict perspectives. This is particularly problematic in a context where community development workers are confronted by the ongoing reality of community protests, which fundamentally destabilise the assumptions implicit in the Parsonian view of power. It may be that Weberian and Marxist perspectives, however challenging, offer community development workers conceptual tools that are more relevant and useful for rethinking their practice.

Some further questions for research

I now briefly suggest an agenda for future research on the nexus of politics, power and community development work that may help to further tease out the practice and theoretical issues posed in this chapter. The following questions might form the basis for such an agenda:

- Can the emergence of mass action and civil strife around service delivery be viewed as an expression of the political practice of community development?
- Do community development workers regard service delivery protests as relevant to their practice roles, specifically in terms of mobilising, mediating, facilitating or defusing? If not, why not?
- Do community development workers see it as legitimate to accompany people in protests against poor service delivery? Do they see a role in facilitating dialogue with the authorities?
- Are these service delivery protests outbursts of spontaneous, often disorganised action, or are they organised events in which community development workers might also play a role?
- How do community development workers see their own roles given the emergence of civil society groundswells of dissent and dissatisfaction? Is there scope to reflect on how they could occupy the spaces between community sensitisation, mobilisation and facilitation, and project implementation?
- Do service delivery protests provide an opportunity to view community development as political action?

Conclusions

Some might regard the emergence of multiple service delivery protests throughout South Africa as positive because it creates a space where ordinary people can claim and demand the democratisation of democracy: for others these rolling community protests are, in themselves, undermining developmental local government. In any case, the protests can be said to provide platforms through which communities can challenge the lack, pace and quality of services at local level, because the poorest of the poor have not visibly experienced the benefits of South Africa's 10-year old democracy. Indeed, service delivery protests could also be viewed as manifestations of an active citizenry where ordinary people cry out for democracy to better realise the prospects for inclusive development. For many, and particularly given the recent history of South Africa, service delivery protests are also a legitimate and efficient means of getting the government to act – in fact, it was through civil strife and local-level protests that the apartheid system collapsed. The 'project' of democratising South Africa remains an ongoing challenge, one where ordinary communities have already mobilised and will continue to mobilise towards improving their quality of life and transforming politics. Service delivery protests are living proof that one can never separate community development and politics, because politics at its very essence deals with issues around power and participation as well as exclusion and inclusion.

One could legitimately ask to what extent the mass occurrence of service delivery protests has improved the lives and livelihoods of poor communities. One positive outcome is that those in power are now forced to listen more to the weaker, excluded and marginalised groups in South African society. In essence, the power elite is obliged to be more accountable for its policy making and decisions. Protests may also result in the decentralisation of decision-making power and there are already some signs that they could lead to improved service delivery (cf Matebesi, 2013). Ultimately, it could be argued that service delivery protests challenge power inequalities because they demonstrate that communities want and intend to be taken seriously by government. They are a meaningful way for underprivileged South Africans to escape the overwhelming sense of entrapment and feelings of impotency; to show agency; to do something to improve their life situations; and to express their discontent through civil strife. Therefore, service delivery protests could perhaps be viewed as an important manifestation of local action that is democratising social, economic and political spaces.

It is clear that the ongoing service delivery protests provide an important but as yet unrealised space for both expanding and embracing the political dimensions of community development work. For a variety of reasons, the vast majority of community development workers do not seem to respond to or engage with the political dimensions of community development work despite the widespread dissatisfaction with service delivery. This may be linked to the particular dilemmas experienced by state-employed community development workers as well as a reflection of the dominant perspectives or views of power that inform professional practice. Critical social analysis and further research may help us to identify alternative conceptions of power as we need to learn more about what is happening in real-life contexts.

Finally, this chapter proposes that a dialogical approach to community development could be a good entry point for community development workers who wish to make sense of service delivery protests and elicit some improvements in the quality and efficiency of service delivery. A dialogical approach can be described as 'other-orientated, humanising attention to the kinds of relationships that enable creative transformation' where community is seen as 'hospitality, as a sense of *communitas* (sense of unity), as ethical space and as collective practice' (see Westoby and Dowling, 2013: 154). This chapter has argued that there is a definite role for community development workers in assisting communities to find a voice and speak to those in power and demand that they be more accountable. Perhaps government officials and office bearers as well as community development workers (both state employed and from the non-profit sector) could look again at the potential for real dialogue with communities. Perhaps the growing service delivery protests are opening up spaces for reconnecting community development and political action but, above all, they provide us with opportunities to create a more just and compassionate society.

Notes

[1] Informal settlements refer to those neighbourhoods which consist predominantly of non-formal houses (houses of corrugated iron, old discarded material, and so on) and often lack many other neighbourhood amenities such as roads, storm water, water borne sanitation, and so on.

[2] South Africa is ranked the fourth most unequal society in the world. The gini coefficient is currently ranging from 0.771 (Primary Gini) to 0.695 (Secondary Gini) (World Bank, 2014) an indication of continued high inequality partly born out of South Africa's divided apartheid past, but also the result of unemployment and dismal primary and secondary education with accompanying highly unequal distribution of incomes, resources and opportunities (Chitiga et al, 2014; Chitiga-Mabugu, 2013).

[3] In Nelson Mandela Bay (Port Elizabeth) poor administration in housing provision and the lack of quality houses were the main reasons for the service protests (Botes et al, 2008a; Botes et al, 2008b).

[4] The ANC, according to Habib (2013: 66), 'following the traditional Marxist revolutionary tradition that sees the state as merely an agency for capture by the party, established a deployment committee to manage the deployment of cadres to the public service. People may argue that deployment is permissible when it is confined to political appointments (ministers, deputy ministers) and the most senior levels of public services. But the deployment of cadres undertaken by the ANC has extended across the entire apparatus of the state'. Local government is the Achilles heel of ANC cadre deployment, which is one of the reasons why service delivery at the local level is in such disarray – people appointed on the basis of whom they know or as part of patronage networks, as opposed to skill sets possessed.

[5] This is not to say that some informal community development workers were not involved in sensitising and mobilising disgruntled and dissatisfied households to rise and claim their space.

⁶ For Hoggett et al (2008), examples of the dilemmatic spaces occupied by community development practitioners include being in and against the state; and being in between an instrumental ethic of programming and a solidarity ethic of struggle.

References

Alexander, P. and Pfaffe, P. (2014) 'Social relationships to the means and ends of protest in South Africa's ongoing rebellion of the poor: the Balfour insurrections', *Social Movement Studies*, 13(2): 204–21.

Alexander, P., Runciman, C. and Ngwane, T. (2013) 'Growing civil unrest shows yearning for accountability', *Business Day*, 27 December, 11.

Amtaika, A. (2013) *Local government in South Africa since 1994: Leadership, democracy, development and service delivery in a post-apartheid era*, Durham, NC: Carolina Academic Press.

Bedasso, B. (2014) *A dream deferred: The microfoundations of direct political action in pre- and post-democratization South Africa*, Economic Research Southern Africa, Pretoria: National Treasury, Working Paper 483, 28 November.

Botes, L., Lenka, M., Marais, L., Matebesi, Z. and Sigenu, K. (2008a) *The cauldron of local protests: Reasons, impacts and lessons learnt*, Bloemfontein: University of the Free State, Centre for Development Support.

Botes, L., Lenka, M., Marais, L., Matebesi, Z. and Sigenu, K. (2008b) *The new struggle: Service delivery-related unrest in South Africa*, Bloemfontein: University of the Free State, Centre for Development Support.

Botha, J. (2012) 'Councillors must get risk cover against service delivery outrage', *Witness*, 27 December.

Checkoway, B. (1995) 'Six strategies of community change', *Community Development Journal*, 30(1): 2–20.

Chitiga-Mabugu, M. (2013) 'The employment effect of economic growth', in U. Pillay, G. Hagg and F. Nyamnjoh (eds) *State of the Nation: South Africa 2012–2013*, Cape Town: HSRC, 169–224.

Chitiga, M., Sekyere E. and Tsoanamatsie N. (2014) 'Income inequality and limitations of the Gini index: the case of South Africa', *HSRC Review*, 12(5): 9–11.

Cull, P. (2012) 'Violence-backed demands become bargaining tool', *The Herald*, 1 December, 14.

Dugard, J. and Tissington, K. (2013). 'What the protesters really want', *Witness*, 10 May, 9.

Giddens, A. (1991) *Modernity and self-identity. Self and society in the late modern age*, Cambridge: Polity.

Habib, A. (2013) *South Africa's suspended revolution: Hopes and prospects*, Johannesburg: Wits University.

Hoggett, P., Mayo, M. and Miller, C. (2008) *The dilemmas of development practice*, Bristol: Policy Press.

Karamoko, J. (2011) *Community protests in South Africa: Trends, analysis and explanations (Report 2)*, Belville: Community Law Centre.

Marais, K. (2014) *Translation theory and development studies: A complexity theory approach*, New York, NY: Routledge.

Marais, L., Matebesi, S.Z., Mthombeni, M., Botes, L. and Grieshaber, D. (2008) 'Municipal unrest in the Free State (South Africa): a new form of social movement?' *Politeia*, 27(2): 51–69.

Marx, K. (1967) *Capital (vol.1)*, New York, NY: International Publications.

Matebesi, S. (2013) 'Social protests and the social fabric: The case of Kuruman and Sannieshof', *Presentation at the Small Towns Symposium at the University of the Free State, South Africa*, 7 November.

Matebesi, S. and Botes, L. (2011) 'Khutsong cross-boundary protests: the triumph and failure of participatory governance?' *Politeia*, 30(1): 51–69.

Max-Neef, M. (1991) *Human scale development: Conception, application and further reflections*, New York, NY: Apex.

Mayo, M. and Craig, G. (eds) (1995) *Community empowerment: A reader in participation and development*, London: Zed Books.

Midgley, J., Hall. A., Hardiman, M. and Narin, D. (1986) *Community participation, social development and the state*, London: Methuen.

Mouton, S. (2013) 'Lack of water service delivery angers all', *The Herald*, 17 September, 2.

Parsons, T. (1939) *The structure of social action*, New York, NY: Free Press.

Pieterse, E. and Van Donk, M. (2013) 'Local government and poverty reduction', in U. Pillay, G. Hagg and F. Nyamnjoh (eds) *State of the nation: South Africa 2012–2013*, Cape Town: HSRC, 98–123.

Pillay, U., Hagg, G. and Nyamnjoh, F. (eds) (2013) *State of the nation: South Africa 2012–2013*, Cape Town: HSRC.

Robinson, J. (1996) *The power of apartheid: State power and space in South African cities*, Oxford: Butterworth-Heinemann.

Sethlatswe B. (2014) *Reflecting on twenty years*, Pretoria: South Africa Institute of Race Relations.

Van Schie, K. (2014) 'Protesters willing to die for their causes', *Star*, 13 February, 5.

Westoby, P. (2014) *Theorising the practice of community development: A South African perspective*, Farnham: Ashgate.

Westoby, P. and Botes, L. (2012) 'I work with the community, not the parties! The political and practical dilemmas of South Africa's state-employed community development workers', *British Journal of Social Work*, (advance access): 1–18.

Westoby, P. and Dowling, G. (2013) *Theory and practice of dialogical community development – international perspectives*, London: Routledge.

Whisson, M. (2012) 'Violent protests: listen to message in fire and stones', *The Herald*, 4 October, 17.

World Bank (2014) *South Africa economic update: Fiscal policy and redistribution in an unequal society*, Washington, DC: World Bank.

Young, K. (1993) *Planning development with women. Making a world of difference: Planning from the gender perspective*, London: Macmillan.

THIRTEEN

Community development and commons: on the road to alternative economics?

Brigitte Kratzwald

Introduction

This chapter explores whether community development can contribute to building alternative economics and for this task it refers to the commons as an economic model. After outlining the concepts of 'alternative economics', 'community development' and 'commons', it looks at their differences, commonalities and mutual learning opportunities. In the chapter's last section several examples show both the possibilities and limitations of community-based economies arising from community development and commoning. From the outset it needs to be acknowledged that considering these issues involves a triple challenge. The first concerns the Austrian context specifically, as the term 'community development' is not widely used in German-speaking contexts. Therefore this chapter must find those fields and concepts that most closely approximate to the theory and practice of community development. The second challenge is to analyse the relationship between community development (or the corresponding German concepts) and 'commons', to highlight commonalities, intersections and differences. The third challenge lies in defining the term 'alternative economics' and relating it to community development. These tasks are complicated by all three terms eluding easy definition: they have different meanings in different contexts and they do not signify 'things' but processes that are dependent on culture and situation. Given this background, the following contribution might be understood as an exploration of a field rather than as a conclusive assessment of this potential relationship.

What is 'alternative' about community-based economies?

Talking of 'economies' in this context does not address a specific sector of society. The 'disembedding of the economy' (see Polanyi, 1957) – its separation from its social context, which was an essential characteristic of capitalist development – is overcome when processes of production are organised by the community. The commons is not only concerned with 'economy' or 'production'; it always reflects ideas about democracy, social relationships and the public sphere where people may organise themselves and act together to defend their interests. Similar aspirations characterise community development. It too aims at establishing a political platform where people 'act together publicly and politically' (Penta, 2007: 7) and can 'continuously and obstinately claim the participatory opportunities of a democracy' (Penta, 2007: 9). If alternative forms of production and reproduction emerge, then 'economy' must be understood more in the sense of a household economy, that is the totality of all the activities needed to reproduce a good life. Thus it is about a 're-embedding of economic actions into the contexts of local communities' (Elsen, 2000b: 234).

Two broad approaches may be distinguished among the discourses on alternative economics. There is the liberal approach, which refers to economies that are developed intentionally in the sphere of civil society *as additional* to the state and market, thus increasing the possibilities of choice. They may achieve considerable improvements in quality of life and greater freedoms for the people involved without challenging the market system. More leftist projects claim to follow a *different* logic to that of the market economy; this is the long-term aim of *replacing* the market economy, which is considered to be unable to achieve a just and sustainable society. Here might be included contemporary forms of the gift economy or peer production. However, while they may allow people to become more independent of the market system, the ability to live off them exclusively is limited to a few exceptions. In practice the distinction between the two economic approaches is probably quite fluid, and one or other consideration will have greater importance for different people.

The revival of the commons

In the last few years it has become increasingly clear that the current economic model offers no way out of the multitude of problems we are facing. The search for alternatives has lost its niche status and has arrived into the very centre of our societies, leading to the rediscovery of the idea of the 'commons', which for a long time was considered pre-modern and outdated. In the following sections some of its essential aspects are considered.

The right to commons in historic England

In England in 1215 the Magna Carta legally established some fundamental political rights and at the same time the right to the commons for those who did not *possess* their own land – at that time the vast majority of the population. This right to the commons made the lowest social stratum more independent in the reproduction of their livelihoods, so that they too could exercise these basic political rights. The use of the commons was organised through a complex system of rules that had evolved through traditional practices, the so-called 'common law'. The king and the aristocratic landowners were subordinated to these rules also and the right to the commons thus gave the poorest more power by limiting the power of the sovereigns. The commons were also a physical space where people could meet in order to organise themselves: rebellion and resistance often started from there. For these various reasons the commons were always contested. Along with the expansion of capitalism came the first great wave of enclosure of the commons (see Polanyi, 1957). Enclosure always involved depriving those entitled to use the commons of their power and consequently they became dependent on wage work to meet their basic needs. However, the labour movement later created new commons in the form of the early social security systems, and housing, purchasing and production cooperatives (see Exner and Kratzwald, 2012).

Design principles for long-lasting commons

Elinor Ostrom and her colleagues at Indiana University in Bloomington have examined many hundreds of commons – old and new – and in doing so have identified some principles that characterise long-lasting commons institutions (see Ostrom, 1990). The most important of these are the following:

- Commons have rules, they are not a no-man's land.
- These rules are made by the users themselves and recognised by external authorities. Compliance with the rules is also controlled by the users.

- The rules are adjusted to the characteristics of the resources and the special cultural qualities of the users and may also be changed, if external conditions require this.
- Easily accessible mechanisms for settling conflicts are an essential prerequisite for commons to function.

In every case the commons involves decentralising power and democratising the economy and society. Consequently the role of the state changes if it assumes different tasks in such commons institutions.

The new commons movement

New forms of enclosure have accompanied neoliberalism and have intensified in the last few years because of crises management, but they have in turn encouraged many people to begin thinking about the idea of commons again. Whether it is about food, energy, public space or information and knowledge, people are resisting increasing control by large corporations and/or international organisations such as the EU or the International Monetary Fund and they are demanding their rights to codetermination. People are questioning the capacity and legitimacy of governments and markets to deal with the challenges we currently face. The diverse discourses of the new commons movement share the conviction that people are capable of communicating and cooperating to solve their problems themselves, frequently doing better than the market or the state. Solutions to social and ecological problems may come from below, if people have the opportunity to take their lives into their own hands. It is essential for the self-understanding and identity of the new commons movement that the commons follow a fundamentally different logic to the market system, and therefore serve as a 'germ form' (see P2P Foundation, 2008) for transitioning to a non-capitalist society.

In English-speaking regions the group of people caring for and using a commons together is often called a 'community'. As this may also stand for conservative values and social control, Peter Linebaugh (2008) proposed the term 'commoners'.[1] In any case the creation of a commons comes down to a group of people, frequently from different social backgrounds and with different interests, being able to communicate and act together: an aim that is similar to that of community development. So, does commoning mean the same as community development? May commons arise through community development? In order to answer these questions we must discuss community development in more detail.

Community development

The idea of an active, professional-led strengthening of communities through particular strategies and methods came to Europe from the US, first as a method of social work after the Second World War. Its aim was to empower socially marginalised groups to pursue their interests themselves. Other terms were used almost synonymously with community development: for example, community work or community organising. In the American-based literature all these methods are defined as 'intervention at the community level oriented toward influencing community institutions and solving community welfare problems. This activity is performed by professionals from a number of disciplines ... as well as by citizen volunteers in civic associations and political action groups' (Mohrlock et al, 1993: 22). The aim of community development is 'the mobilisation of resources in order to meet needs and necessities in the community' (Mohrlock et al, 1993: 30), it is about the 'adjustment between community needs and resources' (Mohrlock et al, 1993: 41). This is achieved through an often long-lasting process of relationship building, bringing into contact and supporting deliberations among the key people from the different groups in a district, but also through the inclusion of influential organisations, such as churches or trade unions (Penta, 2007: 219). The distinguishing feature of community development is that the whole range of inhabitants is addressed and involved, even the weakest and most excluded. This demands professional, trained organisers or developers, but who only become active at the behest of those concerned and withdraw again as soon as local people are in a position to take over tasks themselves. Community development may be guided by social workers and then basically becomes a top–down approach, though it also might develop emancipatory potential under certain conditions. Frequently, however, community development processes emerge beyond or outside social work interventions, arising from the initiative of those directly concerned or from other organisations, such as trade unions, churches or social movements.

Community development in the German-speaking area

As shown above, in the US community development was about 'welfare problems': problems of distribution, and the empowerment of socially marginalised groups such as the unemployed, underprivileged youth, or African-Americans. In European welfare regimes either the state or welfare organisations funded by the state were responsible for many of these tasks, their purpose being mainly support and care and not empowerment. Providing social services through private organisations thus is often perceived negatively and rejected in Germany and Austria (see Penta, 2007: 13). In Austria even trade union struggles were eventually moved to the negotiating table through social partnership processes and structures, which left no space for grassroots organising. Thus there is a limited tradition of people becoming active themselves and this might explain why community development methods are being deployed haltingly in Europe and under different auspices.

When those methods were imported from the US, it was mostly under the umbrella term 'community organising'. It was social workers who first experimented with them and 'Sozialraumarbeit' and 'Stadtteilarbeit' later developed as social work disciplines in their own right: though their emancipatory effect was limited to what the city government and administration would allow. In the face of increasing unemployment, growing social division and exclusion, and the dismantling of welfare state programmes, the pressure increased on social workers to also offer economic alternatives for their clients (Elsen, 2000b: 237). These are primarily concerned with 'regaining socially productive skills ..., enabling people to develop themselves' (Elsen, 2000b: 239). The expropriation of these skills – as a further consequence of enclosing the commons – was necessary for industrial capitalism to develop. Today community-based economies are expected to emerge as '... life-serving economies suitable for maintaining the ability of people to act and contributing to social integration and securing the livelihood of the local population in a long lasting way' (Elsen, 2000a: 192).

Only in the last 20 years have governments in Austria and Germany begun to use participatory methods in order to meet social challenges, such as in Local Agenda 21[2] processes or in urban and regional development projects. However, frequently this is only 'pseudo participation', which mainly serves to legitimise decisions already made. Often the suggestions worked out in this way disappear into some drawer never to be seen again.

Regional development programmes supported by the EU usually deal with questions such as how jobs can be created or investors attracted. Certainly the population is included to some extent but the agenda has little to do with community development and alternative economies. Rather it amounts to outsourcing responsibility for managing the negative effects of neoliberalism to civil society. If in support programmes for 'sustainable communities' citizens are to be given the ability to 'stand on their own feet and adapt to the changing demands of modern life', then this means

> they do not *decline* facing the ongoing transformations that the relentless, ever-changing requirements of the global economy impose. But this idea – with its emphasis on education, training, environment, governance, participation, and, of course, sustainability – amounts to an oxymoronic utopia. It is a vision in which communities never seem to tire of playing competitive games with *other* communities somewhere else in the world in order to overcome the disruptions and inequalities of wealth and income inflicted by competitive markets. In this way *'commoning' is annexed to a divisive, competitive process* in order to keep the whole game going (De Angelis, 2012: 189).

However, in some cases it has been possible to move beyond the preoccupation with job market and competition policy and to get a view of all the problem areas, needs and resources of a region. Thus in the 'New ways of creating jobs' model in the nine federal states in East Germany real citizen participation was put into practice, drawing on methods very similar to those of community development:

> In the day to day work of teams on the spot again and again the activating citizens' surveys give an indication of the complexity of the world the population lives in. They show what it is really about: not women's issues and economic development as segmented areas of an abstract political understanding, it is about developing the infrastructure of rural areas from the viewpoints of men and women, young and old, regional planning, renewal of villages, ... The questions, problems and impulses connected with this ... through bringing together the everyday knowledge of citizens and expert knowledge from politics and administration, rely on mutual exchange, common interests and public action. (Niewöhner, 2000: 159)

Essential aspects of community development

Implementing a community development process needs professional developers or organisers who are not appointed from above, but become active only at the wish of those directly concerned, and who follow the motto 'do not do anything for others that they may do for themselves – to make it possible for many people to take solidarity-based action instead' (Penta, 2007: 103). They can be regarded as 'coordination interfaces' who stay in the background when it comes to identifying strategies and putting them into practice. The prerequisite for successful community development is relationship building in a long phase of personal or individual conversations with key people from all the relevant groups in the district or region. The citizens' platform must be kept free from state or political influence and therefore must seek financing from elsewhere. Mutual trust and listening to each other are crucial if the demands of individual groups are not to be perceived as competing with each other. The hope is that participants will recognise the connections between the problems of different groups and will be able to solve those problems together (see Jamoul, 2007: 173).

Commons and community development: learning opportunities, commonalities and differences

Community development could be a suitable approach for creating sustainable commons: this first part of the commoning process has not been analysed much until now. However, not every community development process produces commons or ends with alternative economies.

New commons projects often start from an explicit critique of capitalism shared by a group of like-minded people, whether they are left leaning and anarchist, religious and spiritual or environmentally oriented. They often find it difficult to link up with other social groups and may themselves reproduce exclusion. Commons approaches could learn from the staying power, intensive relationship building and integrated approach of community development. Both share a commitment to starting out from the needs of people, the aim of self-empowerment, the conviction that people may take matters into their own hands, that a broad range of abilities actually makes it possible to find solutions to community problems, and that experts are needed mainly for the process of organising. However, both also share the experience that collective organisation does not work without the acceptance of politics. It is not enough for people to organise themselves – 'a responsive political system is also needed if such proposals are not to remain a pipe dream' (Wainwright, 2009: 214).

However, differences lie in their understandings of the role of the state and in their visions of society. Commoners are profoundly critical of the system and the state and seek to transform existing structures, particularly the capitalist ownership system: in different manifestations this extends as far as overcoming capitalism. They emphasise the fundamentally different logic of the commons, which is incompatible with the logic of the market system. The right to commons is a right that every person has because of his or her birth, irrespective of achievement, social status and appropriate behaviour.

In community development, on the other hand, the emphasis is on empowering people within the current system, in order to be able to exercise their rights and duties as citizens. Existing market, state and civil society structures are rarely questioned: instead there is a desire to remove 'errors' in the system in order to make it possible for all people to participate satisfactorily. The aims are job creation, the fight for better educational opportunities or higher wages, and to attract businesses. While these may have emancipatory potential they also have the effect of stabilising the system. Therefore, community development could possibly profit from the approach of the commons, particularly regarding the upcoming issues of climate change and energy transition, which demand fundamental and systemic changes.

The emphasis on the active, responsible citizen embedded in the concept of community development complies with forms of market liberalism prevailing in the US, where criticism of capitalism is considerably less socially acceptable than in Europe. In contrast the new commons movement arose out of the deep crisis of contemporary capitalism and its profound ecological problems; therefore a critique of capitalism was inherent in this movement from the very beginning. However, within current community development processes, ideas that are critical of consumption and growth and reach beyond social integration and system maintenance are gaining traction, so that really 'alternative' visions of society may also emerge from this approach, even if it does not always start out with a fundamental critique of capitalism.

There is, for example, an unemployment initiative in Stuttgart, where people have taken over the process of making themselves 'fit' for the primary labour market. In this process people came to realise that wage labour has no inherent value and that whether or not they find employment does not depend upon themselves alone. They overcame the competitive situation of the individual wage worker to think about production cooperatives. 'Alternatives to the wage work system are also discussed against the background of there being no general labour market for many employees who have been made redundant. How is waged labour to be connected with social engagement and mutual assistance?' (Häcker, 2007: 166).

Conversely, commons too may not exist in a pure form in this system. Even if participants claim to develop alternatives to the system, they must make compromises and in the end they also need the acceptance of the state and a supporting legal framework or conditions. Any top-down initiative is only successful if it gains the trust of those directly concerned and if it strengthens people in becoming active around their own demands. Any bottom-up initiative also needs charismatic people and recognition from above. If people really have the opportunity of finding solutions to their problems themselves and of meeting their needs with the means available, the results are obviously quite independent of the different philosophies or visions that underpinned their aims at the beginning.

Commons and community development must both live with these ambiguities. Capitalism always needs resources from outside itself in order to be able to survive (see De Angelis, 2012: 187f); therefore in spite of, or precisely because of, their different logics, commons are always in danger of being coopted. Commons always have two key aspects: they give people more autonomy but also provide capital with free resources. Only the people concerned may determine which aspect prevails.

Community development also has aspects that strengthen the system. Active citizens take over tasks from the state and make the reproduction of labour cheaper. Community development processes may be exploited by politicians. As neighbourhoods are expected to take over the task of social security that the state, allegedly, can no longer perform, politicians also like to invoke the term 'community':

> In Britain, in the midst of the largest cut in public spending (2010 and ongoing) promoted by the conservative and Lib-Dem coalition government the same government is promoting a vision of 'Big Society', that is of community empowerment in solving several aspects of the crisis of reproduction in the context of currently fragmented communities. On the one hand, the agenda of the neoliberal era continues as if no crisis has happened. (De Angelis, 2012: 188)

The dividing line between empowerment and exploitation is a fine one. However, if it is possible to create suitable conditions for self-organisation, if politics reacts to them accordingly and if it takes these processes seriously, then this may lead to real changes in the balance of power and ensure that people become more independent of the system. Some examples of this are given in the following section.

Community development as alternative economics: some examples

The Beutelweg cooperative (Germany)[3]

The Beutelweg cooperative was born in the 1980s out of a long-standing community project in a neglected district of Trier. Many of the residents had already been unemployed for a long time, they were receiving welfare and their homes were run down, they were disheartened and resigned to their situations. When small changes to the estate, such as a play area, were developed together in an equal partnership with the inhabitants, they overcame their resignation and took over the tasks of caring for the park on the estate owned by the city. When the estate was to be sold by the city, the idea arose of setting up a cooperative. The hope was that this would make it possible for residents to remain in their homes, to renovate the houses and thus create affordable living spaces and job opportunities simultaneously.

Today the flats are owned by a residents' cooperative whose members were able to acquire their shares through their own work because they lacked financial resources. They were instructed in the renovations by experienced craftsmen. A craft business was set up, which then took over the renovation work and half of its workforce was recruited from previously unemployed people and youths from the estate. This all became possible because the relevant players from the district and city administration could be brought to the discussion table. It is a prime example of the success of long-standing community work, and certainly a form of 'alternative economy'. Furthermore, with its complex structure creating different roles for public institutions and local enterprises, with responsibility being taken over by those directly concerned, and with its processes of common production, use and maintenance, it is also a prime example of a sustainable commons institution and the practice of commoning.

Marsh Farm in Luton (England)[4]

In Luton's Marsh Farm, a disadvantaged district of a large English town, characterised by high unemployment, particularly among the young, violence on the streets, a large proportion of migrants, and disused industrial plants standing empty, the Exodus Collective began, in the

1990s, organising rave parties for young people in order to get them off the streets. Other leisure outlets and opportunities soon followed. The authorities tracked these activities with varying degrees of acceptance. On the one hand vandalism and violence went down considerably, which spoke in favour of tolerance, but on the other hand the turnover in the local pubs went down drastically too, because hundreds of young people now spent their leisure time in the old building that had been occupied by the Exodus Collective. Therefore there were also loud demands for closure of this semi-legal facility. When a few years after the new millennium the UK government launched its 'New Deal for Communities' (NDC) programme to develop disadvantaged districts, there were some residents of Luton who had emerged from the Exodus Collective with great experience in community work. 'Ex-Exodus members were therefore well prepared for the highs and lows of the NDC process as they struggled to create cooperation, equality and participative democracy in the face of division and conflict' (Wainwright, 2009: 195)

They succeeded in bringing other existing initiatives to the table and set up the 'Marsh Farm Community Development Trust'. In a long process, characterised again and again by setbacks and varying degrees of acceptance by politics and administration, the Trust succeeded in winning the NDC contract. '[R]esidents get organized to set up social enterprises to bid for work now done by private companies and to share services – marketing, physical assets, financial advice and so on – ... a "hub" of social and economic activity' (Wainwright, 2009: 225). The resources from the NDC went to these local enterprises and initiatives and not to professional development offices and housing associations.

These are two examples of classic community development leading to people improving their own economic situation and therefore becoming more independent of the 'free' labour and housing markets as well as gaining independence from state support, taking back control of their own living conditions and at the same time strengthening their own power in shaping the system. These examples were successful because long-standing organising processes met with the necessary support or at least acceptance of the state. Although they were formed before the recent upsurge in the use of the term 'commons' and therefore do not describe themselves in this way, both examples contain commons elements: people taking over responsibility, communicating, cooperating, producing, using and maintaining common resources. To a large extent they managed to make their own rules, which were accepted by the authorities, albeit with all the inevitable restrictions.

New forms of self-organisation from below

In recent years new forms of self-organisation from below have emerged, which are less focused on empowering marginalised groups, and are a reaction to the failure of governments to develop solutions to the problems of peak oil, climate change and energy transition. Here too people want to take matters into their own hands and work for the development of a society beyond consumerism and growth and beyond *homo oeconomicus*. In addition, sustainable living is a way to overcome the isolation, atomisation and individualism of the market system, as people rely on collective forms of organisation and mutual support.

These models explicitly self-identify as 'alternative economies'; their aim is to develop alternatives to market logic from below. People begin to live 'differently' in districts or villages: they grow food themselves or support organic growing through community-supported agriculture, in which they buy 'shares in the harvest'; they rediscover old craft techniques in order to make themselves independent of 'high' technology; they use cars or tools together in order to save resources; and they repair things or pass on second-hand clothes in order to reduce waste. Sharing information and raising awareness about these activities are other important focal points. This is a form of self-empowerment that shows that it is quite possible to make yourself more independent of the market system in some ways. However, such activity remains mostly limited to a certain ecologically aware section of the middle class. One possible reason for this could be that they lack the long-standing commitment to relationship building that might allow them to include many more people across diverse social strata and world views.

It is here that the Transition movement[5] is trying to start. It too begins by raising awareness, but in '[t]he twelve key ingredients to the Transition model' (Transition Network, 2013) there are also many elements of professional 'organising' work to include diverse groups and acquire financial resources. It wants to achieve broad commitment to a phase-out plan for fossil fuel energy within a defined period of time by engaging with city politics. In some towns, particularly in the first Transition Town, Totnes in England, this has already been successful. Here again it appears that aims may only be achieved if there is the necessary acceptance and responsiveness from politicians to initiatives that emerge from below.

It differs from the earlier examples in that its motivation does not come from an experience of social hardship, but from recognising the threats posed by the prevailing economic system. Such initiatives do not pursue integration within the system; rather they work towards overcoming that system. The final example described below combines both aspects.

Detroit (US)

Even during the high phase of industrial capitalism Detroit was already a centre for social movements, particularly the Black Power movement and trade union organisation. When in the 1980s unemployment and poverty increased due to deindustrialisation, population numbers declined drastically and violence was the order of the day, self-organisation took a different direction. The initial situation was desperate: the proportion of black people was about 80% and large industrial areas lay fallow. However, community-based organisations have profoundly influenced social relations and life in the city of Detroit (see Howell, 2006: 64). While official policy still set its hopes on building new industries, local people recognised that the future lay elsewhere. Detroiters Uniting was founded: a broad alliance of community-based organisations, workers, creative artists, church groups and political activists, which represented the diversity of the city. Its aim was 'citizens taking over responsibility for decisions about their city, instead of leaving them to the politicians and the market' (Boggs, 2006: 31), basically organising their district as commons. Detroiters Uniting wanted 'to build local, more self sufficient and sustainable economies, economies that redefine work and our relationships with the earth and build communities again that … were destroyed so recklessly' (Boggs, 2006: 31). It became possible to meet more and more needs as a strong urban gardening movement moved food production into the city. It involved unemployed, and in some cases violent, young people and older African-American women who rediscovered their traditional agricultural knowledge.

But here again one thing led to another: increasing success saw influential and financially powerful people come forward. An Institute of Urban Ecology was established at the university and an architectural institute took part in rebuilding desolate estates, with cultural and artistic activities revived. What happened here connected aspects of commons and community development in an almost exemplary way: it was possible to activate the most excluded strata of the population and this activation was not focused on success within the existing system, but had the aim of building a different, socially and ecologically sustainable city, an aim that was achieved to a certain extent. Obviously Detroit's experience concerns an island of hope within the wider context of the US, which is developing in ever more neoliberal ways.

However, it probably comes closer than any other example to the claim of building alternative economies with the help of community development. And it also shows that alternative economies only work if bottom-up and top-down movements meet and finally pull together.

Conclusion

Community development may produce alternative economies if the community and public authorities can work together on an equal footing. Then it is not so important where the impetus comes, from above or below, or whether criticism of the dominant system or attempts at integration within that system are so clearly defined from the beginning. In any case the prerequisite is the existence of a platform of community-based organisations, along with the engagement of charismatic individuals who will withdraw at the right time and secure at least some recognition from established politics. Such processes take a long time to build trust – both the trust between different groups of residents and the trust between politics and engaged citizens. Such alternative economies are about more than the production of goods or services. First and foremost they lead to the creation of new social relationships and they always include elements of new forms of democracy. However, even successful examples are always balancing acts that may topple over. They may be coopted or taken over by governments and misused to legitimise their predetermined agendas and programmes. Only when they are embedded in a corresponding democratic framework, which must be created first, are such alternative economies sustainable. Wainwright formulates it as follows for the Luton project:

> It is a combination of the micro democracy of interconnected social enterprises and local managed public services, accountable to a wider participatory democracy of the Trust and a regular assembly of residents, and framed by the still-to-be-transformed electoral democracy of Luton Borough Council and, beyond them, regional governments. (Wainwright, 2009: 229)

Notes

[1] Regarding the term commons US historian Peter Linebaugh also coined the terms 'commoner' for people producing, caring for and using such commons and 'commoning' for this process of common production, care and use.

² Agenda 21 is a programme launched by the United Nations Conference on Environment and Development in 1992 to achieve global sustainable development. The action programme for local implementation is called Local Agenda 21 and aims at involving the inhabitants in developing sustainable strategies for the city or region.

³ See Elsen et al (2000) for discussion.

⁴ See Wainwright (2009: 190–231) for a discussion.

⁵ The Transition movement is a bottom-up movement for reducing dependence on fossil fuels and permanent economic growth, to prevent climate change and create a social and ecologically sustainable society by local action.

References

Boggs, G. L. (2006) 'Living for change', in C. Möller U. Peters and I. Vellay (eds) *Dissidente Praktiken. Erfahrungen mit herrschafts- und warenkritischer Selbstorganisation*, Königstein/Taunus: Ulrike Helmer Verlag, 25–37.

De Angelis, M. (2012) 'Crises, capital and co-optation: does capital need a commons fix?', in D. Bollier and S. Helfrich (eds) *The wealth of the commons. A world beyond market and state*, Amherst, MA: Leveller's Press, 184–91.

Elsen, S. (2000a) 'Über den Zusammenhang globaler und lokaler Entwicklungen und die Konsequenzen für die Gemeinwesenarbeit', in S. Elsen, D. Lange and I. Wallimann (eds) *Soziale Arbeit und Ökonomie*, Neuwied/Kriftel: Luchterhand, 179–99.

Elsen, S. (2000b) 'Lokale Handlungskonzepte als Antworten auf Massenarbeitslosigkeit, wachsende Armut und soziale Ausgrenzung', in S. Elsen, H. Ries, N. Löns and H.-G. Homfeldt (eds) *Sozialen Wandel gestalten – Lernen für die Zivilgesellschaft*, Neuwied/Kriftel: Luchterhand, 230–50.

Elsen, S., Ries H., Löns N. and Homfeldt H.-G. (2000) 'Aus der Not geboren: Die Genossenschaft am Beutelweg', in S. Elsen, H. Ries, N. Löns and H.-G. Homfeldt (eds): *Sozialen Wandel gestalten – Lernen für die Zivilgesellschaft*, Neuwied/Kriftel: Luchterhand, pp 261–91.

Exner, A. and Kratzwald, B. (2012) *Solidarische Ökonomie und Commons*, Vienna: Mandelbaum Verlag.

Häcker, W. (2007) 'Myself e.V. in Stuttgart', in L. Penta (ed) *Community Organizing. Menschen verändern ihre Stadt*, Hamburg: Edition Körber-Stiftung, 155–66.

Howell, S (2006) 'Detroit Summer: Wiederaufbau unserer Städte von Grund auf', in C. Möller, U. Peters and I. Vellay (eds) *Dissidente Praktiken. Erfahrungen mit herrschafts- und warenkritischer Selbstorganisation*, Königstein/Taunus: Ulrike Helmer Verlag, 63–72.

Jamoul, L. (2007) 'London citizens', in L. Penta (ed) *Community Organizing. Menschen verändern ihre Stadt*, Hamburg: Edition Körber-Stiftung, 167–83.

Linebaugh, P. (2008) *The Magna Carta manifesto. Liberties and commons for all*, Berkeley/Los Angeles/London: University of California Press.

Mohrlock, M., Neubauer M., Neubauer, R. and Schönfelder W. (eds) (1993) *Let's organize! Gemeinwesenarbeit und Community Organization im Vergleich*, Munich: AG Spak.

Niewöhner, A. (2000) 'Eine andere Form lokaler Wirtschaftsförderung', in S. Elsen, H. Ries, N. Löns and H.-G. Homfeldt (eds) *Sozialen Wandel gestalten – Lernen für die Zivilgesellschaft*, Neuwied/Kriftel: Luchterhand, 155–64.

Ostrom, E. (1990) *Governing the commons. The evolution of institutions for collective action*, Oxford: Oxford University Press.

P2P Foundation (2008) *Germ form theory*, http://p2pfoundation.net/Germ_Form_Theory.

Penta, L. (2007) (ed.) *Community Organizing. Menschen verändern ihre Stadt*, Hamburg: Edition Körber-Stiftung.

Polanyni, K. (1957) *The great transformation: The political and economic origins of our time*, 2nd edn, Boston, MA: Beacon Press.

Transition Network (2013) *12 ingredients*, www.transitionnetwork.org/support/12-ingredients.

Wainwright, H. (2009): *Reclaim the state. Experiments in popular democracy*, Calcutta: Seagull Books.

Index